"I laughed aloud. Those girls have got something there."

—Robert Sean Leonard

"If The Girls from *The Rules* and Miss Emily Post had a clue, they'd put down their tighty whiteys, pull on their leather bustiers, and start paying attention to this ultimate how-to girl manifesto. Oh, that Miss Post is probably spinning in her porcelain, white grave!"

—Marcelle Karp, coauthor of
The Bust Guide to the New Girl Order and
cofounder of *Bust Magazine*

"To her it is not life that matters; it is the etiquette with which one faces it that counts."

—Dorothy Parker, *A Dinner Party Anthology*

"He believed passionately in good form—his choosing of gloves, his tying of ties, his holding of reins were imitated by impressionable freshmen . . . his set was *the* set."

—F. Scott Fitzgerald, *The Four Fists*

Things You Need to Be Told

A handbook for Polite Behavior in a tacky, rude world!

BY THE

Etiquette grrls

Lesley Carlin *and* **Honore McDonough Ervin**

BERKLEY BOOKS, NEW YORK

B

A Berkley Book
Published by The Berkley Publishing Group
A division of Penguin Putnam Inc.
375 Hudson Street
New York, New York 10014

Copyright © 2001 by Lesley Carlin and Honore McDonough Ervin
Book design by Tiffany Kukec
Interior art courtesy Eyewire Inc.
Cover design by Rita Frangie and Lesley Worrell
Cover illustration by Rollin McGrail
All photos of the authors by Michel Delsol

PRINTING HISTORY
Berkley trade paperback edition / October 2001

Visit our website at
www.penguinputnam.com

Library of Congress Cataloging-in-Publication Data

Carlin, Lesley, 1973–
    Things you need to be told : a handbook for polite behavior in a tacky, rude
world! / by Lesley Carlin and Honore McDonough Ervin.—Berkley trade pbk.
ed.
    p.   cm.
    ISBN 0-425-18370-X
    1. Etiquette for young adults. I. Ervin, Honore McDonough, 1975–   II. Title.
BJ1857.Y58 C37 2001
395—dc21

                                                                2001033098

PRINTED IN THE UNITED STATES OF AMERICA

10   9   8   7   6   5   4   3   2   1

CONTENTS

CHAPTER FIVE:
At Work   96

CHAPTER SIX:
Dating and Breakups   121

# ACKNOWLEDGMENTS

The Etiquette Grrls wish to offer Every Token of Our Appreciation to all who assisted us as we prepared This Manuscript. We are Most Thankful for all the Helpful Suggestions, Advice, and, of course, the Copious Gin, offered to us by our Dear Friends. Even our Extensively Large Vocabulary fails to describe how Exceedingly Grateful we are to our Agent, Douglas Stewart, and our Editor, Hillery Borton, for their Good Counsel, Unfailing Wit, Friendship, and Steadfast Support of This Project. Truly, This Book would not exist without them. Mad Props also to our Über-publicist, Kelly Groves, whom we Love to Pieces for all he's done for us, not to mention the fact that he used Random Capitalization Long Before he even met us. And we could never forget the Dear Readers of our website, EtiquetteGrrls.com, who are Unceasingly Devoted.

We are also Deeply Indebted to The Incomparable Phyllis Grann and, of course, Everyone at Penguin Putnam and Berkley for all of their Hard Work. We are Most Grateful also to Letitia Baldrige, Marcelle Karp, and especially Robert Sean Leonard for their Encouragement and Enthusiasm for This Project. Thanks also to Francesca DiMeglio.

Honore would like to thank her Family and her Dear Friends

(who Know Who They Are), all of whom, in addition to their Constant Encouragement, Good Humor, and Invaluable Assistance, are always willing to put in a Good Word for the Etiquette Grrls to anyone who will stand still long enough to listen. Further, many of them kindly provided us with Witty Anecdotes contained within This Book, as well as adding Many Important Words to Our Patois. A Girl couldn't ask for anyone to be Better Sports, or Better Publicists.

Lesley would like to thank her Family and her Dear Friends for their Countless Hours of Good Conversation, their Marvelous Wit and Humor, and their Sage Advice. This book would be Quite a Slim Volume Indeed without the tales they've kindly shared with the Etiquette Grrls! And of course, the "At Work" chapter would not be the same without the Cast of Characters at a Certain Dot-Com which Shall Remain Nameless. Lesley sends special thanks to John and Joan Carlin and to Josh McElhattan.

With much love, we dedicate This Book to All of You.

INTRODUCTION

A young man, a graduate of St. Paul's and Harvard University, takes his first job at a conservative Law Firm. Within one week, this Intrepid Young Barrister is strolling around the office in cutoff shorts and bare feet.

A young couple, out on a Saturday night date at a Trendy Swing Club, are snappily dressed in Vintage Clothing, and they order their martinis with aplomb. However, they chomp on their olives loudly, and make an unseemly production of stealing the bar's distinctive swizzle sticks.

A Girl is staggering under the weight of an air conditioner. It is a very hot day, and she approaches a heavy door, which impedes her progress. A nearby Boy watches with interest as he stands idly by, enjoying a Cold Beverage.

We are appalled.

Something has to be done.

We know what it is, and we know who has to do it.

This is a job for the Etiquette Grrls.

'Fess up now, Dear Reader—in recent months have you committed a glaring faux pas, similar to one of the above-listed scenarios? Have you ever hogged the photocopy machine at work, as a long line of coworkers (even including—gasp!—one of the Big Mucky-Mucks, or, at least, a Bigger Mucky-Muck than you) builds up behind you? Have you ever been tardy to a Social or Work Obligation? Have you had a nonessential conversation on a cell 'phone or failed to turn off your pager in a restaurant, theatre, House of Worship, or other public place? In fact—while we're on the topic—why are you carrying around such electronic gadgets to begin with? (Assuming that you are not a FBI agent, doctor, Terribly Important Hollywood Producer, drug dealer, or member of any other such profession that would necessitate the constant use of such items.) Have you ever canceled a Date at the Last Possible Moment, simply because "something better came along"? Have you ever inexplicably and abruptly gone AWOL for months, maybe even years, at a time, throwing your Nearest and Dearest into unceasing fits of Despair and Worry as to your Health and Well-Being? Shame on you, Dear Reader. However, we know you didn't really mean it—you just didn't know any better. Luckily for you, the Etiquette Grrls are here to remedy the situation. It won't hurt, we promise.

It is indeed a Tacky, Rude World which we inhabit. We, the Etiquette Grrls, have decided that things are simply getting out of hand, and thus we have Taken It Upon Ourselves to step in and provide you, our Esteemed Peers, with a helpful guide that you may carry with you, and refer to frequently, as you encounter Etiquette Quandaries in your day-to-day life.

And who are we, you ask, to be writing such a book? We are graduates of Prestigious Colleges and New England Preparatory Schools; we are throwers of Great Parties; we can hold our liquor; our expertise on fashion and makeup—and especially Subversive Nail Polish colors—knows no bounds; we wear Doc Martens with our cashmere twin sets; and, most important, we know what the hell we're talking about.

So, gather 'round, all you Kats and Kittens, and listen up. We wouldn't want to have to repeat ourselves. After all, it would be Terribly Rude of you not to pay attention.

CHAPTER ONE

In Your Apartment

Chez Toi

Just because you are in your own home is no reason to neglect Good Manners and become a noisy, inconsiderate, slothful, unhygienic, and Rude Creature. You have neighbors; you have guests; perhaps you have roommates. None of these should be subjected to Unforgivable Etiquette Faux Pas, no matter how much you dislike them or how rude they are to you. As always, Dear Reader, you should attempt to rise above the Lowest Common Denominator. By doing so, we can only hope that you will bring others along with you, out of the Depths of Rudeness.

You Don't Have to Love Thy Neighbors, but You Shouldn't Drive Them to the Brink of Insanity, Either

The Etiquette Grrls are not hypocrites. We admit, shamefacedly, that even we have been guilty of occasionally playing music at a level that neighbors might find irritating. But this is unacceptable when it becomes a Daily Occurrence. Nobody, but nobody, wants to be subjected to the reverberating *thumpa-thumpa* of the bass line of rock music 24/7. Even the more tuneful and innocuous sounds of classical music or Frank Sinatra can become irksome when they are incessant. Now, Dear Reader, we're not saying that you should use headphones when listening to your stereo—this can make moving around your apartment rather limiting, and besides, we've been told that constant headphone use can permanently damage your hearing. But try to remember that most apartment walls are about as thin and sound absorbing as, say, an Onion Skin, and undoubtedly, your neighbors are able to hear everything that goes on in your apartment. So just try to keep the noise level down to a Dull Roar, please. We think that you will be able to get away with playing your music at a decent level and still not disturb everyone on your block.

INDOOR SPORTS

Naturally, the same goes for any potentially noisy activity of which you might partake in your apartment. If you are a devotee of energetic activities such as aerobics, for instance, you should refrain from engaging in such exercise in your apartment, especially if you live above the first floor. In the condition that most apartment buildings are kept these days, even in the higher-rent districts, all your jumping around may dislodge the plaster in the ceiling of the apartment below yours, causing one of those inexpensive and hideous 1950s overhead light fixtures which (much to our chagrin) we all have, to fall, seriously injuring that Terribly Attractive downstairs neighbor whom you've been keeping your eye on. You might even kill their cat, goldfish, or other Small Pet. (And no, Dear Reader, you may not use this behavior as a method to introduce yourself to him or her.) As for other Athletic Activities in Your Apartment, Impromptu Games of touch football, basketball, or hockey are never permissible, even if you do have Fabulously Slippery Hardwood Floors and no Pesky Furniture to get in your way. Although we all appreciate your efforts to shield us from seeing you in sweaty, unflattering clothing and ungraceful, embarrassing positions In Public, unfortunately, exercising at home will have to wait until you have your own house, in which you may build a fabulous exercise room. Every city is filled with many pleasant, clean, and affordable gyms. If you wish to follow a daily exercise routine, we suggest that you join one.

PRACTICING YOUR DO-RE-MIS

While the Etiquette Grrls deeply admire those who have been graced with Musical Talent, and we understand that These Things do not Come Easily, and musicians must practice diligently in order to Perfect Their Talent, you should probably refrain from practicing your instrument of choice in your apartment at any and all Ungodly Hours. Most especially if you are not a professional, or at least very, very good at it. (It doesn't matter if *you* think you're very, very good at it—the question is, do other people who are qualified to make such a judgment think you are very, very good?) We guarantee you, Dear Reader, even if you are of the opinion that you are the next Pavarotti, Yo-Yo Ma, or even Jimi Hendrix, your neighbors are not likely to share your opinion if you endlessly practice in your apartment, no matter how great your talent. Awakening all in your building at six o'clock every Saturday morning with a screeching, off-key, unrecognizable rendition of "Flight of the Bumblebee" on your violin will not win you any votes for Mr. or Miss Popularity. In fact, as there is no guarantee that the other tenants of your building will have read this Informative Publication, you can probably expect some Nasty Retaliation from your more imaginative and short-tempered neighbors. In the event that you cannot afford your own Studio, you might want to inquire at a Local University or Arts Center about the availability of practice rooms. Often, such institutions will allow you to use practice spaces for little or no cost—a truly worthwhile investment that will keep you and all your neighbors on Friendly Terms.

APPROPRIATING SPACE: COMMON AREAS

You also should not treat the Public Areas of Your Building, such as the lobby, hallways, and stairwells, as an extension of your Personal Living Space. These areas are to be used by all the tenants, and should be kept clean and quiet. You may not deposit your garbage in the hallways, leaving it there for weeks on end, filling the Entire Building with the piquant scent of rotting Pad Thai. You should deposit your garbage in the rubbish bins which are, undoubtedly, located either in the basement of or outside your apartment building. You also should not use the hallways as your living room. That is to say, you may not place your couch or other furnishings in the hall or on the landing; nor may you lounge in the above-mentioned locations, carry on telephone conversations, or otherwise Socialize. If you have pets or Small Children, they should not be permitted to play in Common Areas, either.

The exterior of your door should also be considered part of the Public Area of the building, and you should keep this in mind should you choose to decorate it. Of course, the Etiquette Grrls prefer an undecorated door, save for the Holiday Season, when one may hang a simple evergreen wreath. You should, at all costs, avoid any such decoration that might cause offense to your neighbors, such as Pentagrams or Velvet Paintings of Jesus. You should also steer clear of any signs bearing offensive pictures or text. And while there is nothing offensive, per se, in pennants supporting your favorite sports team or posters of Elvis, we strongly feel that these items might be better housed inside the safe confines of your residence. After all, you wouldn't want someone to make off with your beloved *X-Files* poster that boldly proclaims, "The Truth Is Out There," do you?

STICKY FINGERS

Naturally, it goes without saying that stealing mail, laundry, or anything else that you might find lying around your building is Absolutely Impermissible. (Even if you are attempting to Enact Revenge.) The Etiquette Grrls fully understand that the rudeness of others can Drive One Mad, but you should try to refrain from stooping to such childish and rude behavior.

Roommates: The Necessary Evil

We have learned from experience that having roommates can be Quite Trying, even if you are all Good Friends. Throwing two or more young people into cramped living quarters leads to a situation that is rife with possibilities for creating a minefield of Potential Etiquette Faux Pas and, thereby, short tempers, lost friendships, and (although we sincerely hope not) Dark Plots to murder said roommates. By following some simple Ground Rules, all in your house can become kind, considerate, and conscientious about paying their share of the bills on time, and therefore, we hope, no one will plan ways to act on any of the suggestions of "101 Ways to Drive Your Roommate Crazy" that circulate on the Internet, nor will there be any unnecessary, messy bloodshed.

All shared areas, such as the living room, kitchen, and bathroom, should be kept clean and tidy. Don't leave your clutter all over every flat surface. This is what your bedroom is for. Don't leave your food to get moldy in the refrigerator. Take the garbage out before it begins to overflow; it will be a long, long time before the life-forms in the trash bin evolve to the point of taking themselves out and closing the door behind them. The responsibility of keeping these rooms in order should not fall on any one person—the duties should, of course, be shared equally between all who reside in the apartment.

Perhaps one of the most difficult things about living with other people is making an honest effort not to "hog" any of the household's common rooms or appliances. Lying on the living-room couch all day and insisting that the television be tuned to the Country Music Channel 24/7 will not endear you to anybody. We (and your roommates, who have undoubtedly Had Their Fill of Shania Twain) suggest that you purchase a small television and watch it in your room. You also should not spend inordinate amounts of time in the bathroom, if you merely have one, nor should you be on the telephone so much that everyone thinks that it must be Surgically Attached to your ear. And while we're on the topic of the telephone, you should, of course, be conscientious about passing on messages to your roommates—write them down lest you forget. You should also notify the necessary parties should you be aware of messages left on the answering machine that are meant for them. (More on telephone etiquette—taking and passing on messages, etc., in chapter 4, "Staying in Touch.")

Another area of frequent contention among roommates is the Food Supply. Oftentimes, staples, such as milk, are communal property, and roommates agree to take turns purchasing them. If you have agreed to such a system, you and your roommates really *should* take turns. It may seem like a Little Thing, but if it falls on your roommate Penelope's shoulders to purchase the milk every single week for months on end when she does not habitually eat cereal and takes her coffee black, it will undoubtedly lead to resentment on the part of the One in Charge of Dairy. If special food items (unusual, expensive, or difficult-to-find culinary delights that you know were Specially Purchased by a roommate for his or her own consumption) appear in the pantry, you should ask before Chowing Down upon them. The Brie and green grapes sitting on a lovely Fiestaware platter in your otherwise empty refrigerator were probably purchased by your roommate as a special treat for herself; do not treat them like common chips. If you are dieting, or even if you are not, and have stocked the pantry shelves with all manner of low-fat, low-sodium, low-taste "goodies," you really ought not to continually forsake these items in favor of your roommate's Entenmann's Chocolate Chip Cookies. She will undoubtedly be livid when she goes to the pantry in search of a yummy cookie to consume with a tall, ice-cold glass of milk (which she personally lugged from the grocery store to your pied-à-terre), and she only finds fifty varieties of rice cakes. If you're really dying for a cookie (and even if you are dieting, a cookie or two won't kill you, by the way—you'll be happier and healthier in the long run if you have one really yummy cookie or brownie rather than a boxful of bland and tasteless low-fat knock-offs), either ask if you may have one from your roommate's stash of Pepperidge Farm goodies, or better yet, hop over to that nice bakery around the corner and bring some back for everyone in the house. (This goes for anyone—if you're buying a treat, it's nice to bring enough for everyone. Remember, Dear Reader, generosity is *always* stylish, and stinginess is not!) You should also proceed with caution when "borrowing" your room-mates' clothes, cars, or other belongings. You should always, always ask permission before taking anything, and nothing should be "borrowed" on such a Permanent Basis that it could be con-strued as Theft. Everything should be returned in Immaculate (and, if applicable, Working) Condition. We recommend that if you are in the habit of tearing, stretching, maiming, or spilling things on your clothes, books, or other items, or of wrecking auto-mobiles, that you refrain from borrowing these items from your roommates (or from *anybody*, for that matter, as such behavior will undoubtedly make you Most Unpopular).

When one is splitting the rent and other assorted bills with a group of people, it is Terribly Important to pay one's share of what one owes Promptly, and in the Full Amount. No one likes a Free-loader. Should you fail to pay Your Share of the bills, the Entire House may be deprived of telephone or electrical service, or even, perhaps, evicted. Causing other people to become homeless is The Height of Rudeness (THOR).

When you have guests, especially someone who spends a great deal of time at your residence, such as a boy- or girlfriend, you should attempt to be respectful of the other members of your household and not intrude upon their space. Everyone is likely to become resentful if Joe Boyfriend is, for all intents and purposes, part of your household, eating all the food, running up the 'phone bill, running his "courier business" from your home, Napping Constantly upon the settee, and not paying a penny of rent. If you want to live with your Significant Other, then we suggest that you actually sign a lease together.

Entertaining at Home

The Etiquette Grrls love to entertain, and you should, too! There's nothing more enjoyable than arranging a Swanky Cocktail Party chez toi for your witty, fascinating, stylish friends. Entertaining at home is often far more enjoyable than your usual Friday Night Pub Crawl of Local Watering Holes, as you know you will enjoy the company of all present, you are not likely to be approached by Rude and Boorish Strangers, and you are guaranteed to have a Plentiful Supply of your favorite beverages and foodstuffs.

"Having people over" can range in levels of formality from an impromptu visit by your best friend to a semi-formal dinner party. However, the same set of basic etiquette guidelines should be adhered to, no matter what the situation.

MEALS

Sit-down luncheons and dinners are Tricky Territory. The Etiquette Grrls recommend that beginners keep it simple. Only invite the number of people to dinner that can be Comfortably Seated at your kitchen or dining-room table. Nearly everyone, including the Etiquette Grrls, becomes uncomfortable when faced with the near-impossible task of cutting food served on a paper plate, which is balanced precariously upon the knees, without spilling anything or sending a fusillade of peas flying across the room, pelting an Unsuspecting Diner. One of the Etiquette Grrls was once invited to A Holiday Dinner at the apartment of several intelligent, handsome, witty, well-bred, and theretofore Extremely Polite Boys. Much to her annoyance (as she feared spilling gravy on her fetching, new, navy-blue lightweight wool shift dress), she was required to eat an entire Traditional Holiday Feast off a plate in her lap, with the only utensil provided being a fork. Her water glass stood precariously on the floor, in Constant Danger of being kicked over by many feet. In addition, this particular meal was served in front of the television, which eliminated all possibility of Conversation. After maneuvering through the Tricky Dinner Obstacles, this Etiquette Grrl was left to her own devices while all in the house went their Separate Ways to complete homework and other tasks. Further, unable to locate the remote control, she was subjected to several hours of Atrocious Television Programming before someone reappeared to entertain her. Which brings us to another important point. If you have invited people to dine with you, it is presumed that you actually want their company, and you should make an effort to converse with them. If the only company you are interested in at dinnertime is that of Tom Brokaw reporting from NBC Studios in Rockefeller Center, then we suggest that you refrain from inviting others to join you at meals.

If you feel that you would enjoy the company of others for a meal, you should be thoughtful about what you serve to eat. Obviously, if your guests are vegetarians, then serving your grandmother's wonderful recipe for meat loaf would not be wise. When in doubt, keep things simple. We have found that an uncomplicated meal, such as a salad, good-quality pasta, and some nice fresh bread, is always a good choice and is enjoyed by everyone. On the other hand, if you are a dinner or lunch guest, you are obligated to be polite about what is served, even if you do not care for it. There is no need to make your feelings known by shrieking, *"I WON'T EAT THAT!!!!!!!!"* like a spoiled and ill-bred four-year-old without even trying what you have been offered. Simply take a bite or two of everything that is served, eat what you do like, and leave the rest of it alone. Your host will undoubtedly take the hint and not serve you the same dish again. If you or many of your friends are Finicky Eaters, then we suggest that you consider eating out rather than dining at home. That way, everyone may order exactly what he or she likes, and everyone will be happy. (More on this in the Dining Out section of chapter 2, "Out and About.")

Should you find that friends have dropped by at mealtime, you ought to offer them a little something to eat. Even if your cupboards are bare, you should at least offer to send out for something. Many of today's food establishments, most notably Pizza and Chinese Restaurants, will deliver food directly to your door for no Additional Fee! This is most convenient should you find yourself with an Unexpected Dinner Guest, and far preferable to having to revive a friend who has fainted on your living-room floor from Lack of Nourishment.

TABLE MANNERS

Even if you are The Wealthiest and Most Powerful Person in The World, Dear Reader, you will appear to be An Uncouth Boor if you have Poor Table Manners, and the Etiquette Grrls simply will not tolerate it! Work hard at cultivating Good Table Manners, Dear Reader; it's as important as, say, maintaining a Clean and Tidy Personal Appearance. Here are some Quick Pointers:

- Don't slouch; slump; sprawl; or sit cross-legged, especially not Lotus-fashion, on the chair (see page 66 for directions on How to Sit Properly); or fling an arm across the back of the chair.

- Put your napkin on your lap as soon as you sit down at the table, and don't remove it until the end of the meal. And for heaven's sake, don't tuck your napkin into Your Collar! (Incidentally, as an aside, Any Adult ought to be able to eat Lobster without the aid of one of those Silly Bibs!)

- Get those Elbows off the table! And stop asking the Etiquette Grrls why, just do it! (Do you want to tip the table over because you are leaning heavily upon it? No, you don't, Dear Reader. Trust the Etiquette Grrls.)

- Don't Dig In until Your Hostess has been seated and Begun Her Meal.

- If you are Dining avec A Family who is in the Habit of Saying Grace before a Meal, you must respect this, even if you do not participate in such a ritual yourself. If you are unsure how to

act, simply bow your head and remain respectfully silent, or follow others' behavior. It is especially Poor Form to begin eating
while Everyone Else is Saying Grace.

- Take Small Bites. Chew thoroughly before swallowing.

- Don't chew with your mouth open. Yuck, yuck, yuck!!! This
  drives the Etiquette Grrls *crazy!!!*

- Don't slurp, either. And this goes for both beverages and
  soups. There is absolutely no reason whatsoever why you are
  unable to consume your Cream of Butternut Squash Soup
  without slurping, Dear Reader! The Etiquette Grrls really
  don't understand why some people, as soon as they sit down
  at the Dinner Table, seem to adopt many of the characteris-
  tics of a Vacuum Cleaner. What's so tricky about eating soup
  silently?

- Don't talk with your mouth full.

- Is there bread? Tear, do *not* cut, it into Small Pieces before consuming. Butter, which is spread on each of these Small Pieces,
  and never on the Entire Slice all at once, should be first placed
  on your Bread Plate (or the side of your Dinner Plate if there
  isn't one) before you spread it on the bread.

- Don't Play with Your Food. It is Not At All Amusing when Small
  Children sculpt their Mashed Potatoes into a model of Mount
  Rushmore, and it is Even Less Amusing when Adults do such
  things.

- Don't push things onto Your Fork avec Your Fingers. If you need
  assistance getting Your Peas to sit tidily upon Your Fork, then
  you may prod them along a bit with Your Knife.

- Hold Your Utensils in A Graceful Manner, not in A Fist, or in
  any Odd Way whatsoever.

- Take care not to scrape your knife/fork/spoon on the plate, as this causes a Wretched Noise, much like that of nails on a chalk-board, and it Sets the Etiquette Grrls' Teeth on Edge.

- Boys, when A Lady arrives at or departs from The Table, you should stand up. This is most important at Formal Meals, but the Etiquette Grrls don't really think it could hurt to Practice at the Family Dinner Table.

- At the end of the meal, don't leave the table until you have been Given Permission. (Or when Your Hostess prepares to Leave the Table, often by suggesting that you Retire to the Drawing Room, or some such.)

THE PROPER PLACE SETTING

Have you ever wondered about Cream Soup Spoons, Dear Reader? No? Well, how about Gumbo Spoons, then? Bonbon Spoons? Five o'Clock Spoons? Asparagus Tongs? Waffle Knives? Olive Forks?? Lemon Forks??? Strawberry Forks???? Well, suppose you Think About It for a while, and then come back, and the Etiquette Grrls will be happy to tell you All About It, Dear Reader. Believe us, the above utensils are Really Keen, and you ought to know about them! In the meantime, allow us to just tell you A Few Things You Need To Know right away, before you Set The Table.

If you're lucky, you've inherited Grandmama's silver, and you have, say, service for twenty-four, and All Sorts of Cunning Pieces like those mentioned above. If you do have Family Silver, and you feel you must Augment the service, there are many places, such as Replacements, Inc., where you can purchase Discontinued Patterns. (And even if your pattern is not discontinued, it's nicer, the Etiquette Grrls think, to acquire Old Pieces rather than new, because Old Pieces often have a pretty patina and a nicer feel than Brand-New ones.) Sometimes silver is monogrammed on the handles; don't worry your pretty little head about things like Mismatched Mono-grams—of course The Silver has been in Your Family for Simply Ages, and so *of course* there are going to be Different Monograms!

The Etiquette Grrls won't tell on you if that Jelly Knife inscribed avec a *B* actually just arrived chez toi via UPS last week! Lastly, if you do have Real Silver, you shouldn't be afraid to use it. Silver is *meant* to be used, and the Etiquette Grrls think it's so tragic to let Pretty Things sit there in the Sideboard, never seeing The Light of Day!

But what if you're moving into Your First Apartment, and Grand-mama isn't prepared to part avec her service from Tiffany's just yet? Rather than making do with shoddy odds and ends, or, horrors, plastic, you should acquire a Small Service of Stainless-Steel Flatware. Many Stainless-Steel services are very high quality and attractive, and if you choose wisely, this service will last forever, and if necessary, can even substitute for Real Silver, should you neither inherit any nor be able to afford your own. (In the Etiquette Grrls' opinion, High-Quality Stainless is far superior to Silver Plate.) You should select a pattern that is Plain and Traditional in appearance; Trendiness is something that is to be avoided always, but especially in something which is intended to last A Lifetime. Avoid handles which are Too Skinny or Too Fat, as they are Uncomfortable to Hold. Although "architect-designed" flatware may be aesthetically pleasing, beautiful even, avoid it. It's a Funny Thing, but those who are good at designing Big and Famous Buildings are Notoriously Bad at designing Small and Practical Things like Forks. Go figure. Stay far, far away from anything which is electroplated avec gold, or which has any sort of Ornate, Gaudy, Baroque Design. Lastly, Your Stainless should be of the best quality that you can afford . . . you don't want to Waste Money on some Flimsy Set which will bend at the Slightest Provocation. (Naturally, you should keep all these things in mind should you be choosing a Silver Pattern as well . . . just because something is Expensive, it doesn't mean it should be Flashy, Dear Reader!) You won't often run into this problem when purchasing Stainless Steel, Dear Reader, but you should know that in Silver, even Standard Utensils come in Two Sizes: Luncheon and Dinner. We feel that it's Much More Useful to first acquire the Luncheon Size, which are somewhat smaller than the Hefty Dinner Size, because you may use them at Any Meal—breakfast, lunch, or dinner—whereas Dinner

Forks/Knives/Spoons are really only appropriate at Dinner. To begin Your Flatware Collection, you should acquire The Following Service For Eight (you can Expand Upon This later):

- 8 Forks
- 8 Salad Forks (may also be used as Dessert Forks)
- 8 Knives
- 8 Soup Spoons
- 8 Teaspoons (but try to get 16 if you can; they're Very Handy, and can also be used for cereal, dessert, grapefruit, etc.)

Some pieces which are Optional, but Very Handy to Have are:

- 8 Butter Knives
- 1 Butter Spreader
- 2 Serving Spoons
- 1 Serving Fork
- 1 Ladle
- 1 Sugar Spoon

In addition to Flatware, you should have a nice set of China, and Your China, like Your Flatware, should be The Best Quality You Can Afford. Here, too, you should avoid anything Gaudy or Trendy. Also, the Etiquette Grrls think that it's safer to stick to patterns which are mainly white or ivory, as they will look attractive in almost every décor, and more important, food will always look nice on them. Those square cobalt-blue-and-yellow plates you saw at the store may be Striking, and Look Great upon the shelf, but ask yourself, Dear Reader: Will they be so pretty with Thanksgiving Dinner or, say, Your Famous Lasagna? Probably not. Also, if you cannot have both Informal and Formal China, then you should select a Pattern which will be

Suitable for Any Occasion—the Plainer the Better, but avoid anything Overly Rustic, as such things are Too Casual to serve as Good China.

You should start off with:

- 8 Dinner Plates (ten-inch diameter)
- 8 Salad/Dessert Plates (eight inch; as with Teaspoons, double this amount if you can, because they're Very Useful, and after all, you may have occasion to serve Eight People salad *and* dessert at One Meal!)
- 8 Bread Plates (four to six inches)
- 8 Soup Plates
- 8 Soup Bowls (also good for cereal, ice cream, etc.)
- 8 Teacups and Saucers
- 1 Sugar Bowl
- 1 Creamer
- 1 Teapot
- 1 Coffeepot (these last four pieces may be either Ceramic or Silver)

You should also acquire some Serving Pieces—several sizes and shapes of Platters, open and/or covered vegetable dishes, and a casserole, for instance. Later on, you should also think about getting Luncheon Plates (nine inch) and Demitasse (after-dinner) Cups and Saucers. (At which point, you will also have to purchase Wee Demitasse Spoons, which are The Most Adorable Things Ever!)

Your Glassware, like Your China and Flatware, ought to be Simple and Tasteful. Even Very Inexpensive Plain Glass is much, *much* more elegant than El Cheapo Glass which is striving to look like Waterford! Here again, Avoid Like the Plague anything with Gold Trim, and you should also steer clear (har, har) from any colored or tinted glass, as any beverage which is not clear will look Utterly Putrid in it. You will need:

- 8 Highballs (tall and skinny)
- 8 Old-fashioneds (short and fat)
- 8 Wine Glasses

Other things which are Nice to Have are:

- Water Goblets (because at Formal Dinners you will want to have water *and* wine at each Place Setting)
- Champagne Flutes
- Juice Glasses
- Martini Glasses (because they're Pretty)

Now that you have all the Accoutrements to have a nice little Dinner Party, Dear Reader, you may well be asking how you Set The Table. It's actually Quite Simple, and the Etiquette Grrls are sure that you'll Get The Hang of it in No Time! First of all, you never, ever use Placemats at a Formal Dinner. The Etiquette Grrls have seen Many Cute Placemats in their time, but these should be relegated to the Most Casual of Tables. Likewise, do not use Napkin Rings—which, incidentally, are only to be used with Cloth Napkins, which are reused for several meals before they are washed, never with Paper Napkins! In either case, napkins should be folded into tidy triangles or rectangles, and placed to the left of the plate. Never, ever Stuff A Napkin into a Water Glass or practice your Origami on it!!

Now that you have a nice, bare table and your napkins folded properly, Dear Reader, you may move on to The Flatware. This is placed to either side of the plate—forks on the left, and knives and spoons to the right. You only put out utensils for courses which will actually be served. For instance, if there will not be a Soup Course, then you would not put out any Soup Spoons. The Etiquette Grrls think this seems Rather Obvious, especially given that if they put out *all* of Their Silver for each meal, then there would be Hardly Any Room on the table at all! You place the utensils for each course from the outside working in toward the plate. For instance, you might have, looking from left to right, the Salad Fork, the Regular (dinner/luncheon) Fork, the Plate, the Knife (blade turned toward the Plate, please), and then the Soup Spoon. The Dessert Fork and Spoon are placed horizontally above the plate, with the fork closest to the plate, with its tines pointing to the right, and the spoon above it, its bowl pointing to the left. (After dinner, you will bring out another spoon—tea or demitasse—with the Coffee, so that people may Stir It without using the same spoon they will use to eat their Chocolate Mousse.) The Water Glass or Goblet is placed directly above the Knife, and the Wine Glass, if there is one, is a little bit to the lower right of this. The Bread Plate is placed above the Forks, with the Butter Knife placed horizontally across it, blade pointing downward (toward you), and handle pointing to the right. Got all that, Dear Reader? Whew, even the Etiquette Grrls are getting a Wee Bit Confused! Please refer to the Diagram the Etiquette Grrls have drawn for you (below), and maybe it'll help Clear Things Up.

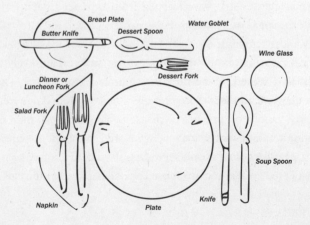

Anatomy of a Place Setting

ARE HOT HORS D'OEUVRES A HERESY?: PARTY FOOD

At any sort of party, you should serve food—which should be something more Imaginative and Filling than a bowl of potato chips. However, any foods served should be in easy-to-manage, bite-sized portions, and should not require the use of a knife and fork. You may offer only savory items, or you may have a mix of sweet and savory. The Etiquette Grrls have found the following items to be popular with everyone at parties, and all are easy to make:

- Stuffed Mushrooms

- Small Finger Sandwiches

- Small Cream-Puff Shells filled with chicken, tuna, or salmon salad

- Brie (or other high-quality cheese), served with a Variety of Fresh Fruit (like grapes or strawberries) and Good-Quality Crackers (the Etiquette Grrls are Rather Fond of Carr's Water Crackers)

- Artichoke Dip

The Etiquette Grrls have learned from experience that for parties held in the Heat of Summer, it is perhaps best to stick to cold hors d'oeuvres. Attempting to make hot hors d'oeuvres will make your kitchen Uncomfortably Warm and Steamy, and you are likely to look Flushed and Wilted by the time your guests arrive. When it is above ninety degrees, hot hors d'oeuvres are a heresy. Hors d'oeuvres made with any variety of processed cheese, bologna, those mini-hot-dog things, or anything that is artificially flavored should be Avoided At All Costs. Regardless of what you serve, you should, of course, have a large supply of small plates and attractive cocktail napkins within easy reach.

YOUR BAR

Your Bar should be well stocked with the best quality you can afford of all the major varieties of liquor (at minimum, Gin, Vodka, Rum,

Scotch, Vermouth, Red and White Wine, and Bottled Beer; other liquors such as Bailey's or Grand Marnier are nice extras but cannot stand in for the Gin) and Mixers. You should also have plenty of ice on hand. (If we wanted drinks served without ice, we'd all move to England.) It is also imperative that you have all the necessary glasses (old-fashioned, highball, cocktail, pilsner, and red and white wine). And we cannot emphasize enough that they should, in fact, be glass. Paper and plastic cups are only appropriate for Frat Parties, and perhaps Informal Picnics. (And even then, only for soda. Alcoholic beverages always deserve to be served in Real Glasses.) You should also familiarize yourself with the ingredients of common Mixed Drinks and keep a bartending guide handy for reference.

WHOM TO INVITE
Your Guest List should consist of a variety of people, but try to ensure that all invited will get along. Should a fist-fight occur at your soirée, it will put Quite A Damper on the festivities. However, we assume that all of your friends and acquaintances are as well-bred as you, and no such behavior is likely to occur. It is particularly nasty of you to invite Potentially Explosive Former Couples, especially if you intend for them to serve as Party Entertainment. Also, you should try, if you can, to invite a fairly even mix of Boys and Girls. While there's certainly nothing at all wrong with Having The Girls (or Boys) Over (nay, the Etiquette Grrls are All For such evenings), if you invite nine Girls and only one Boy to your wee soirée, or vice versa, the Odd One Out is liable to feel un peu overwhelmed, and it is, of course, THOR to make any of Your Guests feel uncomfortable. Likewise, if you plan to have a sit-down dinner party, it is always best to invite an Even Number of people. First of all, having a lopsided table is Terribly Unpleasing, aesthetically speaking, and also some Poor Soul is bound to feel as if he's been seated out in Left Field. This is especially true if you are adhering to Strict Formal Dinner Party Protocol and "turn the table," which requires The Hostess to spend the first half of the meal conversing with the gen-

tleman on her right, and the second with the one on her left. Guests should watch The Hostess and follow suit, and if you have an odd number of guests, someone will obviously be left Extremely Lonesome. That said, however, the Etiquette Grrls feel that it is nice to converse freely with *all* dinner guests, as long as they are seated within earshot.

SMOKE, SMOKE, SMOKE THAT CIGARETTE

If you are unsure as to whether you are allowed to smoke at a party, you should wait until your host has given you Express Permission before Lighting Up. However, if you are the host, we think that you ought to allow smoking at your party. After all, many people feel that drinking and smoking go hand-in-hand, and if they are not permitted to smoke, they are unlikely to stay at your party for a very long time. They are also likely to grow fidgety, restless, and cranky. Many smokers are clever, witty people with Dryly Ironic senses of humor, and they will be a good addition to any party. It would be a shame to ostracize them. Place many ashtrays around your apartment to discourage the extinguishing of Burning Materials in potted plants, empty vases, carpeting, etc. Should you find yourself a nonsmoking guest at a party where there are smokers, you should keep your views on smoking to yourself. It is particularly Bad Form to screech at your hostess, "Ohmigod! *SMOKE!!!* I can't *bear it!!!!*" while making unattractive gagging sounds. Nor should you start spouting statistics about the many Adverse Effects of Smoking or the Evils of the Tobacco Industry to everyone holding a cigarette. They undoubtedly are already aware of these facts, and they don't care. You will only annoy them, and it is unwise to anger anyone who is holding anything that is On Fire. You should realize that in any gathering of Young People, whether it be at a bar or a private party, there undoubtedly will be smokers. If you really feel strongly that smoking is wrong, then you should throw your own party, and you may then certainly send the smoking guests out onto the balcony to smoke, and of course they may not complain, no matter how frigid the temperature may be.

Smokers should turn to page 191 for advice on how to light up politely and with style.

MISS OTIS REGRETS: INVITATIONS AND R.S.V.P.-ING

If you choose to send out Written Invitations for your party, you should be sure to include the obvious . . . the date, the time, the location, and the kind of party that it is. There is nothing More Embarrassing for a guest than to arrive at your party in Informal Dress, only to find everyone else Dressed to the Nines.

R.S.V.P. is an acronym for *répondez s'il vous plaît,* which is French for "Tell Me If You Plan to Attend My Party So That I Know How Many Batches of Artichoke Dip to Make." Should you receive an invitation with the letters R.S.V.P. written in the lower-left corner, you must immediately apprise your future host or hostess of your plans to attend. Should you fail to do so, you might well find yourself at a party where there is a Serious Shortage of Liquor, which will make no one happy. You should, of course, also send Your Regrets if you are unable to attend, but we assume that your friends, like ours, throw such Excellent Parties that you wouldn't dream of missing one.

WHAT YOU SHOULD WEAR TO A SOIRÉE

It saddens the Etiquette Grrls that so many of their peers feel that it is acceptable to arrive at a party in jeans, tennis shoes, a dirty old college sweatshirt, and the ubiquitous (and dreadful) baseball cap. Not only is this attire unflattering, unstylish, and most unimaginative, it implies that you care so little about the Great Pains that Your Hostess has gone to in order to provide you with an abundance of Delicious Food, Expensive Liquor, and Constant Entertainment that you did not even feel the need to bathe and change clothes before arriving at her doorstep. And this, need we even say, is Terribly Rude.

The Etiquette Grrls remind their Dear Readers that one is almost never overdressed. It vexes us that we live in such an Informal Era, and we long for the bygone glamorous days when everyone Dressed for Dinner. We realize that most Young People don't have the sort of wardrobe to support this sort of lifestyle in our minimalist day and age, but one can still make an effort to look elegant and put-together for parties. Please, *please,* Dear Reader, save the jeans and the khakis for your weekly Trip to the Grocery Store! For Special Occasions or Holidays, you may (and indeed, should) pull out all the stops and Dress to the Nines, naturally. We remind our readers who might hesitate at the thought of getting dressed up out of fear of embarrassment at being the only one at the party attired in such a manner, that if other people are ignorant of how they should dress, it is their problem, not yours. You should set a Good Example for the Poor Dears.

THE WEEKEND GUEST

Having houseguests for a weekend can be a practically hallucinogenic lot of fun, if one uses just a bit of Common Sense. Both host and guest ought to be on their Best Behavior, and if both are thoughtful and considerate, a good time will be had by all.

Before your guests arrive, you should make sure that your place of residence is clean and tidy, and that you have fresh towels and sheets ready for your company. Coordinating sets are a pleasant touch. It is also nice to provide them with two pillows. The Etiquette Grrls cannot tell you, Dear Reader, how many times they have arrived at their friends' summer cottages only to be forced to go in search of a linen closet containing towels and sheets in the Dead of Night. We never were able to locate any pillows. Rest assured, Dear Reader, that the Etiquette Grrls did not darken any of these doorways again!

You should also make sure that the fridge and the pantry are well stocked with a variety of food products, including snack food. Your guests are on holiday, and everyone knows that when one is on holiday, eating Vast Amounts of "junk" food is Perfectly Acceptable. You should offer your guests a meal or snack every couple of hours or so. You should also have a variety of breakfast foods on hand, even if you are not generally in the habit of taking this meal. Merely offering your guest a small bowl of Rice Krispies (with skim milk) for the morning meal will not suffice. If you are not one to get up at the

Crack of Dawn to start baking Tasty Breakfast Pastries, prior to your guests' arrival you should visit the best bakery in your area and purchase some tempting breakfast and brunch items. We especially approve of brioche, croissants, muffins, doughnuts, coffee cakes, delicious raisin bread, and the like. You should also familiarize yourself with the art of making Light and Fluffy Scrambled Eggs, and perhaps of mixing up some Mimosas or Bloody Marys. Also, should you have leftover hors d'oeuvres from a cocktail party that you gave in honor of your houseguests during their stay, keep in mind that these Tasty Tidbits can make quite a delicious and filling brunch. And, of course, it goes without saying that you should always have a bountiful supply of good-quality, freshly-brewed coffee at hand.

When you have houseguests, you should not, under any circumstances, force them to partake in activities that they will not enjoy. If they easily get seasick, or have an Irrational Fear of Water, for example, you should not force them to go sailing, insisting that they'll "like it once they're out there." Should, God forbid, your guests become ill or overtired while visiting you, you should allow them to sit quietly on the Verandah and read magazines, and not drag them kicking and screaming to the tennis court to "hit the ball around" for hours on end.

The houseguest's responsibilities are to be good-tempered, easygoing, and friendly toward any member of the family or other guests who are also in residence. Upon your arrival, you should present your host or hostess with a small gift. If you cannot think of an item which your host would particularly like, then a box of chocolates (preferably from La Maison du Chocolat, or, at least, Godiva) is Always Appropriate. (For more information on How to Be a Good Houseguest, please see pages 159–161.)

THE WELL-STOCKED PANTRY

We all have our Culinary Foibles, even the Etiquette Grrls. However, the Etiquette Grrls think that their particular foibles are indicative of their Proper Upbringings, and, therefore, have chosen to embrace, nay, Publicly Proclaim them. We encourage you to adopt our preferences as a matter of course and abandon your own silly preoccupation with brown rice, which the Etiquette Grrls know that in your Heart of Hearts you understand is, if not downright vile, at least bland, chewy, and Completely Uninteresting.

Many Girls of our generation appear to subsist entirely on yogurt, iceberg lettuce, and bottled water. This is quite impolite, as it connotes that they do not have The Proper Appreciation for Really Good Food that all of us who were not raised by wolves or on ashrams have. Yogurt is a slimy substance that is, to the best of the Etiquette Grrls' knowledge, a Revolting Mix of sour milk and bacteria enhanced with a Flashy Marketing Campaign. The Etiquette Grrls know better than to consume such things. Iceberg lettuce, similarly, has no flavor whatsoever, is frequently not even cleaned very well, and the Etiquette Grrls know that no one really likes it at all, despite their protestations. Those who grow iceberg lettuce for our Supermarket Chains could certainly switch to Boston lettuce, red leaf lettuce, or adorable and pricey mesclun, and we would all thank them. Finally, bottled water is not a food at all. The Etiquette Grrls get entirely enough water in the tonic water they consume, which, unlike Evian, also offers protection from Malaria. The slightly dehydrating effects of the Gin mixed with the tonic water are, obviously, offset by the Healthful Properties of Quinine. Bottled water is also not a Fashion Accessory and should not be toted around as one would tote a fuzzy handbag. Well-bred people can sit through an hour-long lecture on Keats' Aesthetic Vision without dying of thirst, and, if they should find themselves at this lecture at an Ungodly Hour like 8 A.M., would derive more benefit from a Good Cup of Coffee.

However, once one has ventured into the Brave New World of foods beyond yogurt, lettuce, and water, how does one choose from the Dizzying Array on display at your local supermarket? Fear not; the Etiquette Grrls will lead you through the aisles held firmly by the hand.

Certain foods are best avoided. For instance, the Etiquette Grrls are especially suspicious of the minuscule dehydrated marshmallows which are often found in packaged hot chocolate mix. If the Etiquette Grrls wanted small bites of pumice floating in their beverages, we would collect some pumice the next time we find ourselves near the Ring of Fire. There is no need, ever, to make your own labor-intensive versions of such perfectly good packaged foods as Triscuits, hard candy, chewing gum, fruit leather, sun-dried tomatoes, peanut butter, deviled ham, etc. To do so does not mean you are any sort of Gourmet Chef, but rather that you simply Have Too Much Time on Your Hands.

The Etiquette Grrls think that people allow Saltines to run around in far too many foods where they obviously do not belong. Saltines, indeed any cracker, are meant to be used as a base for Good Cheese, and should never, never find themselves inappropriately included in omelettes, cakes, puddings, on top of macaroni and cheese, or accompanying any sort of vegetable side dish. Cornflakes, similarly, are only eaten with milk at breakfast, and are not intended to be part of any sort of breaded coating (which should, as the name suggests, be made from bread crumbs), etc.

We also remind you that grits are not a real food. Should you have a sudden craving for a bland, white, rather tasteless mush, then it is clearly time to prepare a bowl of Cream of Wheat.

Maple syrup is a wonderful food which the Etiquette Grrls particularly enjoy, and you should enjoy it, too. However, you must remember that what is marketed as "pancake syrup" is not maple syrup, just Brownish Sticky Stuff, and should never, ever be purchased by a well-bred person. If you are served this pseudo–maple syrup in a restaurant, the Etiquette Grrls give you permission to Complain to the Manager. What you must have on hand at all times for the Impromptu Pancake Breakfast chez toi is "Grade-A Vermont Maple Syrup," either dark or light amber, depending upon your personal preference. "Reduced-calorie maple syrup" is vile and is not permissible. Similarly, you should cultivate a taste for maple sugar candy, which is one of the Etiquette Grrls' favorite Autumnal Foods. Like all True New Englanders, the Etiquette Grrls think this substance is fabulous, and particularly enjoy how it is frequently molded into Cunning Little Maple Leaves and Wee Pilgrims.

We also wish to remind you that none of us, even those living in, say, places like the Wilds of Montana, are Pioneers on the Frontier, and these days we all have access to a wide variety of fresh, or, in the worst-case scenario, frozen, fruits and vegetables. Therefore, we feel there is absolutely no call whatsoever to purchase any sort of tinned fruit or vegetable. The only exception to this is in the instance where the item may not be easily prepared by oneself, such as baked beans, tomato paste, or artichoke hearts. There is never, ever any excuse to purchase, let alone consume, any variety of tinned green vegetable, such as peas or haricots verts.

Also, even in their fresh incarnations, some vegetables are Simply Vile and should never be purchased. We particularly dislike vegetables which tend toward the mushy, slimy, stringy, or licorice-flavored, such as collard greens, okra, fennel, and celeriac. We're also not too fond of sweet potatoes, due in no small part to the frequency with which they are served with a marshmallow topping. We strongly feel that vegetables are vegetables, and artificial sweet things are artificial sweet things, and the two should not intermingle.

The Etiquette Grrls are also Rather Suspicious of any sort of liquid that can be purchased in powdered form. We understand that such items might be useful for people such as Astronauts, who must conserve space and weight in their pantries, but we don't understand why the rest of us need to purchase powdered alfredo sauce for our fettuccini when we have ready access to fresh cream, butter, Parmesan, etc.

There are some foodstuffs which you should always have on hand, even if you do not particularly enjoy them yourself. Unless you are a True Hermit in the Sense of Arthurian Legend, you may have guests in your home to whom you should offer food. One should have coffee, tea, and the ingredients for ice water. Cream (for coffee) or milk (for tea—one does not put cream in tea) are nice additions; one should also have sugar. If you take your coffee black, you should still have on hand a wee box of Parmelat milk to offer your guests. The Etiquette Grrls think that even if one does not do much Cooking From Scratch, one can stock a Decent Pantry with snack foods and a variety of condiments which, in a pinch, can augment or substitute for a Real Meal. Imported Parmesan cheese, various fruit jams, good mustard, peppercorns in a mill, good-quality olive oil, and balsamic vinegar are all particular favorites of the Etiquette Grrls because they are flavorful and, frequently, pretty.

The Etiquette Grrls believe you are always better off buying the best-quality traditional foods you can find and avoiding anything which reeks of the trailer trashy (e.g., corn dogs), or on the other end of the spectrum, the nouveau (e.g., wasabi-encrusted lemongrass kebabs). Also, sometimes it's best to Send Out for dinner, especially if you have a hankering for something which might be tricky to make yourself. Are you a Trained Sushi Chef? The Etiquette Grrls don't think so, and we don't think things such as Raw Fish should be Left In Your Hands. Giving tapeworms and parasites to others is Terribly Rude.

How can you tell, Dear Reader, if a food is likely to be enjoyed by everyone? The Etiquette Grrls know that everyone enjoys those foods with a high ratio of butter, eggs, chocolate, or cream to their other ingredients. We recommend Walker's Shortbread, which is mostly butter, and can also be found with diminutive chocolate chips. Everyone who is worth knowing loves Walker's Shortbread. Also, high-quality ice cream, such as Häagen-Dazs, is superb. Almost anything that tastes good on its own tastes even better wrapped in puff pastry, which increases the amount of butter it contains. Artichoke Dip, for example, is a top-notch food in its own right, but when it forms the filling for small puff-pastry turnovers, it is really Too Clever By Half.

The Etiquette Grrls' Recipe for Delicious Artichoke Dip

1 can Artichoke Hearts. Not the marinated kind, the other ones.

Enough mayonnaise. (The Etiquette Grrls are partial to Hellmann's—
    the Regular, Full-Fat Kind.)

Fresh lemon juice.

2–3 cloves garlic, minced.

Lots of imported Parmesan cheese, grated.

Blend everything in a Cuisinart, or cut it all up and mix it by hand. (The Artichoke Hearts can be mashed up with the back of a fork.) Spread it in a casserole dish and bake at around 375°F until the top is golden and the dip is bubbly.

Serve hot with fresh, crusty bread or Carr's crackers.

CHAPTER TWO

Out and About

At the Bar

The Etiquette Grrls adore ending a Difficult Week (or even a week-day) by going out and Knocking Back a Few. We love Swanky Bars, and we even love some Divey Bars—not the kind where Scary Biker Gangs are likely to be habitués, but the kind where there's Elvis on the jukebox and the drinks are Strong and Cheap. However, we've noticed that even at Our Favorite Bars, there's almost always a Drunken Slob who ruins it all. Let's have a Moment of Flashback. All the Etiquette Grrls remember about the ridiculous sex-and-sub-stance-education class at Prep School is that "alcohol is a disinhibi-tant." Well, perhaps we also remember the Dean of Students squirting contraceptive foam into someone's Diet Coke can, but really, we've repressed most of this. At any rate, it is a Scientific Fact that drinking makes you silly, or rowdy, or talkative. However, this is still *NO EXCUSE* to be Rude! For instance, should you happen to knock over a Girl's full G&T as you carelessly reach behind a sofa for your coat, you *must* send over a Fresh Drink to her (and preferably one to all in her party). You may *not,* under *any* circumstances, offer her your half-empty, warm, *vile* bottle of Rolling Rock. (As an aside, the Etiquette Grrls are happy to report that perhaps the Goodness of

Barflies Everywhere is not an entirely lost cause. The above incident did, in fact, happen to the Etiquette Grrls, and we were Absolutely Outraged. However, a Delightfully Polite Boy witnessed the event, and was so outraged himself that *he* sent over a New Round of Drinks to the Etiquette Grrls. And did not feel that this Good Deed was then license to Bother Us. The Etiquette Grrls at this very moment are Raising Their Glasses to that Young Gentleman!)

Let's also have a Moment of Presumption, in which the Etiquette Grrls assume you understand basic principles of safety: i.e., do not believe the Boy at the bar who tells you the little capsules he's dropping in your drink are just "fizzy vitamins." The evening news and most women's magazines can make you Suitably Paranoid about all manner of Frightening People and Situations and educate you about how to extricate yourself from them. Dear Reader, we value your safety and well-being, but we're crediting your intelligence when we say that the Etiquette Grrls are not qualified (or for that matter, inclined) to give you a crash course in Self-defense for Women. We are not the Karate Grrls, or the Take Back the Night Grrls. We do, however, give you our permission to Raise Hell if you are honestly scared.

But back to business. Below we outline some Rules of the Road for first, choosing The Bar at Which You Should Become a Regular (and more importantly, those at Which You Should Not); second, how you should behave once you get there; and third, how to get rid of Undesirable Sorts.

ARE YOU IN THE RIGHT BAR?

It's wonderful to have a Neighborhood Bar with Strong Drinks, Good Music, and a Pleasant Crowd—but should you find yourself in a strange locale, how can you tell if the bar which beckons so appealingly from across the street is an appropriate place to have five or so Martinis? Hint: If you notice any of the following, consider yourself warned:

- *Sign:* Mall hair, an overabundance of fringed clothing, women in tight jeans and white pumps. *Meaning:* You have either thwarted the space-time continuum and are inexplicably in 1984, or, more likely, you are not in the sort of bar that will be able to serve you a French 75. Keep walking, unless you're *really* in a mood to go slumming.

- *Sign:* Recognizable athletes. *Meaning:* A riot will soon ensue.

- *Sign:* There's a brisk market in glowing necklaces outside and/or there are mimes. *Meaning:* You're either in Disneyland or East Berlin. Neither is an Ideal Place to Get Plastered.

- *Sign:* A black banner outside reads "Miss Goth Pittsburgh! Finals TONITE!" *Meaning:* This is both the Wrong Place and the Wrong Time.

- *Sign:* A preponderance of sorority sweatshirts with the snazzy little floral Greek letters. *Meaning:* You're in luck, if you're a minor.

You should also Keep Your Distance from any bar that advertises on the radio, has special "Promotion Nights" for various brands of cheap beer or tequila (or, horror of horrors, "Tequiza"), purports to be a "Beach Bar" (especially if it's in a land-locked city like Omaha), has an open deck (especially one that's open well into Autumn, with the help of Heat Lamps), or has Theme Nights—especially Theme Nights which require that you come in Costume when it's not Halloween.

Ideally, The Perfect Bar is within walking distance of your apartment (and those of your friends). While there are, undoubtedly, potential hazards of stumbling home after Last Call (particularly if you are a Girl wearing very tricky shoes or if a small Ice Storm has come and gone while you've been Hoisting the Demon Drink), and while stumbling home drunk can make one look somewhat less than one's usual, poised self, the Etiquette Grrls heartily endorse this way of capping your evening. We quite genially forgive packs of glazen-eyed boozers when they make spectacles of themselves in the street, because, let's admit it, public drunkenness is somewhat amusing, and, more seriously, because at least they're not driving. Should you not be so fortunate as to live around the corner from your favorite *boîte de nuit*, you must select one of your crowd to stay sober and drive the rest of you home. Being the Designated Driver is never as much fun as getting Sloppy Drunk, so everyone should be *extremely* conciliatory to the person who's agreed to drive. Under no circum-stances should the driver have to buy his or her own soft drinks! Fur-thermore, if you frequently go out with the same group of friends, you must take turns driving. Even if you do not own a car, you should still offer to drive (assuming, of course, that you have a license). Not to do so is Quite Rude and will likely result in your friend with the Convenient Car finding a new group of drinking bud-dies, leaving you Lonely and Sober. And the Etiquette Grrls don't want *anyone* to be Lonely and Sober. Heavens, no.

DRINKING GAMES

The Etiquette Grrls are a bit puzzled at the popularity of drinking games. We have never needed props, elaborate rituals, small tests of memory, etc., to encourage us to Drink Up. However, if it is *de rigueur* in your circle to engage in such diversions, you must remem-ber that it is Quite Rude to take the competition seriously. One of the Etiquette Grrls was mildly amused when a group of her supposedly intellectual graduate-student colleagues spent an evening playing the Celebrity Initials game—yet her amusement turned to shock when she realized several participants were nearing blows over whether "Q-Bert" qualified as an acceptable celebrity. (Blows actually were reached over whether "Q-Bert" should be treated as one word or two, but by that time she had hastily repaired to the kitchen to assist her hostess in setting out fresh hors d'oeuvres.) The Etiquette Grrls firmly believe that drinking is *intrinsically* an Entertaining Activity, and we encourage you to enjoy it sans Distracting Games. Furthermore, if your drinking is taking place in a bar, games should not take place. This is just juvenile, and accordingly, if you don't want to invite the whole class to your party, you can't have a party at all. No drinking games in public unless the Scary Bikers at the end of the bar can join you. Basically, you must conduct yourself at all times as if you were Comfortably Ensconced at the Café Carlyle. Would you play Blow Pong there? No. Then you are not allowed to do so at the Hi-Ho Beer Barrel Tavern, even though you are (clearly) slumming.

IS IT A REAL DRINK?
The Etiquette Grrls are Firm Believers in the Excellence of Traditional Drinks, like Gin and Tonics (G&Ts), Scotch and Sodas, Gin Fizzes, Gimlets, Manhattans, Mint Juleps, Tom Collinses, Screwdrivers, and the like. That is to say, if a drink was "invented" anytime in the last sixty years or so, chances are it is not An Appropriate Drink. You should not drink anything that sounds either "cute" or frightening. For instance, you may not drink anything named after candy (e.g., a Tootsie Roll), anything that may be purchased at a drugstore (e.g., Crest, Dentyne, Windex), or, indeed, drugs (e.g., Liquid Heroin, a Quaalude). To help you determine what you should and should not be drinking, we've provided you with the following checklist. You're not consuming an Appropriate Beverage if any of the following statements applies:

- Pop Rocks are present in any shape or form.
- The name of the drink mentions one or more Caribbean Islands.
- The "drink" is not, in fact, a liquid.
- It is served in an IV bag suspended from a Wheeled Holder—or in any container other than a glass.
- It contains anything which can be construed as "alive," such as blue-green algae.
- It is blue.

- It is on fire.
- Its main source of alcohol is not Gin, Scotch, Vodka, and/or Bourbon.

Also, we feel we should mention that occasionally even Real Drinks are not necessarily Appropriate Beverages to be drinking at a bar. For instance, no one should go out on a Late-Night Pub Crawl and order Bloody Marys or Mimosas, as these are only consumed at brunch. Should you be Slumming one evening and find yourself at a dingy Dive Bar, don't ask for a Gibson. Unless you're Looking For A Fight.

M IS FOR MARTINI

All right, Kats and Kittens. We're only going to say this once, so listen up, and listen good. The Etiquette Grrls are sick to death of everyone going around calling any sort of beverage that is served in a Martini Glass a "Martini." The Etiquette Grrls can hear F. Scott Fitzgerald (or, as we know him, Scott '17), Cary Grant, and James Bond collectively Turning Over In Their Graves (never mind that James Bond is fictional and Not Dead) at the thought that somebody out there thinks that something called an "Espresso Martini" is a *real* Martini. You want espresso? Go to Starbucks, not Your Local Watering Hole. Just because the Etiquette Grrls drive Volvos, that doesn't make them Swedish, does it? Of course not. Well, Dear Reader, the same goes for drinks. A Martini does not include chocolate, coffee, any variety of juice, curaçao, or anything else that is colored among its ingredients. A Martini is cold, a Martini is clear, a Martini is very, very strong, and a Martini is very, very dry. A Martini consists of Gin, Vermouth, and a couple of Big Damn Olives (green and pitted, please) that have been impaled on a darling glass toothpick. And nothing else. Anything else, and it is not a Martini, it is a cocktail. (Which, might we add, is nothing to be ashamed of. In most cases.) Substitute a cocktail onion for the olives, and it ceases to be a Martini. It is a Gibson. We concede that a Vodka Martini (which is served with a twist of lemon in lieu of the olives) might possibly be a Martini, but we're of the opinion that Vodka Martinis are a little nouveau, and thus you probably shouldn't be drinking one anyway. A Martini is also properly served "up." If you avail yourself of a nifty stainless-steel cocktail shaker, fill it up with lots of ice cubes, and shake everything up in it, your drink will be plenty cold, and you will have no need to have ice cubes floating around *in* your drink, taking up space. Besides, if a Martini is served "on the rocks," you may not serve it in one of those snazzy glasses, which is really the best, if not the only, reason to drink a Martini anyway.

"HAS ANYONE EVER TOLD YOU THAT YOU LOOK JUST LIKE GWYNETH PALTROW?": PICK-UP LINES AND HOW TO AVOID THEM

Good heavens, Dear Reader, the Etiquette Grrls have heard some doozies of Pick-Up Lines in our time. We've noticed that one of the more popular "lines" seems to be approaching a Girl (or a Boy; we suppose perhaps some Dreadful Girls might use this same Tactic) and telling her that she looks just like A Celebrity. If she actually *does* closely resemble say, Grace Kelly, then she's probably so used to hearing it, you're not saying anything novel. And no one likes someone who goes around Stating The Obvious. Otherwise, insisting that the Girl over in the corner looks *exactly* like "the chick from No Doubt" is Utterly Outlandish. Furthermore, you will run the risk of being Highly Insulting by choosing a celebrity to whom no one really wants to be compared. The Etiquette Grrls, for instance, bear no resemblance whatsoever to say, Tori Spelling or Emily Dickinson, and we don't appreciate being informed by Drunken Slobs who can hardly stand on their own two feet that we do. You also should not approach someone and try to guess their Ethnic Background. Again, you could end up being Wildly Insulting to your victim. Furthermore, you should not *argue* with your target about it if they do wind up telling you what their heritage is. After all, they would know best, and in any case, do you really need to know this information? Nor should you amble up to a table and make some inane remark like "So, uh, are you guys grad students? 'Cause you *look* like grad students." You *"look"* like grad students"? Overworked, tired, and run-down? Bitter, Penniless, and Marxist? Great. We want to go out with *you*. Similarly, it is not kind to tell the Etiquette Grrls, or, indeed, anyone, that "You guys would make really good Goth Chicks. You're so, uh, pale."

So what to do, Dear Reader, if some Obnoxious Person is bothering you in a bar? Sometimes it's sort of fun to humor the idiot for a while and then Have a Good Laugh at his expense later. Otherwise, it's best just to ignore the Foolish Chap. The Etiquette Grrls say that when the situation is Simply Hopeless, and the Would-Be Picker-Upper just Isn't Getting The Hint, it's okay to be Icy. Whatever it takes to be able to enjoy your G&T in peace. Should someone undesirable attempt to join you at your table, you may say something along the lines of "If you don't mind, we're having a Private Conversation."

Being a Regular at a particular bar has many advantages, but perhaps the most valuable is the extra options it offers you in your quest to Avoid Riff-Raff. If you spend a great deal of Quality Time at one bar, chances are a Kindly Barkeep will step in to shoo the Riff-Raff away from you (and, of course, you will Tip Accordingly). And, if worst comes to worst, you will probably know the location of the Back Exit, and can slip out unnoticed.

The Etiquette Grrls feel one is always safest dating Within One's Social Circle. Therefore, if you are Awestruck by the Attractive Stranger seated at the Far Side of the Room, we feel your best tactic is to Obtain an Introduction to him or her. This is yet another reason, Dear Reader, to frequent one particular bar where you know a Good Portion of the Crowd. Surely, then, you will know Someone who will know Someone who will know the Attractive Stranger, and after a series of Proper Introductions, you will be able to have a Polite Conversation avec him or her.

WHERE AND WHEN TO PASS OUT, AND WHAT YOU SHOULD WEAR
Okay, kids. This is important. The Etiquette Grrls absolutely, positively *insist* that as long as you are in a Public Place, you attempt to maintain a Sense of Dignity. This means no passing out while still at the bar (even if there's a comfy couch with your name on it), or

worse, on the street. The Etiquette Grrls don't like having to step over prone bodies on their way home after a tough night of Heavy Drinking. After you are in the Safe Confines of Your Own Home, and *only* then, you may get as sloppy as you wish, and pass out on the bathroom floor if you so desire.

If you'll be participating in a night of Binge Drinking, and anticipate getting Un Peu Loaded, you should keep your ensemble comfortable, sleek, and, as always and above all, stylish. You're probably going to be in the same clothes come Noon Tomorrow, so try to wear something that doesn't wrinkle easily, doesn't pick up lint, and will look appropriate for brunch. We think stretch-wool pants or a skirt with a nice fitted tee (and perhaps a little cardigan if it's chilly) are always a safe bet.

At the Movies, Theatre, and Concerts

The Etiquette Grrls adore going to the theatre, to concerts of both the classical and the rock varieties, and even to the movies. But increasingly, we've encountered such flagrant flouting of the Basic Rules of Etiquette at all of these venues that frankly, we'd rather Stay Home. Cell 'phones are ringing! Someone brought snacks wrapped in crinkly cellophane! People are carrying on Full-Fledged Conversations smack in the middle of Act II! The woman behind us feels the need to give everyone within earshot a Running Commentary on the plotline! The guy in the seat over by the wall is hell-bent on making his way to the center aisle right *now*, no matter how many toes he treads upon! Horrors! Oh, Dear Reader, it makes the Etiquette Grrls want to cry out of rage!

KEEPING QUIET
With the exception of *The Rocky Horror Picture Show,* movies are not interactive. (And you can probably guess what the Etiquette Grrls think of *The Rocky Horror Picture Show,* Dear Reader.) You should never attempt to shout things at, or otherwise communicate with, the actors on the screen. They are unable to hear you, and you will

only irritate the other members of the audience, perhaps to the point where you will make yourself vulnerable to a Lynching. In live theatre, it is also unacceptable to attempt to speak to the actors, even though they *can* hear you. Their job is to pretend you are not there. Help them to do this by being as still and quiet as possible.

You also must not attempt to converse with other audience members during a film, concert, or other Theatrical Event. This means at any time when the houselights are lowered, including the previews at a movie theatre. We suggest you save your comments until you are in a location more conducive to talking. Such as your own living room.

WHAT YOU SHOULD WEAR
While informal attire is perfectly acceptable for attending the movies (except for premières, which are Formal Events) and rock concerts, you should take more care with your appearance at theatrical productions or concerts of the nonrock variety. What you wear depends greatly upon the time of day—matinées are more informal than evening performances, and for these, a skirt and sweater or simple day dress are fine for Girls, and a nice coat and tie are acceptable for Boys. You should get more dressed up for an evening performance, however. A Girl might wear a semi-formal dress and high-heeled shoes, and Boys should wear suits.

FOOD AND BEVERAGES
In the theatre, the consumption of food items is not appropriate. The actors are working, and are unable to break for a snack, so it is Quite Rude to eat in front of them, as even if you were to offer them some of your watercress finger sandwiches, they would be unable to accept. Therefore, you must wait until Intermission, when you may go to the lobby and purchase a drink, which will contain cocktail olives, which you may munch upon to quell your hunger. Ideas concerning food and drinks are more relaxed in a movie theatre, and here, you are invited—nay, *expected*—to purchase some Overpriced Snack Items and a drink. However, you should not take this as an invitation to

engage in food fights, either with other audience members, the Projectionist, or the Movie Screen—no matter what you think of the Overrated American Ingenue's horrendous "British" accent. You should also shy away from any foods that are intrinsically noisy (e.g., "Kettle Style" Potato Chips) or packaged in materials that make any sort of irritating rustling sound (e.g., Twizzlers, individually wrapped Caramels, etc.). You should also carefully place any garbage that you accumulate during the movie on the floor by your feet until the film has ended, at which point you should drop it in a trash receptacle on your way out the door. You may not, under any circumstances, have a contest to see who in your party can toss their crumpled-up napkin or blow the paper covering of their straw the farthest.

SITTING STILL

You should not, at either the theatre or the movies, repeatedly get up, leave, and come back, especially if you are not sitting in an aisle seat, as you will consequently force an entire row of people to get up and move for you. This will cause a great deal of shuffling around, shifting of coats, handbags, etc., and in general, be A Great Annoyance. If, however, you are forced to climb over a row of people, you should take great care not to tread on any toes, or to hit anyone in the head with your Kate Spade bag. This is not An Acceptable Method to get people to Move Out Of Your Way.

Also, you should wait until the event is over before you leave. It is very rude to leave a play before the actors have taken their Curtain Call. Also, if you are at the movies, and sitting in the inside of a row, you should not pressure the people on the aisle to leave early if they should want to stay and watch the credits. Nor should you step over them, or throw their coats at them, shouting, "Move it!" On the other hand, should you not care to watch the credits, you should rapidly move into the aisle and out of the way rather than standing in your row, blocking the view of others. Nor should you unexpectedly stop in your tracks in the aisle to have a conversation or to watch the movie credits, as this will undoubtedly cause someone to run into you, and the person behind them into them, and so on, creating the human equivalent of a ten-car pileup on I-95 during Rush Hour.

ROCK CONCERTS

The Etiquette Grrls vociferously regret that many people feel attending a rock concert is license to conduct oneself in a Drunken, Obnoxious Manner. This behavior puzzles us. Are you attempting to emulate Rock Musicians, who are notoriously Rude People? If this is the case, we remind you, Dear Reader, that you are not, in all likelihood, a Rock Musician, at least not a Famous one, in which case you have no business Breaking Guitars, Screaming Obscenities, or Throwing Glass Bottles at people's heads. Naturally, the Etiquette Grrls have issues with even Famous Rock Stars behaving in such a manner, but we will take this up personally with ill-mannered bands, and you need only concern yourself with your own deportment. You especially should not scream obscenities, or throw things, particularly heavy, dangerous things like batteries or Croquet Mallets, at the band who is performing. The Etiquette Grrls remind you that you have paid money to see these people, and if you dislike them so much you feel it is necessary to toss steel-toed Doc Martens at the keyboard player, then we suggest that you might do better to conserve your Hard-Earned Money and stay at home. (Also, this would be a terrible waste of Perfectly Good Doc Martens.) The Etiquette Grrls also do not understand Mosh Pits. We would have thought it perfectly clear that to intentionally bruise or otherwise injure other people is Incredibly Rude. Moreover, if we wanted to be pushed around and trod upon by big, heavy, sweaty, unpleasant people, we could do so on the New York City subway, where we could then proceed to Bergdorf Goodman's and then to a quiet, swanky bar to recuperate.

The Etiquette Grrls also feel that the vast majority of Rock Concerts should be over-twenty-one shows, as we were not especially fond of mingling with teen-agers when we *were* teen-agers, let alone now that we are adults. Also, we have found that at concerts where alcoholic beverages are available for purchase, we, as members of society who are Of Age, are usually forced to corral ourselves in Remote Areas where we are often unable to see or hear the band. Now, the Etiquette Grrls are no experts in Retail Strategy, but we know that a Real Drink costs more than a Soft Drink, and since we are providing the venue with more income than those who are too young to purchase Alcoholic Beverages, we ought to have the better seats. Also, we think that all venues ought to have a Well-Stocked Bar, as we do not care to be forced to drink watery, warm, overpriced beer. Not that we particularly care to drink beer in the first place.

From McDonald's to Tavern on the Green: Dining Out

As much as the Etiquette Grrls adore throwing Wee Dinner Parties for Their Dear Amis, sometimes Venturing Out to a Local Restaurant is a Smashing Good Idea. It provides a Change of Scenery, and not only do you not have to cook, but at a restaurant all guests can get just exactly what they want, and you, personally, don't have to worry about everyone's allergies/dislikes/etc. And sometimes that's Quite a Relief. However, the Etiquette Grrls have noticed that many people have absolutely no idea of how they should behave while dining at a restaurant. They are, perhaps, invited for dinner at a swanky restaurant by Their Boss, or a wealthy Great-Aunt, or a Family Friend. They panic, they freeze; chaos ensues. Well, Dear Reader, the Etiquette Grrls are here to Set You at Ease. There's really nothing to worry about. Herewith, a Brief Guide to Dining Out.

WHERE YOU SHOULD DINE

Of course, we all love going for a Malted and a Cheeseburger and Fries at our favorite local Burger Joint. (The Etiquette Grrls especially like the sort of establishment that has a Vintage Flair—decades worth of initials carved into the tabletop, and those darling wee individual jukeboxes.) However, we feel that everyone should, from time to time, Venture Out and try something a little more interesting and/or elegant. We like restaurants that have excellent food, and that are swanky, but not so swanky that your dinner is likely to turn into a Spectacle (i.e., the sort of place that is trendy for about ten minutes, during which time everyone in Hollywood rushes there to Be Seen). You should avoid Chain Restaurants if you possibly can, as they are usually noisy, sans ambience, and the food is nearly always mediocre at best. However, Dear Reader, remember: As with just about Everything Else, just because a Restaurant is Expensive does not mean that it is Good. Beware, especially, of New Restaurants, no matter how Snazzy they seem—most Restaurants need a bit of time to Work Out the Kinks. If you truly care about having a Pleasant Meal, and not just Being Seen Somewhere, always read a few Trustworthy Reviews of a Restaurant first, or consult Friends Who Have Dined There.

WHAT YOU SHOULD ORDER, AND HOW YOU SHOULD ORDER IT
The Etiquette Grrls would like to remind you, Dear Reader, that when one is dining at A Restaurant, one is not, in fact, dining At Home. This means that you may, and indeed, should, seize the opportunity to order something which you would not be terribly likely to make for yourself at home. For instance, why order Steamed Carrots (at twenty dollars a plate) from a restaurant, when one could treat oneself to something scrumptious, like Chicken Kiev, or even (if you really want vegetables that much) some Garden Vegetable Crêpes? One should regard restaurants as places where one may try dishes which are interesting or complicated, and thus not things which the Novice Cook is likely to attempt to create herself in her tiny apartment kitchenette.

Should you happen to be on some sort of Special Diet, you should try to avoid rambling on about it at the Dinner Table. The Etiquette Grrls think it's fine if you've Gone Macrobiotic, but we remind you that we have not, nor in all likelihood has Anyone Else at the Table, and thus we don't really need, or want, to know why what *we* happen to be dining on does not fit into Your Dietary Limitations. Similarly, one should never attempt to make anyone else at the table feel Guilty about what they have ordered, whether it be dessert, or Red Meat, or

Veal, or what-have-you. It is very, very rude to Ruin Someone Else's Meal.

"Now," you ask, Dear Reader, "how shall I go about ordering this yummy-sounding dinner I've decided upon?" The most important thing, of course, is to be kind and courteous to your waiter or waitress. Nothing looks more ill-bred than being unnecessarily rude to The Help. And if your waiter seems a little harried, well, how would you like to be carrying around all those heavy trays all night? Perhaps he just needs a Kind Word. When your waiter comes to take your order, you should be as clear and concise as possible—"May I please have the Angel Hair with Artichokes and Salmon?" not, "Can I get that pasta thing with the stuff?" You should also avoid, if at all possible, all sorts of odd "special requests" that so alter the nature of the dish you have chosen that it becomes Something Unrecognizable. It's far better to find something else on the menu more to your liking. Also, no matter how the waiter or chef has misinterpreted what you have ordered, you should never, ever screech so loudly at the poor waiter that your dulcet tones carry to every corner of the restaurant. Simply call over the waiter, and in a Quiet Voice explain that you "believe there has been some confusion, as [you] did not order a Porterhouse Steak, but rather, the Cheese Soufflé." The waiter, no doubt, will be Most Apologetic, and bring you the Proper Item, possibly at No Charge.

ADVANCED MATH: SPLITTING THE CHECK AND TIPPING

There are probably few things more amusing than watching the Etiquette Grrls and their Literary and Artistic Cohorts attempting to Divvy Up the Bill and Figure Out the Tip when they're all Out for Lunch. For this reason, we try to always bring a Math Person with us wherever we go. However, should you happen to be Good at Math, and find yourself in charge of Figuring Out the Bill, you should not calculate what everyone owes down to the Last Penny. It is not terribly gracious to proclaim, "Including tip, you owe $14.32, you owe $17.04, and *you*, because *you* had A Drink, owe $25.76." Nor should you split the bill evenly if one person only had an Appetizer and someone else had a Steak. In both of these instances, one should divide the check equitably, but in Round Figures (e.g., "Sally owes about seven dollars, Bob owes thirteen, and Celia owes twelve"). If everyone ordered Similarly Priced Items and/or split several dishes among themselves, it is easiest to simply divide the bill evenly among everyone, and no one should quibble over a nickel or two.

The Etiquette Grrls don't quite understand why everyone finds the concept of Tipping so perplexing. It's really not difficult at all. If the service is excellent, leave 20 percent of your Total Bill. If it's passable, you may leave 15 percent. The Etiquette Grrls have heard people say that if the service is Less Than Spectacular, you shouldn't leave anything at all, or only a few pennies, but truthfully, we've never been that distraught by the service at a restaurant. We try to remember that everyone has a bad day now and again, and while perhaps we're momentarily annoyed if the waitress brings us a Ginger Ale instead of a Coke, we don't really feel the need to begrudge her a couple of dollars. Especially as we know that *we* wouldn't want to spend our evenings waiting on Fussy, Rude, Cheap People!

"THE SERVICE AT THIS PLACE IS LOUSY!":
DEALING WITH SURLY WAITERS

Sometimes, however, Dear Reader, one does get Mistreated while at a restaurant. Maybe the place is Unbearably Chic, and some Snooty Waiter thinks that because you are a Young Person, you don't deserve to be there, or you won't be able to pay the bill. This is, of course, Utter Rubbish, and you needn't stand for it. You should not Create a Scene, however, as this is always THOR. You should, instead, cheerily attempt to Kill Him With Kindness, which will (one hopes) make him feel Incredibly Guilty, and he'll Shape Up. Or, perhaps your waitress is un peu AWOL. If you've been sitting at your table for forty-five minutes, and seen nary a breadbasket nor a glass of water, you have the Etiquette Grrls' permission to get up and leave, and have a Quiet Word with the Management on the way out.

CHAPTER THREE

Your Personal Appearance

Good Grooming

Oh, Dear Reader, do the Etiquette Grrls have a mouthful to say on this topic! It is Simply Criminal that so many slovenly, smelly, gum-snapping, two-inch-long-artificial-nailed Misguided People wearing mendhi, purple lipliner, and/or a full-body coating of glitter are allowed to Walk the Streets. Forgive us if you're already taking exemplary care of your skin, applying discreet and flattering makeup, dressing well, and bathing regularly. The Etiquette Grrls commend you! However, the rest of you, listen up. These are the ultimate Things You Need To Be Told.

BASIC CLEANLINESS

First, one must wash. Every single day, preferably twice a day; and it is absolutely mandatory that one wash after any sort of sweat-engendering activity. There is a plenitude of lovely, expensive, pretty soaps, many of which smell divine, and you should use them. Frequently. Furthermore, everyone is required to use deodorant. *Especially* anyone in the same Time Zone as the Etiquette Grrls. Perfume or cologne does not replicate the function of deodorant. In fact, Kats and Kittens, the combination of the rank smell of sweat mixed with the trenchant aroma of drugstore cologne is a vile, vile thing. Take a whiff the next time you are a passenger on a commuter train, and you'll understand why the Etiquette Grrls sometimes think they would do well to carry wee pomanders around with them.

The Etiquette Grrls thank their lucky stars for their clear, smooth, nearly translucent complexions! While we realize that some people are not quite as blessed with Good Genes, we remind you that this is what Dermatologists are for. It doesn't matter what the problem is; the Dermatologist can help. Make an appointment immediately. It is very important to attain good skin so that one can use Fun Makeup to its best advantage. After all, Dear Reader, it's no fun to spend hours having to blend The Perfect Shade of Concealer to cover that pulsing boil on your forehead, is it? It's much, much more fun to play with sparkly eye shadow, and you should make this your goal.

Teeth must also be clean, and, preferably, white and straight. However, they should not be so white that they appear to be made out of Bathroom Porcelain. If your smile approaches the wattage of any of the stars of *90210*, you should cut back on the Eterna-White. Nowadays, there is no excuse whatsoever for Truly Hideous Teeth. Braces are readily available and provide those who wear them with Something to Complain About. Indeed, many Teen-age Friendships involve bonding over the trials of wearing unattractive wire on one's teeth. However, when one gets braces, one gets either the run-of-the-mill silver ones or the new-fangled clear ones. Technicolor braces frighten the Etiquette Grrls. Also, it is not permissible to festoon your teeth with gold caps. Are you a Pirate? The Etiquette Grrls don't think so.

Nothing screams, "Unkempt and Lazy!" like dirt under one's nails. You should keep your nails as clean as possible. If you are not wearing nail polish (and why aren't you, unless you are a Boy?), you should get one of those white pencils to make the edges of your nails look even cleaner. However, the Etiquette Grrls want to make absolutely clear that you should keep your nails *short,* and you should never, *ever* have scary, claw-like fake nails applied. This is especially true if you are a Cashier, a Pianist, or an Obstetrician. Trim your nails at home, in private, with a clipper or scissors (we do not bite nails off or, worse, tear them—this makes the Etiquette Grrls cringe) and *throw the clippings away.* Do not leave them on your cocktail table for your guests to admire. This is disgusting.

Hair must also be kept very clean and snarl-free. Whatever your God-given hair type, you must simply Accept It and Take It From There. The Etiquette Grrls find it so very sad that Girls devote so much time and money over Why Their Hair Is Too Straight or Why Their Hair Is Too Curly. Hair color, of course, can be changed, but we think this must be done with great care. Unless you are a Trained Beautician, it's probably not a keen idea to color your hair at home— particularly if you are attempting anything like Highlights. Further- more, home hair coloring is a time-consuming, smelly, messy process which will undoubtedly end in Your Best Towels becoming spotted with "Sunny Moonlight Copper" or whatever you're using.

Your Hair is not an Art Project. You do not need to have a Wee Army of barrettes in your hair at any single time, ever. You do not need more than one (1) ponytail or braid, unless you are dressing up as Pippi Longstocking for Halloween. You should not attempt to cre- ate a Wee Replica of the New Getty Museum on top of your head using a pound of gel—if you fancy yourself An Architect, the Eti- quette Grrls humbly suggest you acquire Formal Training.

Cosmetics: Use and Abuse

The Etiquette Grrls simply *adore* makeup, Dear Reader! Nothing cheers us up when we're suffering from A Serious Case of Ennui like popping into the nearest Sephora and buying a pretty and/or quirky new Urban Decay lipstick! However, the Wide World of Cosmetics is a confusing, and often chaotic one, and as with Most Things, one must proceed avec A Great Deal of Caution. Thus, the Etiquette Grrls have Set Forth to delineate Some Simple Guidelines for you to follow, Dear Reader.

WHAT LOOKS GOOD ON EVERYONE

During the day, you may wear a bit of foundation to cover wee flaws in your complexion. Obviously, this foundation should match your Actual Skin Tone. No matter how much you fancy yourself a Bronzed Goddess, if your natural hue is Ghostly White, "Golden Tahitian Tan" base is not going to Accomplish a Miracle. Furthermore, the effect will be somewhat lessened by the comparative pallor of your neck, hands, etc. The Etiquette Grrls recommend shopping for foundation in a department store with good light.

Most Girls also look good with a touch of mascara—black or brown, please, never, *ever* Electric Blue. Blue mascara is only about fifteen years out of date, so steer clear. Also, be sure not to glom the mascara on so as to make thick, scary, gloppy spikes of your lashes. If it requires effort to blink, you are wearing Too Much Mascara. Use one of those Minuscule Combs to separate your eyelashes—however, be very careful to avoid Poking Your Eye Out. The less-steady-of-hand should simply go lightly with the mascara.

It's extremely important to have Nice Eyebrows, and you should make every effort to achieve a pretty brow line. Use a Brow Brush as part of your Regular Makeup Routine. Also, stray hairs should be removed, and yes, you should have two (2) distinct eyebrows with a space between them. Even Brooke Shields does not actually have Brooke Shields Eyebrows anymore, and this is a very good thing. Be very, very choosy, however, in allowing an Aesthetician to wax or tweeze your brows. You may end up with a very bizarre Dietrich look, which, while retro, is rather difficult to Carry Off at 8:30 A.M. when you're wearing a Conservative Suit.

For day, you may apply some lipstick or lipgloss in a shade that suits your coloring. If one does not have A Steady Hand, one should probably stick to light, transparent lipglosses in order to avoid the Robert Smith look. (Which, the Etiquette Grrls admit, is Quite Adorable on Robert Smith, whose mopey Cure lyrics carried the Etiquette Grrls through many a Dark Day in Prep School. But Not So Adorable on anyone else.)

WHAT LOOKS GOOD ON NO ONE

- Obvious lipliner. Only permissible if you are, in fact, a Circus Clown.

- The hideous blue-on-the-lid, brown-in-the-crease, white-on-the-browbone eyeshadow look that, like blue mascara, was already dated in 1985.

- Thick foundation, all over your face, covered with a good inch of powder. If you fancy wearing Greasepaint, you should consider taking Acting Lessons.

- "Contouring." This never works. You may look decent straight on, in your mirror, but you are not a Television Personality who only needs to face forward all the time. From the side, you surely will appear streaky and freaky.

- Bright yellow makeup of any sort. No, yellow lipstick isn't Quirky. It's Wrong.

- "Nail art." No. No, no, no, no, *NO!!* No sunsets, no shamrocks, no holiday stockings, no flowers, no School Mascots and/or School Colors, no rhinestones, no hoops through the nails.

- Glitter Overdoses. Just because Drew Barrymore puts it on her shoulders doesn't mean you have to smear it all over your face, hair, and body. You may use a *tiny* bit on your eyes, but that's it, and the rest of your face should be simply made-up. And if you do this, it had better be very fine sparkly stuff, not the kind of glitter we all enjoyed playing with in elementary school.

- Mendhi (a.k.a. henna tattoos), or bindi, those wee forehead dots which ladies in India sport. Isn't this over yet? Come on, people. Even the No Doubt Girl has Moved On. While mendhi and bindi are Perfectly Acceptable if you are, say, a Practicing Hindu, it's simply ridiculous if you are a Congregationalist born and raised in New Hampshire. It is as disrespectful for you to be prancing around avec these items while you're drunk as it is for you to be wearing a Rosary as jewelry.

- Blue eyeshadow *plus* red lipstick. Cameron Diaz, who lets you out of the house like that, much less onto the Talk Show Circuit?

WHAT LOOKS GOOD WHEN APPLIED VERY, VERY CAREFULLY

When one is an Old Hand at the Art of Makeup (as the Etiquette Grrls obviously are), one may experiment a bit with colors and application methods. However, you should only do *one* wacky thing at one time. This shows everyone that while you're Hip and Adventurous, you're not just Following All the Magazine Instructions Simultaneously. The Etiquette Grrls recommend that if you are going to be trendy, you buy your Trendy Makeup someplace where the Trends are actually on the shelves at the same time they're in style, such as at Sephora or Barney's. By the time the glittery, loose-powder eyeshadow filters down to Maybelline, the rest of us will have Moved On. Urban Decay, Stila, and BeneFit are very good sources for Trendy Makeup. (As an aside, the Etiquette Grrls think it is Very Important for cosmetics companies to give their products Witty Names. Of course we want to wear a lipstick called "Manic-Depressive"! We do not, however, want to wear one called "Ice-Blue Pink.")

Only venture outside of your apartment wearing any of the following things if you have 1) perfected the application technique, and 2) have been assured by a Very Stylish Friend that you do not, *honestly*, Look Ridiculous: false eyelashes; loose glitter; fake tattoos/body paint; hair mascara; liquid eyeliner; that Benetint stuff; self-tanner; or lipstick as blush.

THE IMPORTANCE OF SUBVERSIVE NAILPOLISH

What a sad, inexpressive, sorry, predictable world it was before the advent of Urban Decay! The Etiquette Grrls find it difficult to look back upon the ante–Urban Decay years because they were so frightening, and after Urban Decay, our lives were Forever Changed. Then we saw as through a glass, darkly; but now we have such an array of adorable, sparkly, wacky-colored makeup strewn across our vanity that the glass itself is inconsequential! Hurrah, Urban Decay!

How does one use Urban Decay? It's most effective as a subtle dig against the Norms of Society. Do most women in your office wear modest pink nailpolish? Then you arrive for the Big Meeting sporting "Cult," a feisty, glittery blue-green flecked with gold. Does the family picnic grate upon your nerves? Then you show up with toenails polished with "Plague," an iridescent red-violet shade. The fun is endless! (Of course, one should exercise Moderation with Urban Decay, lest one take on the colorful appearance of a Transvestite on Halloween . . . not so appropriate at Breakfast Avec the New CEO.) The Etiquette Grrls also love Urban Decay because of the clever names of the products. Why yes, we absolutely want a foundation called "Apparition"! We *are* pale as, well, Ghosts, and for Urban Decay to acknowledge this in the shade name is Fabulously Cool. And how ironic is it for the Etiquette Grrls, Of All People, to go bar-hopping wearing "Litter" eyeliner? It's too funny for words! And everything comes in adorable, vaguely industrial bottles! Tee-hee! We love you, Urban Decay! Please send our gift baskets to us c/o The Berkley Publishing Group, A Division of Penguin Putnam Inc., 375 Hudson Street, New York, NY 10014!

Clothing

There are Few Things the Etiquette Grrls like more than Pretty Clothes, Dear Reader! We think that we could probably be Perfectly Happy spending all of our days perusing SoHo for Betsey Johnson frocks, Charming Beach Towns for Lilly Clamdiggers, Funky Boutiques for Vintage Ball Gowns, and Scotland for Cashmere Sweaters. Your Wardrobe is one of the things that can make or break Your Total Appearance, Dear Reader! Wandering though the day looking disheveled or Wearing The Wrong Thing may not do you any harm per se, Dear Reader, but in the Etiquette Grrls' opinion, it's likely not to do you any good, either. So why risk it? Have a seat while the Etiquette Grrls give you some Pointers on What You Should Be Wearing.

GENERAL ADVICE ON FIT

While the Etiquette Grrls enjoy attending stylish soirées too much to become *total* recluses, we are occasionally so offended by What Other People Wear that we are tempted Not to Leave Our Flats. Recently the Etiquette Grrls have encountered men with "muscle" shirts loitering in the lobby of the Algonquin, and let us not even *start* to describe the horrors we have witnessed at Church.

First of all, Dear Reader, you must learn what cuts and styles of clothing flatter your body (the body you actually *have*). For both men and women, nothing you put on should be tight, ever. "It fits fine as long as I wear control-top stockings and suck in my tummy" does not equal "flattering." Your clothing should not be tight when you move, sit down, stand up, reach overhead, etc. This is not to say you cannot wear fitted clothing—there is a Great Difference, Dear Reader, between a fitted blouse and a tight one.

Everyone needs a Good Tailor or Seamstress! And as these Talented Folks are, sadly, Few and Far Between, you must ask all of your Close Friends, right now, to whom they take their clothes for alterations, and find someone immediately. A Good Seamstress can make your clothes fit smoothly and easily, and the Etiquette Grrls would never dream of buying, say, an Expensive Suit without Having It Altered. Make sure you are measured by the Seamstress and that your clothing is taken in or let out accordingly. Trust the Etiquette Grrls on this one. Maybe we all can't afford Bespoke Suits, but we can and should take our Banana Republic suits to be tailored.

FAUX PAS OF FIT WHICH MUST BE AVOIDED

- Cleavage. In any way, shape, or form, especially during the day. Unless you can wear a scoopneck top without looking like a St. Pauli Girl, don't wear one. You should especially not try to create cleavage which you do not actually have, as this looks obvious, trampy, and, above all, uncomfortable. If you are going, say, to the Academy Awards, you may wear a dress which is a bit more décolleté. But if you choose to do this, you must exercise restraint: Nothing may bounce, nothing may be horribly jammed together, nothing may threaten to fall out. You know what the Etiquette Grrls mean.

- Too-short sleeves or pant legs. Now, the Etiquette Grrls are not talking about bracelet sleeves, which are obviously intended to be shorter than the wrist, or deliberately ankle-length pants. However, if your arms or legs are un peu too long for your jacket or pants, you risk looking like a Small Child who has Outgrown His or Her Clothes.

- Too-long sleeves or pant legs. As for sleeves, are you trying to go for that "I'm dressing up in my mommy's clothing!" look, or perhaps that "ready to be tied up in a straitjacket" look? And with pants, do you want to look as if you're in a Gang? You should not have to roll up your sleeves in order to hold a pen, nor should you wear your pants so long that they drag in the mud and threaten to trip you.

- Visible underwear. Whether it's peeking out *from* clothing or visible *through* clothing, this is not acceptable. Visible bra straps are, thank heavens, over. Remember that it is called *under*wear for a reason.

- Too-short skirts or shorts. When the Etiquette Grrls were At School, their entire wardrobes reflected the School Dress Code, which mandated that nothing be more than two inches above the knee. How we wish the Entire World were subject to the rules of Prep School, and we could give Demerits to those women who insist upon wearing scandalously short skirts or hot pants in public! We think it is a Crime Against Humanity that major stores like J. Crew would even *make* shorts that have no discernible inseam, as this sends a message that it is perfectly acceptable for people to Wear Them Around! Tacky, tacky, tacky!

GENERAL ADVICE ON STYLE

After fit, of course, we come to style. We know that for many people, style is somewhat of a personal thing, and yes, the Etiquette Grrls are aware that this is a Free Country and that you can, in fact, wear whatever the heck you desire. However, do remember, Dear Reader, that this is also a Judgmental Country—there are general bits of advice you would do well to follow so you are not perceived as a Fashion Train Wreck or, worse, considered Inappropriately Dressed.

To be, as the Etiquette Grrls are, Always Correct, you must first develop a Healthy Amount of Skepticism toward Trends. To quote the Etiquette Grrls' Mothers, just because everybody else jumped off a cliff, Dear Reader, would you, too? Trendy Things are fun, but it is always, *always* a smarter move to wear mostly classic pieces and incorporate *one* Trendy Item into your outfit. Instead of wearing a handkerchief top avec a picture of The Buddha embroidered on it, capri pants with decorative stitching and spangles, a head scarf, a baguette bag, and ponyskin mules, you might choose to wear a classic Little Black Sheath Dress and carry the baguette bag. This shows that while you are aware of current fashion, you have not been made its victim. Read on to find what elements of clothing should compose Your Basic Wardrobe, and if you must purchase Trendy Things, do so only after you have acquired all of the following.

ITEMS OF CLOTHING ALL GIRLS SHOULD OWN

- A Little Black Sheath Dress, in silk, cotton, lightweight wool, or, for hot climates, linen. This should have the neckline and skirt length most flattering to you, and no decoration. None. At all.

- Black shoes to go with this dress, in good-quality leather and with your favorite style of heel.

- Black mid-calf or knee-length boots. These are what you wear in winter when it's snowy in the city.

- A long coat, in cashmere, wool, or a cashmere/wool blend, if you live anywhere that gets cold in the winter. Remember, more people will see you in this coat than in any outfit you may have on beneath it, so you should spend accordingly. Black, charcoal grey, or camel (if it suits your coloring) are all nice. If you must have a coat in a trendy color, too, make sure you acquire a classic one first.

- A raincoat. Burberry and Aquascutum ones have pretty plaid linings!

- Cashmere sweaters in as many colors and styles as you like and can afford. Yes, cashmere is pricey (especially *good* cashmere), but it's sooooo soft and lasts much longer than wool sweaters, which are itchy to boot.

- Doc Martens. Because sometimes, you just *need* to wear them with your cashmere sweater.

- A suit, in a dark color and which is tailored perfectly. You will need this for Job Interviews, and, of course, for Wakes and Funerals. The Etiquette Grrls think you'll get more mileage out of a skirt suit or dress-and-jacket suit than a pantsuit, if you can have only one, but pantsuits are nice for travel, among other activities requiring Ease of Mobility.

- In hot climates, a Lilly Pulitzer sundress. Preferably in a print featuring Alcoholic Beverages.

- A good watch, on a metal or leather band.

- A good handbag in a neutral color, made of leather for winter or possibly cloth for summer.

- A small evening bag. Vintage bags are fabulous!

ITEMS OF CLOTHING ALL BOYS SHOULD OWN

- A really well-fitted suit in a dark color, e.g., navy blue or charcoal grey, made of lightweight wool.

- Several shirts, of finely woven cotton, in solid, unwacky colors and/or subtle stripes. The Etiquette Grrls really prefer Boys in point collars, but button-down collars are preferable to those horrid "dress shirts" without collars (which no one should ever, ever wear). Make sure the shirts actually fit and are not just S-M-L or XL.

- Several ties, made of silk, to complement the shirts and suit. Small patterns or rep stripes are nice. Silk-screened prints of comic book characters, faux tie-dye, and sports-team logos are not nice.

- A pair of black leather shoes that tie. *Not* those weird, faux oxford shoes that look intended for Jazz Dancing. Ugh. You are allowed to have nice leather loafers, too, but must have the black leather tie shoes. Avoid shoes with any Weird Ornamentation. Wing tips are nice.

- If you live in a cold climate, a cashmere, wool, or cashmere/wool-blend overcoat. It should be big enough to wear over your suit, and should be in a dark color, like black or charcoal grey.

- Thin black socks. These are worn with the black shoes. The only form of patterned socks you are allowed to have are Argyle Socks, but you must have a Certain Degree of Gatsby-esque Flair in order to Carry Them Off. Polka dots, stripes, and weird patterns are a big no-no.

- A belt of black leather with a plain silver or leather-covered buckle.

- Charcoal-grey wool pants.

- A sports coat in navy or a nice tweed pattern.

- For summer, lightweight cotton piqué or knit polo-collared shirts.

- Flat-front khaki pants made of good-quality cotton.

ARTICLES OF CLOTHING WHICH ARE NEVER, EVER ACCEPTABLE ATTIRE

- Tank Tops, or, worse, Tube Tops.

- Items with any sort of team or band logo written upon them.

- Athletic shoes worn at any time when one is not participating in athletic activity.

- Short shorts or hot pants, on anyone, anywhere.

- Cutoff shorts.

- Anything made of polyester knit.

- Items bearing the name of a college or university which you did not attend, unless they were a gift from a Dear Friend who does, in fact, attend the school in question. It is most uncool to wear a Harvard tee shirt that you bought at the mall in Peoria.

- Acid-washed jeans.

- White shoes, unless you are a Bride or a Nurse.

- Items festooned with Religious Symbols, or, indeed, Large, Diamond-Encrusted Religious Symbols worn as Evening Jewelry (as seen on Donna Martin on the Second *90210* Prom Episode). This goes beyond rude into offensive, particularly if you do not espouse the beliefs of whatever religion's symbols you think look really cool with your new Missoni sweater.

- Construction boots, unless you are a Construction Worker or a Lumberjack and you are currently engaging in work directly relating to your profession.

- Anything Day-Glo, phosphorescent, or which changes colors in response to sunlight.

- Anything with rhinestones or metal studs applied to its surface with a glue gun.

- Anything made out of Artificial Leather.

- Anything which could be mistaken for a bathing suit, lingerie, or pajamas (or, worse, any clothing actually in these categories not being worn for its intended purpose).

- Socks worn with sandals.

- Evening dresses or shoes worn before 5 P.M.

- Flip-flops, other than in gym showers, on the beach, or at the pool.

- Anything torn, stained, or wrinkled.

- Sheer, flimsy, or clingy clothing, worn without the appropriate undergarments.

- Puffy down-filled parkas, unless you live in Maine, Minnesota, Wisconsin, or another Northern and Extremely Cold Climate, and it is the Depths of Winter.

- Anything with cats, ducks, bunny rabbits, horses, or any other animal pictured on it in any manner, especially if it is painted by hand onto the fabric.

- Anything Lycra. A touch of Lycra in, say, a cotton blouse is acceptable; a blouse made of 100 percent Lycra is not.

- Anything with text upon it that is written in a language you do not understand. The Etiquette Grrls sincerely hope that all those trendy Chinese-character tee shirts really say something to the effect of, "I am a Fashion Victim!"

LAST-MINUTE CHECKS

The Etiquette Grrls remind you that before you Set Foot outside Your Apartment, you must examine every item you have put on your body to make sure that it is clean (and by "clean" we mean *actually* clean, not "I've worn these jeans five times, but you can't really see the mustard stain"), pressed, and devoid of holes, runs, lint, etc. A full-length mirror will serve you well. Be sure that your shoes are clean and polished!

CHOOSING AN APPROPRIATE OUTFIT

Assuming all your clothing fits correctly, and is presentable, then what do you wear to particular events? It saddens the Etiquette Grrls to no end that, seemingly, everybody and their brother is running around in khakis, short-sleeved tee shirts, and sandals, no matter where they are going! Surely you, too, Dear Reader, have been aston-ished to see Young People wearing, say, tube tops and capri pants In Church, or to witness tourists in sweatpants and fanny packs striding down Park Avenue! We must band together in order to vanquish Our Common Foe, the Inappropriately Casual Dresser. It has always been the Etiquette Grrls' belief that you are much better to be slightly overdressed than underdressed, for any occasion. Yes, we are aware that it is probably, in the Larger Scheme of Things, not the End of The World to board a plane wearing snap-bottomed track pants. Similarly, although one certainly will not get Sent Home from, say, an Internet Start-Up Company if one were to show up in ratty jeans, one should choose not to wear them.

Elsewhere in this book, you can learn What You Should Wear at Concerts, Theatre Performances, Your Workplace, Parties, While Traveling, While Writing Letters, and While Composing E-Mail. And in our next section, we will explain Formal, Semi-Formal, and Casual Dress, as indicated on invitations. However, Dear Reader, *we beg of you,* dress nicely! All the time! Everywhere! Our Country—nay, Our World—will be a More Civilized Place!

DEFINING OUR TERMS: FORMAL, SEMI-FORMAL, ETC.

How abjectly frustrating that the lines have become blurred between Formal, Semi-Formal, and Casual Clothing! If Truth Be Told, the Eti-quette Grrls aren't All That Fond of these categorizations, as we think everyone should simply *know* that if it's a Cotillion, one must be For-mally Attired. However, in order for everyone to know this, someone has to tell everyone, which is where the Etiquette Grrls will Step Up to the Podium. We would suggest, also, that if you are the Hostess, you employ your Network of Close Friends to Spread the Word as to how formal your party is, rather than adding it to your invitations.

Formal

To simply use the word "Formal" is not specific enough. Do you wish your guests to wear White or Black Tie? The Etiquette Grrls have found (through our Extensive Research) that "Formal" Dress in this country usually means Black Tie. However, Dear Reader, if you get invited to a State Dinner, you will need to know what constitutes White Tie, because, dammit, you will be required to wear it.

Of course, we are talking about Evening Clothes here. About the only occasion for which one might be required to wear Formal Daytime Clothes would be a Wedding (or, perhaps, Ascot), and, surely, if you hang out with a crowd that is accustomed to Formal Daytime Weddings (or Attending Ascot), you already know What Is Appropriate Attire.

White Tie This is the most formal category of dress. One wears White Tie to, say, an evening reception at the White House.

GIRLS	BOYS
·Long evening gown	·Tailcoat (black, naturellement)
·Long gloves (Which, of course, come off while you are Eating. You also never wear rings over gloves!)	·Matching trousers
	·White shirt, tie, and waistcoat
	·Black patent-leather evening pumps (Which, despite your snickering, Dear Reader, is how one refers to men's evening shoes. Also, you should own these, not rent them—ugh.)
·Stockings	
·Evening Shoes to match the gown	
·Tiny, adorable Evening Bag to match Your Outfit	
·Really Good Jewelry	·Black socks

Black Tie Black Tie means, "Formal, but not White Tie." It is worn to evening weddings, cotillions, balls, opening nights, the Academy Awards, etc.

GIRLS	BOYS
·Long evening gown	·Black dinner jacket (In Resort Towns, at the Country Club, or at the Yacht Club, one may, during the summer months, wear a white wool jacket, in lieu of the black. Trousers and tie stay black, however.)
·Stockings	
·Evening Shoes to match your gown	
·Tiny, adorable Evening Bag to match Your Outfit	
·Really Good Jewelry	
	·Matching trousers
	·White shirt
	·Black bow tie that you tie yourself (Please note that you do *not* wear the bow tie with a wing collar! Those are for White Tie—you shouldn't ever be able to see the back strappy part of the tie.)
	·Black cummerbund or black waistcoat (*never* both at once; the Etiquette Grrls rather prefer Boys in waistcoats.)
	·Black patent-leather evening pumps
	·Black socks

Boys should have Nice Cufflinks, preferably handed down from, say, Their Grandfather, and should wear no other jewelry (except a Wedding Band, if they are Married). Girls may carry an Evening Wrap if the night is chilly, but should not sport a Down Parka or other casual outerwear over their Evening Gown.

Semi-Formal

This is what you wear to a typical cocktail or dinner party, and to some college dances (most notably, the second evening of Houseparties at Princeton). Semi-formal attire is also appropriate for dinner at a Nice Restaurant, at weddings which do not require Black Tie, etc.

GIRLS	BOYS
·Long or short (but not *too* short) dress (of dressy cut and fabric)	·Suit or sports coat with dress pants
	·Button-down shirt with point or spread collar
·Nice shoes to match dress	
·Stockings	·Tie
·Tiny, adorable Evening Bag to match Your Outfit	·Black lace-up shoes
	·Black socks
·Really good, but subtle jewelry	

Boys are not allowed to interpret "semi-formal" as "formal from the waist up, casual from the waist down." We have seen horrorshow outfits of blue sports coats, dress shirts, and ties worn with khaki shorts and sneakers. Once and for all, yes, long pants are required whenever you are wearing a tie.

Casual

This is what you wear when you are not wearing Black Tie, White Tie, or Semi-Formal Attire. Casual Attire goes to casual restaurants, shopping, to movies, etc.

GIRLS	BOYS
•Blouse (or dressy tee) and skirt; or blouse (or dressy tee) and nice pants; or dress	•Button-down shirt and nice pants; or (if it is very warm out or the event is *very* casual) polo-collared shirt and nice pants
•Sweater or Twin Set	•Sweater
•Nice shoes (no sneakers or flip-flops)	•Nice shoes (no sneakers or flip-flops)
•Subtle jewelry	•Dark socks (no tube socks, ever!)
•Daytime bag (made of leather or cloth; not sparkly)	

Other Categories of Dress

The Etiquette Grrls do not approve of the following pseudo-categories of Dress, but we define them here for your benefit, Dear Reader. After all, before you accept an invitation, you ought to know what you're getting yourself into.

- **"Business Casual"**—The Etiquette Grrls have a bit of a difficult time with "casual" in places like The Office, but since Business Casual is everywhere, we're trying to Work With the Concept. This means "Don't Wear a Suit, But Don't Look Like You're at a Frat Party or at the Gym, Either." No sneakers, no clothing with holes, nothing wrinkled, no tee shirts, no shorts. Not that you *would* go out In Public sporting any of these things, anyway; we're just reminding you.

- **"New Media Business"**—Break out the funky eyeglasses and the cropped pants, grow some skinny sideburns (if you're male) or put your hair into little ponytails (if you're female), and walk around with a lollipop in one hand and a blue "martini" in the other. Yes, the Etiquette Grrls think this is Rather Amusing.

- **"Cocktail Attire"**—There's something Inherently Sleazy about this. You wear semi-formal dress to a cocktail party if it is held in the evening at a suitably swanky location. You do not wear "cocktail attire," which seems to imply clothing which might be worn by a Cocktail Waitress. And you most certainly do not want to emulate that look.

- **"Smart Casual"**—To the Etiquette Grrls, this is Redundant. Even in casual clothes, of course you should look smart. Basically, this is a manner of making what should be the Lowest Common Denominator explicit to our Uncivilized Neighbors.

- **"Festive"**—Ugh. What, exactly, does this mean? "Festive" describes a *mood,* not a dress code. The Etiquette Grrls have seen this *far* too often on corporate holiday party invitations, and frankly, we interpret it as giving Guests free rein to wear sweaters with appliquéd wreaths, dreidel earrings, and all manner of horrid Santa and Elf Hats.

- **"Black Tie Optional"**—This means "The hostess is indecisive."

THE SEE YOU IN HELL LOOK AND HOW TO CREATE IT

Dinner with Your Ex-Boyfriend. The day you hand in your resignation. A wedding at which the Bride is Younger Than You, and you're still Single. For these occasions, there is only one dress code: See You In Hell.

See You In Hell is about looking better than any other Girl in the room. Achieving this takes about as much effort and advance planning as D day, but it is well worth the pains. You will need The Perfect Outfit, preferably one that's Striking (one cannot say See You In Hell in khakis or sneakers, ever), is Exceedingly Flattering, and has a bit of an edge to it (e.g., you should wear knee-high boots with Serious Heels; you should not wear ballet flats). For example, the Etiquette Grrls have said See You In Hell in a sleek, ankle-length dress by Betsey Johnson, and, for another occasion, a gray beaded skirt worn with an ever-so-slightly sheer black boatneck top, black camisole, and tall black boots. Accessories are equally important. You cannot, for example, be truly See You In Hell if you are carrying a beat-up old L.L. Bean knapsack. You need a very angular, take-no-prisoners, Little Black Bag. If you will be Seeing Someone In Hell in public, you should take great pains to Create An Entrance. A leopard coat, an excellent vintage necklace, a burgundy cashmere sleeveless top in the Dead Of Winter (*not* all at once, please)—these are all workable pieces. Of course, you will have Perfectly Manicured Nails in a gutsy Urban Decay color; flawless skin, courtesy of a facial (which, naturally, you've had well before SYIH Day, to give any Unfortunate Reaction time to Go Away) or, at least, very carefully applied makeup; and very, very good shoes. Also, one hour before the Big Event is not the time for a last-minute Highlight Fest at home in your bathroom with the Sun-In and the Hair Dryer. Visit your Usual Hairdresser for a good blow-out and, at most, a trim. If it's really worth a new See You In Hell Haircut, you should get the haircut at least a week in advance. This way, should it be hideous, you may try to have it remedied in another salon, or, in worse cases, you may cancel.

Basically, the impression you are attempting to convey is that you are a Flawless, Impeccably Dressed, Impossibly Hip, Badass Girl avec Perfect Hair and a Very, Very Cool Life. This will surely make whoever lays eyes on you extremely intimidated by your Very Presence and sorry for whatever wrongs they have done you. Of course, the See You In Hell look is Rather Time-Consuming and, thus, difficult to maintain for extended periods. Unless you are one of the Etiquette Grrls, for whom See You In Hell is second nature.

You Must Have Studied Dance:
Posture and Movement

Well, Dear Reader, now that you're immaculately made-up and Dressed To The Nines, you'll be sure to transfix everyone at the swanky cocktail party you'll be attending tonight, n'est-ce pas? Not if you slouch like a vulture, sit with your legs madly splayed, and hide behind a curtain of your hair!

POISE

No matter how tall you are, it is important that you Stand Up Straight. The Etiquette Grrls know that Your Height will not be An Issue unless you Draw Attention to it. Far better to be a six-foot-five girl and stand, straight-backed, head and shoulders over the rest of the party than to be six-foot-five and attempt to be five-foot-ten! And by "straight-backed" we *mean* straight-backed: head high, spine extended in a nice, long line perpendicular to the Oriental Rug. Other forms of postural overcompensation are, like slouching, quite obvious and quite silly looking. Girls who stick out their meagre chests look not only sway-backed but Un Peu Desperate, and, Dear Reader, the Etiquette Grrls know you don't ever want to appear Desperate!

The Etiquette Grrls often wonder why Chairs seem to present such a Grand Problem to many people. Many of our acquaintances seem to feel that one should feel free to Drape Oneself over all parts of the Chair. Indeed, we've seen too many a Young Person putting his Doc Marten–clad feet on the seat of a nicely upholstered Chair, or sitting on its arm. Dear Reader, it's true: *you sit* in *the damn seat.* And your feet go on the floor! Your arms go on the arms! It's really quite easy! Also, no tipping backward, no sitting backward, and no feet on the coffee table. Tables are not ottomans.

However, even if one puts the appropriate parts in the appropriate place on a chair, one can still appear ungraceful. Girls, the Etiquette Grrls are adamant about this: You *must* learn how to cross your legs nicely, especially if you are a devotee of above-the-knee skirts.

Do not:

- Cross your legs more than once. You will look like a Twizzler.
- Dangle one shoe from Your Toe. If your Blahniks are that uncomfortable, you shouldn't be wearing them.
- Endlessly, annoyingly, kick the crossed leg back and forth, as if it were part of a wee Rockettes show.

- Cross your legs and drape one over another person's leg (or any other part of their body). Especially if you have not been Formally Introduced.

In fact, the Etiquette Grrls recommend that you Take a Bit of Time, put on Your Shortest Skirt, set up a chair in front of a mirror, and practice sitting down, crossing your legs, uncrossing them, and standing up again. (Of course, it goes without saying that you should do this in The Privacy of Your Own Home.) At worst, you'll realize that you do quite the unwitting Sharon Stone impression (heaven forbid); but at least you can work to rid yourself of this dreadful, dreadful tendency! The Etiquette Grrls remind you: Well-bred Girls know that sitting with their legs crossed at the ankle is always an excellent option, and, frequently, a more attractive one than crossing one's legs at the knee.

Finally, no matter where you are, how tired you are, or how boring the Mandatory Lecture on "Visions and (Re)Visions: Prufrock the Ophthalmologist" is, *do not fidget*. Nothing, but *nothing*, is more annoying in a quiet room than the sound of someone endlessly rocking whilst seated in a Very Squeaky Chair (and, as we all know, all Auditoriums have nothing but Very Squeaky Chairs) or drumming his fingers upon an armrest. The Etiquette Grrls remember well how Frightfully Tiresome it was to remain in a classroom after having finished An Examination, but we did not take advantage of that time to practice Our Percussion Skills, and neither should you. Any sort of habitual behavior that others could possibly see, hear, feel, or smell (or, we suppose, taste, though the thought horrifies us) must be avoided at all costs. This includes knuckle-cracking, whistling, tapping one's foot on the floor, examining one's Split Ends, doing that pseudo-baton-twirling trick avec a pen, etc. Well-bred People do not fidget, *ever*, and neither should you!

CHAPTER FOUR

Staying in Touch

The Internet

The Etiquette Grrls feel that electronic mail, or e-mail, is one of the Greatest Inventions of the Twentieth Century. We love being able to send Well-Written, Thoughtful Messages to our Dear Friends, and receiving equally Well-Written, Thoughtful Replies in short order. E-mail is an easy, inexpensive way to stay in touch with all your friends, family, and acquaintances, and has become integral to our Busy, Post-Post-Modern way of life. E-mail should not, however, be used as a means to send one letter to your Dear Friends En Masse. It is fine to send out a Group Mailing to update your acquaintances of a change of telephone number or address, but it is no more acceptable to send a message describing the trivialities of your Daily Life to everyone all at once than it would be to photocopy a Handwritten Letter and send that out in lieu of a Personal Note. And the Etiquette Grrls know that our Dear Readers wouldn't *dream* of doing that, not even at Christmas. If you have an e-mail account, you are under an obligation to a) check your incoming mail frequently, and b) reply with Reasonable Promptness. To fail to do so defeats the purpose of e-mail (the ability to communicate quickly), and in that case, you might just as well write an old-fashioned, pen-and-ink letter.

FORWARDED MAIL AND ATTACHMENTS

E-mail is not something to be abused. There is nothing More Disappointing than to think you have a message from one of your Dear Friends, only to open the message and find a Chain Letter, the author of which demands that you send it along immediately to twenty-six of your Closest Friends within five minutes, threatening you and/or your computer with Dire Consequences should you fail to do so. Forwarding Chain Letters will not, under any circumstances, miraculously cure a Small Child Residing in Kansas of A Fatal Disease, Entitle You, or Anybody Else, to A Check From Bill Gates, Grant Any Sort of Wish, Stop Racial Violence, or otherwise result in any form of Windfall and/or Social Improvement. Furthermore, we shouldn't even need to tell you that threatening anyone with a Fate Worse Than Death should they fail to carry out Your Directions is never Good Manners.

Sometimes Forwarded Mail does not contain any instructions for sending it on to others, but these messages can be equally tiresome. These messages tend to be jokes, lists of 101 Pick-Up Lines/Dumb Things Men Do/Ways to Kill Your Roommate, or any one of a number of other topics of a similar nature. The Etiquette Grrls find nearly all of these types of messages to be Quite A Bore. They are rarely amusing, and the few that have been circulating for so long that we have received them in Our Mailboxes monthly for the past five years. If you do, however, feel Overwhelmingly Compelled to forward one particular message you are sure is not in Mass Circulation, you should take Great Pains to ensure that the little ">" characters that typically indicate "quoted" text are not present to the extent that they interfere with the legibility of the message. Let's look at the following example together.

        >>>>>>>>>>>
        >>>>>>>>>>>[begin quoted text]>>>>>[on July 19,
        sharon@peoplewithtoomuchtimeontheirhands.com
        wrote]>>>>>>>>[snip]>>>>>hey dude i thought you'd get
        a kick out of this check it out>>>>>

>>>>>>>COLLEGE LIGHTBULB JOKES 1) How many
Dartmouth>>>>>
>>>>>>>students does it take to change a
lightbulb?>>>>>
>>>>>>>None. They don't have electricity in Hanover.

As you'll have noticed, there are Several Indications that this message has been Around The World Quite A Few Times. Your friends have, surely, all seen it already. And you would not want to appear to have been Hiding Under A Rock since the long-ago time the rest of us saw the Lightbulb Jokes list, would you? If there are more than two of the ">" characters around any line of text, you should not bother to forward that message, as it is clearly already in General Circulation and your e-mail buddy will have already seen it Quite Enough, Thank You.

You also should be Discriminatory about sending file or picture attachments with your e-mail. Only do so when Absolutely Necessary, and never attach anything which might contain A Virus, take an hour to download, fill all the space in the recipient's mailbox, or cause her computer to Crash. You also should make sure that the recipient will be able to open and read the variety of file which you are sending. Hint: If you cannot open a file yourself or *suspect* it may have Some Sort of Computer Virus, you should not forward it to Unsuspecting Dear Friends. Is it a good idea to Tempt Fate by sending an attachment named "deadlyvirus1.exe" to Your Boss? The Etiquette Grrls don't think so. The Etiquette Grrls aren't stupid enough to *open* something called deadlyvirus1.exe, so they Particularly Resent messages (which they receive, oftentimes, by the score) warning them to Watch Out for Such a Virus. We think that most Writers of Nefarious Computer Viruses are A Bit More Intelligent than to name their chef d'oeuvre something which calls attention to the fact that it is, indeed, a virus, so such warnings are an Insult to Our (and Their) Intelligence. The Etiquette Grrls think it would be splendid, if we were to take up Writing Deadly Computer Viruses as a Weekend Hobby, to embed a Deadly Computer Virus in the middle of an e-mail message encouraging all of Cyberspace to prevent the spread of Deadly Viruses by forwarding this warning immediately to their Entire Social Circle. And the Etiquette Grrls might just have to do this if we become annoyed enough with the stupid forwarded messages, Dear Reader, so you must stop forwarding things, *right now*.

SOME THOUGHTS ON CLARITY: THE WELL-WRITTEN MESSAGE

E-mail can also be quite a handy tool for arranging plans with Your Dear Friends, should either party be Un Peu Difficult to reach by telephone. But we remind you, Dear Reader, that, as with all other forms of communication, you should be clear about the plans which you make, or Terrible Confusion may result. The Etiquette Grrls will give you An Example of this vagueness, Dear Reader, in the Following Example.

> To: Puzzled Polly <polly@perplexingmail.com>
> From: Omniscient William
> <william@godlikeinhisomniscience.com>
> Sent: Wednesday, April 24, 2001 3:27 PM
> Subject: Tomorrow
> Dear P. P.,
> What're you doing tomorrow?
> O. W.

Polly's prompt response was as follows:

> To: Omniscient William
> <william@godlikeinhisomniscience.com>
> From: Puzzled Polly <polly@perplexingmail.com>
> Sent: Wednesday, April 24, 2001 4:16 PM
> Subject: Re: Tomorrow

Dear O. W.,

Well, I have a Dentist's Appointment in the morning, and I
have Some Errands to run in the afternoon, but I guess I'll
be home in the evening. Why?

P. P.

She then received this reply:

To: Puzzled Polly <polly@perplexingmail.com>

From: Omniscient William
<william@godlikeinhisomniscience.com>

Sent: Wednesday, April 24, 2001 4:17 PM

Subject: Re: Re: Tomorrow

P. P.,

Okay.

O. W.

Now, you see, Dear Reader, it is entirely unclear as to *why* Omniscient William wants to be informed of what Perplexed Polly's plans
are for tomorrow, or indeed, what part of the day he is inquiring about.
A Vague Message such as this encourages a reply which contains The
Recipient's itinerary for what she habitually does on a Thursday, which
is probably not what The Author intended. But things only get worse
in Omniscient William's second message. Not only did he fail to reply
to Polly's query about why he was inquiring about her plans for the following day, he also failed to Clearly State whether he was actually
attempting to make plans with her or not. Okay *what*? Okay, he will
drop by? Or does he mean, okay, he won't drop by? Her Planned Activities are okay with him? Consequently, Poor Polly is left wondering
whether she can expect to see Omniscient William tomorrow or not—
and is he going to come to her apartment, or does he expect her to
meet him somewhere, or what? The Etiquette Grrls remind you, Dear
Reader, that even if *you* are Un Peu Omniscient, your Dear Friends and
acquaintances may not be. Thusly, in order to avoid Terrible Confu-

sion, it would be wise to Articulate Your Thoughts. The above exchange of correspondence would have better read like this:

> To: Puzzled Polly <polly@perplexingmail.com>
> From: Omniscient William
> <william@godlikeinhisomniscience.com>
> Sent: Wednesday, April 24, 2001 3:27 PM
> Subject: Tomorrow?
> Dear P. P.,
> I was Just Wondering if perhaps you would be free to have dinner at Bernard's Bistro around 7:30 tomorrow evening? I've been Terribly Anxious to see what it's like—the *Times-Herald* gave it that Smashing Review, you know. Let me know if you'd like to come with me.
> O. W.

The proper response would be:

> To: Omniscient William
> <william@godlikeinhisomniscience.com>
> From: Puzzled Polly <polly@perplexingmail.com>
> Sent: Wednesday, April 24, 2001 4:16 PM
> Subject: Re: Tomorrow?
> Dear O. W.,
> Why yes, I am free tomorrow night, and I would very much enjoy meeting you for dinner at Bernard's. That would be lovely, indeed, O. W. Thanks for asking; I've been wondering about Bernard's myself.
> P. P.

To which Omniscient William would reply:

> To: Puzzled Polly <polly@perplexingmail.com>
> From: Omniscient William

<william@godlikeinhisomniscience.com>
Sent: Wednesday, April 24, 2001 4:17 PM
Subject: Re: Re: Tomorrow?
Dear P. P.,
Great, I will pick you up at your apartment tomorrow
evening at 7:30. See you then!
O. W.

See how much better that was, Dear Reader? In a Quick and Pain-less Fashion, and in only a few short sentences, everything was made clear, and Firm Plans were made!

The Etiquette Grrls have noticed that many people seem to feel that because e-mail is deemed an Informal Mode of Communication, all rules of grammar, spelling, and punctuation may be Completely Ignored. This annoys the Etiquette Grrls to No End, Dear Reader! It is Extremely Tiring to attempt to decipher a Stream-of-Consciousness Message that contains no punctuation, capitalization, or separation of paragraphs, as if it were composed in a Joint Effort by James Joyce and e. e. cummings. And, just as one should Shy Away From a cummings-esque Lack of Capitals, one should never, ever use solely Block Capitals. Not only does this connote Shouting, which is, of course, Rude, but it makes you look a bit like you have been Possessed by THE SPIRIT OF OWEN MEANY. The rules delineated in the *Chicago Manual of Style* apply to *all* Written Material, whether it be electronic or on paper. What follows is an example of poorly written e-mail message. Note especially the absence of a greeting or signature.

To: Winifred Cummings <WinifredC@girlscollege.edu>
From: Elspeth Smyth-Jones
<ElspethS-J@biguniversity.edu>
Sent: Thursday, October 18, 2001 5:26 PM
Subject: Re: Re: Re: Re: Re: Re: hi

hi whats new not much here I had an exam this morning
ineconomicsclas im sure I probably failed god I hatethat
class not much
else is new me and my roommate went to themall bought
rely cool new shoes at 9west for the fall dance do you
have a fal dance at you're schools areyougoing
whatsup
time for diner gottago
winifred

This is the above message translated into Legible Prose:

To: Winifred Cummings <WinifredC@girlscollege.edu>
From: Elspeth Smyth-Jones
<ElspethS-J@biguniversity.edu>
Sent: Thursday, October 18, 2001 5:26 PM
Subject: Re: Re: Re: Re: Re: Re: hi
Dear Elspeth,
Hi! How are you today? Anything new and exciting with
you? Things here are, I'm sorry to report, as Tedious As
Ever. I had an exam today in that Terrible, Horrible
Economics Class my department is forcing me to take,
and I'm quite sure I did Very Poorly. That class is so
discouraging!
Life here at Girls' College is otherwise Fairly Uneventful.
Yesterday, my roommate Anne and I hopped over to the
mall so I could look for shoes to wear to the Autumn
Formal--I found a pair I think will look nice with my navy
blue velvet dress. I can't remember if you told me, Elspeth
dear, is there an Autumn Shin-dig at your school? Do you
plan to go if there is one?
Anyway, how's your week been? Is everything going all right?
Well, I'm Positively Famished, so I think I'm going to toddle

over to the Dining Hall and see what's on offer for tonight.
More later!
TTFN,
Winifred

See how much clearer the second message is, Dear Reader? The
Etiquette Grrls encourage you to embrace the rules of punctuation
and to use spell-check often!

CHOOSING AN E-MAIL ADDRESS AND USERID
One of the wonders of e-mail is that it allows one to hide one's iden-
tity. One can assume virtually any userid one wishes, so one should
look at a new e-mail account as an opportunity to Forge A Brand-
New Personality. The Etiquette Grrls highly recommend using free
e-mail services such as hotmail.com, so that one may open a Suffi-
cient Number of accounts with names to suit All Facets of One's Personality. However, usernames containing any of the following words
should be Avoided At All Costs: Bunny, Unicorn, Rainbow, Kitty, or
MissThaaang. One would, after all, be Quite Embarrassed to use an
address like iluvunicorns4ever@hotmail.com on one's Résumé.

WHAT YOU SHOULD WEAR WHILE ON-LINE
Dear Reader, just because you are at home alone is No Excuse not to
be dressed appropriately for whatever activity you may be engaging
in, and this includes e-mailing and web surfing! You should treat the
composition of e-mail much as you would A Real, Live Conversation, and you should remember that Appearance *Always* Counts. We
tell you this now because the Etiquette Grrls understand that in A
Few Short Years, everyone will have video e-mail, and when this happens, you *certainly* aren't going to want to be seen in your Flannel
Pajamas and Pink Bunny Slippers by everyone in Your Address Book,
are you? Thusly, it is best that you attempt to break the habit of
Dressing Sloppily while at the computer right now, Dear Reader!
Your Technological Wardrobe ought to be appropriately Sleek and

Modernistic, with perhaps a bit of a Cyberspacy look to it. This is not to say that Tout le Monde should run out and buy skin-tight, holo-grammy hooded catsuits—as ever, Know Your Limits. Clothes in shades of black, grey, and white (for the Summer) are always Quite Nice, and any jewelry you wear ought to be Silver or Platinum, of course. (Gold is *very* unmodern.)

The Telephone

Dear Reader, the Etiquette Grrls are Big Fans of the Telephone! Not only have we found it to be a handy instrument with which to make plans with our Social Circle, but we have many Far-Flung Dear Friends with whom we *adore* to talk on a Regular Basis. E-mail is nice for this, as are letters, but after all, the next best thing to an in-person conversation is a Good, Long Chat on the 'phone.

CALL WAITING

Unless it is a genuine emergency, do not hang up on Caller Number One in order to talk with Caller Number Two. This is an abuse of Call Waiting, and also (more importantly) rude. You will undoubt-edly make your first caller feel as if they have been "blown off." In fact, we're not even sure anyone should have Call Waiting at all. The beeps are Irritating In The Extreme, as they almost always occur while one is in the midst of a Crisis-Mode Conversation. Obviously, in a case such as this, you should not only not take the Second Call in favor of the First Call, but you should not even pick up the Call Wait-ing. We recommend subscribing to the type of voice mail that picks up if the line is busy. If the Second Caller has anything Truly Impor-tant To Say, he or she will either leave a message or call back later.

OTHER ACTIVITIES WHILE ON THE TELEPHONE

One should not engage in Other Activities while on the 'phone, espe-cially Noisy Ones (washing dishes, vacuuming, skeet shooting, etc.). Quiet activities that require your Full Attention, such as writing let-ters, reading, or watching television are also a No-No. It is Highly

Disconcerting to be Gabbing Away and suddenly realize that The Person on the Other End of the Line is paying so little attention to you, she fails to realize that you have just asked her A Question. Nor should one be eating; Crunchy Foods like chips and Chewy Foods like caramels should particularly be avoided. (Drinking, however, is okay, as long as you don't slurp.) Also, you may not "take a break" from a phone call to have a twenty-minute conversation with somebody who is in the room with you. Where you place a call *from* is also Extremely Important; in this day of portable and cellular phones, try to avoid calling from a location so loud that the party you are calling will be unable to hear you. And of course, while at home, do not, we repeat, *do not* place calls from the bathroom. This is Disgusting.

WRONG NUMBERS
If you accidentally dial a Wrong Number and you realize as soon as someone answers, apologize ("I'm terribly sorry, I'm afraid I have reached the Wrong Number. Is this the Smith residence?"); do not simply hang up. If you are informed that you have the Wrong Number by the person you have called, again, apologize. Do not get belligerent. It is not the callee's fault that you have the Wrong Number, and, we promise, he is *not* lying to you. Eleanor really *doesn't* live there. Do not repeatedly redial a number that you know is wrong. This will undoubtedly anger the person you keep calling, and remember, many people have Caller ID. They will Know Who You Are, and they will Get You.

WHEN NOT TO CALL
There is a difference between calling someone at a College Dormitory or An Apartment Full of Young People and calling someone at Her Parents' House. In the case of the latter, it is generally best to avoid calling at Dinnertime and late at night—which, to folks of Our Parents' Age, means after 10 P.M. Also, even if calling a Young Person living alone, try to be considerate of his or her schedule. If your friend must arise at 5 A.M. for her two-hour commute to work, she probably doesn't really

want you to call her "just to chat" at 3 A.M., no matter how much she loves you. This may also apply to Peak Telephoning Hours. If you know that your friend religiously watches *Law and Order* every Wednesday night at ten, and has done so for years, then for heaven's sake, don't call during that time! Nevertheless, if someone calls you during a show you hate to miss, and you do, in fact, answer the 'phone, you are *not* allowed to Zone Out on your caller because you're being Sucked In by the action on the tube. This is what Caller ID is for.

ANSWERING MACHINES AND VOICE MAIL

In this Day and Age, everyone must have either an answering machine or a voice mailbox, so that one's Dear Friends may leave Cheerful, Polite Messages when one misses their calls. Not to have voice mail or a machine tells Your Dear Friends you really don't care that they have taken the time out of Their Busy Day to telephone you, and the Etiquette Grrls assure you, they will soon cease to call, and you will become a Social Pariah.

Your Outgoing Message should be simple and straightforward. No one wants to listen to ten minutes of music/iambic pentameter/dogs barking until they get the beep. This should particularly be avoided if you are likely to be receiving calls relating to work. (Do you really want your boss to hear your Marilyn Monroe impression, Dear Reader? The Etiquette Grrls Highly Doubt It.) On the opposite end of the spectrum, there should *be* a message of some sort. It is always very confusing to suddenly be confronted with A Loud Beep with No Outgoing Message Whatsoever, before you have had the time to Collect Your Thoughts about What You Want To Say in the message you are leaving. Here is a sample of An Acceptable Outgoing Message:

> *"Hi, you have reached 555-3069. No one is available to take your call at the moment, but please leave a message after the tone, and we will return your call as soon as we can."*

A note to Single Girls Living Alone: It is not a Good Idea to leave any indication on your Outgoing Message that you are, in fact, A Single Girl Living Alone. Use the plural, and do not give your name. You never know what sort of Psycho might somehow get hold of your number. We know some Girls who have a Boy record their messages for them, but this is apt to Cause Confusion, and quite possibly, in the case of parents, grandparents, and the like, Alarm, when some Strange Boy purporting to be A Member of Your Household requests that they "please leave a message, and we will get back to you as soon as we can." Finally, any answering machine on which the "beep" is not a mere beep but a piercing, atonal rendition of "Für Elise" should be Avoided At All Costs.

TAKING A MESSAGE

People who are unaware of how to take and/or pass on a message Drive the Etiquette Grrls to Distraction. If you are, for some reason, Unwilling to Take A Message for Your Roommate, you should subscribe to Caller ID, and if it is evident that the call is not for you, you may simply not answer the 'phone. Otherwise, you are obligated to be kind and courteous to the caller, and to pass along the message to the person whom they are calling. You should not merely hang up the 'phone as soon as you have ascertained that the call is Not For You. What follows are examples of how you should and should not take a message. This is what you should *not* do:

'Phone rings.

RUDE TELEPHONE MANNERS BOY: Hello?

TERRIBLY POLITE CALLER: May I please speak to Charles?

RTMB (*mumbling*): He's not here. (*Hangs up.*)

Again, the 'phone rings.

RTMB: Hello?

TPC: RTMB, this is TPC. I just called. I wanted to leave a message for Charles.

RTMB (*mumbling*): Not here.

TPC (*Interrupting, before RTMB can hang up again.*): I *know*. You *said*. I wanted to leave a *message*. Will you please tell him that I will meet him at Starbucks at seven?

RTMB (*mumbling*): Ummmph. (*Hangs up.*)

Do we even need to tell you, Dear Reader, that Charles never got the message? Not only is behavior like this THOR, but it might be truly detrimental to your roommate's General Well-Being. What if you behave in this manner and the caller is Your Roommate's Boss, or Mother, or Very Wealthy Great-Aunt Who Insists That You Always Return Her Calls Or She Will Cut You Out Of The Will, or anyone else who will Not Look Kindly upon such rudeness, not to mention the failure of the person to whom they wished to speak to Return Their Call? Perhaps you think that failing to pass on a message is unimportant, but the Etiquette Grrls remind you that every time you are Rude on the telephone or fail to pass on a message, you Might Be Ruining Someone's *Entire* Life. And that certainly wouldn't be very nice of you.

Here is an example of how the above conversation *should* have gone.

'Phone rings.

NICE TELEPHONE MANNERS BOY: Hello?

TERRIBLY POLITE CALLER: May I please speak to Charles?

NTMB: I'm sorry, he's not in at the moment. May I take a message?

TPC: Yes, could you please tell him that TPC called?

NTMB: Oh, hi, TPC! This is NTMB. How are you?

TPC: Hi, NTMB; I'm fine, thank you. And you?

NTMB: Very well, thanks. Well, nice talking to you, and I'm terribly sorry Charles wasn't in, but I will have him call you as soon as he gets back.

TPC: Thanks . . . 'bye!

NTMB: 'Bye! (*Hangs up. Fifteen minutes later, TPC's call is returned.*)

You do not need to engage in A Long Conversation with the caller if you do not wish to do so. However, should you speak to the caller for a length of time, you should still remember to pass on the message to the person to whom the caller originally wished to speak. Just because the caller talks with you for twenty minutes doesn't mean that the Original Purpose of her call is null and void.

Also, the Etiquette Grrls recommend that when you ask for someone on the telephone, you should phrase the question as "May I please speak to so-and-so," rather than the dreadful "Is so-and-so there?" Not only does the former *sound* more gracious, but it is a more direct question. The latter leaves open the possibility of a one-word response of "Yes," or, worse, "Yes, but she won't talk to you."

The Facsimile ("Fax") Machine

The Etiquette Grrls aren't too fond of fax machines. They clatter and beep to No End, and often faxed messages are Utterly Illegible. However, if you can't avoid sending a fax, we offer a few guidelines. First, clearly indicate whom the fax is meant for. If you fail to do so, you will have absolutely no right whatsoever to Get Angry when the Intended Recipient fails to receive it. Second, type, don't handwrite, your message. Handwriting often does not transmit very well. Also, no cutesy-pie cover sheets are allowed. Just as borders of adorable kitty cats are Not Permissible on Your Writing Paper, they also are Not Appropriate on faxes.

Also, if you have a fax machine at home, the Etiquette Grrls *beg* you to please, *please* get a Second Line! It is *so* Terribly Annoying to attempt to call someone and be greeted with the high-pitched beep of a fax machine. If this happens more than once, the Etiquette Grrls will be forced to stop telephoning you, Dear Reader, and we know you wouldn't like that at all.

Portable Communications Devices

These days, with the aid of Portable Communications Devices, it's possible to be in touch with everyone 24/7. The Etiquette Grrls aren't so sure this is such a Grand Thing. The Etiquette Grrls like our privacy, and you should, too, Dear Reader. This means there should be times when you are Simply Unreachable (Your Wedding, Your Honeymoon, and Your Funeral come immediately to mind). Nevertheless, we know that there's No Going Back Now, and thus, we offer our thoughts on the use and abuse of various Electronic Gadgets.

CELLULAR TELEPHONES

Are you a Hollywood Director, Dear Reader? We didn't think so. While engaging in Social Activities in Public Places, turn off your cell 'phone. Nothing looks More Pretentious than a person on their phone while in the middle of a meal in a restaurant. (Additionally, if you are on a date, and spend half of it on your cell 'phone, you are very likely to anger your date, probably with disastrous results. See pages 121–123 for more information on How You Should Behave on a Date.) Certainly, there are times when a cell 'phone comes in handy—say, when your car breaks down in the Middle of Nowhere, and there isn't a pay 'phone within a fifty-mile radius. Otherwise, there's really no need to tote a cell 'phone with you everywhere you go. The Etiquette Grrls find it Incredibly Annoying to have to listen to Your Telephone Conversation while they're attempting to shop for a new Betsey Johnson frock, or while they're trying to Improve Their Minds by taking in the new show at the Met.

If, however, you are in possession of a cell 'phone, it should be As Small and Sleek As Possible, and you should purchase a darling Coach carrying case for it. Both should, of course, be black. Although Nokia's ads would have you believe differently, you should *not* strive to color-coordinate your cell 'phone with Your Outfit. And you should always, *always* Turn The 'Phone Off while you are In Church, or At The Theatre. If, during the dénouement of *The Blair Witch Project,* your 'phone rings, and you take the call and carry on a long conversation, do you know what's going to happen to you? The Etiquette Grrls will *personally* take you out to the middle of the woods and *leave you there*. And if you had been paying attention during the movie, as you *should* have been, you would know what Horrors await you.

ATTN.: DOCTORS AND DRUG DEALERS—SOME THOUGHTS ON PAGERS AND BEEPERS

The Etiquette Grrls realize that, unfortunately, there are some professions which necessitate the use of a pager. We know (from watching *ER,* not to mention our innumerable med-student beaux) that doctors are apt to be paged at Any Moment and summoned to the hospital to take care of some Dramatic Emergency. Our Dear Computer-Techie Amis also inform us that they need to have pagers so they can be informed at once if a Server Crashes or something of a Similarly Horrific Nature occurs, which requires their Immediate Attention. We don't like it at all when our e-mail Goes Down, so we suppose, albeit Somewhat Grudgingly, that perhaps this is a Legitimate Excuse to Have a Pager. We also understand that Drug Dealers find them to be quite useful, but really, the Etiquette Grrls don't know anything about this, and nor do we want to. There is no reason, at all, *ever,* for anyone else to have a pager. Why are there so many high-school and college kids walking around with pagers? The Etiquette Grrls sincerely doubt, if you are fifteen years old, that you are so important someone might need to reach you at Any Given Moment. Worse, in these incidences, the pagers tend to be pink, or clear, or of some other Hideous Design. Which, of course, need the Etiquette Grrls even say, is Utterly Unacceptable.

PALMTOP COMPUTERS

The Etiquette Grrls think palmtop computers are Simply Darling! Like your cell 'phone, your palmtop should be small and sleek, and you should purchase a Coach case for it. And also, like your cell 'phone, your palmtop should be used Avec Discretion. For instance, it is Rather Rude to start taking notes on your computer while at, say, a Small Cocktail Party, where your actions would surely be noticed. Furthermore, and perhaps, most importantly, we remind you that palmtop computers are Actual, Functioning Machines. They are not to be used merely as A Status Symbol. If you don't know how to use your palmtop computer properly, and you've only purchased one because you think it's Cute, or Neat, or Trendy, then you shouldn't have one. Remember, while the Etiquette Grrls think palmtop computers *are* Cute, and Neat, and Trendy, we're also Computer Wizzes, and we use our palmtops for more than just playing Minesweeper.

Letters

As much as the Etiquette Grrls love sending their Dear Friends witty e-mail messages and talking on the telephone, it saddens us that we rarely get real, old-fashioned, pen-and-ink letters in the Post. Receiving a good, long letter always Brightens One's Day, and tends to make one feel Well Loved. And, the nice thing about getting letters is that the other people in your apartment building and your postman will think you are Very Popular when you have a stack of intriguing-looking, Handwritten Letters sitting in your mailbox every day! They will probably be very jealous, as they receive only bills and Annoying Flyers from the Local Department Stores, and they will wish they also had lots of Interesting, Literate Acquaintances. Also, although one may print out copies of e-mail, a thick stack of billet-doux, tied with A Lovely Silk Ribbon, is far more romantic than a pile of $8\frac{1}{2} \times 11$-inch computer paper, which is likely to get mistaken for a Term Paper or something equally Dull and Boring. If you wish to send sweet little notes to your Petit(e)-Ami(e), Dear Reader, you *must* do so in pen and ink.

EQUIPMENT FOR LETTER WRITING

Now that you've Heeded Our Advice and wish to take pen to paper and compose A Real Letter, you must acquire the Proper Accoutrements. If you think scribbling in Purple Ink on Lined Paper torn from a Spiral-Bound Notebook constitutes A Letter, then you needn't bother. Nor should you attempt to write letters on Post-its, or on the backs of grocery lists, receipts, or anything else which has been Previously Used. Your Writing Paper (which is never to be referred to as "stationery") should be of Heavy Stock, preferably from Crane's. The Etiquette Grrls love Crane's paper because a) it is always beautiful, b) it is manufactured in Massachusetts, and c) it is the paper on which United States currency is printed. If the Department of Treasury thinks Crane's paper is good enough for American Greenbacks, then it's good enough for you. The color should be white or ivory (we prefer ivory), or if you are a Girl, perhaps pale blue. Any other color is Highly Suspect, and you should proceed avec A Great Deal of Caution (even if Crane's is the Manufacturer). You may, if you wish, select a paper with a Colored Border, with Envelope Linings to match. However, when selecting a shade for your envelope linings and/or trimming on your paper, some colors should be avoided at all costs, such as gold, silver, and red, unless, of course, you are writing from A Bordello.

We also highly recommend that you invest in Writing Paper engraved with your monagram, your Full Name, or your Full Name and Address. Engraved paper is usually less expensive than you might think, and is Far Superior to the more common thermographed variety, which often looks Rather Tacky. The engraving should be in a simple, plain, smallish font, and should be in blue or black ink only. The Etiquette Grrls understand that their Dear Readers might be hesitant to purchase such an item while they are leading Rather Transient Lives, and are apt to move often, but we really think that you ought to go ahead and order some good Crane's engraved writing paper. *Right now*. You never know when you might really need it, and if you should happen to move before you have finished the box, we have found that engraved paper with out-of-date addresses (of which the Etiquette Grrls have stacks and stacks from their boarding-school and college years) is Quite Useful for writing grocery lists or to use as Scrap Paper by the telephone.

You should only ever use dark blue or black ink—no other colors, *ever*. And we do mean Real Ink, not ballpoint. Fountain Pens are preferable, of course, but the Etiquette Grrls will permit you to use a

Good-Quality Rollerball Pen if you find it easier. You should never, under any circumstances, write any sort of missive in crayon, colored or regular pencil, Magic Marker, or highlighter. Nor may you cut out Wee Letters from magazines or newspapers and paste them onto blank paper unless you are composing a Ransom Note, in which case, the cut-and-paste method described above is not only Perfectly Acceptable, but really, we think, the Only Option You Have.

Letters other than those of the business variety should never be typed, no matter how wretched your handwriting, Dear Reader. Typed personal letters are Cold and Evil. If you really must insist on typing all Your Personal Correspondence, we think you are Probably a Lost Cause, and you might as well stick to e-mail.

ENCLOSURES

You should also never enclose any variety of Small and Potentially Messy or Annoying Items, especially confetti, in any sort of correspondence. The Etiquette Grrls are continually trying to eradicate the Etiquette Flat of tiny sparkly hearts, shamrocks, pumpkins, flags, and all manner of other Holiday Symbols that their Rather Inconsiderate Acquaintances insist upon inserting in all of their correspondence with the Etiquette Grrls. Should you absolutely *need* to use confetti, perhaps in an invitation to a *really* smashing party, then we suggest you use Cunning Little Translucent Envelopes through which the recipient may see the confetti, and will, thereby, be forewarned and not inadvertently send Tiny Two-Dimensional Martini Glasses skidding across the Beautifully Polished Hardwood Floors.

SEALING AND STAMPING THE ENVELOPE

Nor should you plaster your letters with stickers—neither on the letter itself nor on the envelope. There is absolutely no need for this whatsoever. The Etiquette Grrls will permit you to place one small, pretty sticker on the outside of the envelope, if you wish, to aid in sealing it, especially if you are writing to one of your Small Nieces, Nephews, Godchildren, or Young Siblings. Even when writing to

Small Children, though, you should never use scented, glittery, or puffy stickers, as these are always Rather Tacky, and you ought to be setting a Good Example for Your Young Friends. For correspondence with adults, the Etiquette Grrls would rather you use sealing wax should you feel the need to augment the Adhesive Matter already extant on envelopes. Sealing wax is Rather Distinguished; a letter that has been sealed with wax connotes matters of Great Importance and Intrigue. And *everyone* likes to receive Important, Intriguing Letters. You should probably not, however, go around dunking all your rings in Hot Melted Wax, as unfortunately, rings these days are not meant to be used in such a manner, not even so-called Signet Rings. This saddens the Etiquette Grrls, and we are afraid we shall have to take this up with Our Favorite Jewelers. In the meantime, you may purchase Nifty Little Devices that will imprint a design in the melted wax at your favorite purveyor of writing implements.

You also ought to consider the variety of postage stamp that you use. Occasionally, one may find a stamp that is particularly well suited to either the interests of your correspondent or to the topic of your letter. For example, if one is hosting a fabulous Roaring Twenties party, one could use the F. Scott Fitzgerald (or, as the Etiquette Grrls call him, FSF '17) stamps which were issued in the Recent Past.

THE THANK-YOU NOTE

Your Grandmother was quite right about one thing, Dear Reader: It is Terribly Important to write Thank-You Notes to everyone, for everything. (In fact, the Etiquette Grrls are awaiting *your* Thank-You Note for providing you with all the Useful Information you have gleaned from this volume, Dear Reader!) Not only is it polite to formally thank people when they have done Something Nice for you, but it could also be Life-Altering, especially when elderly, rich relatives are concerned. Wouldn't it be Just Terrible if you were cut out of Great-Aunt Ethel's will simply because you failed to religiously write her A Gracious Little Thank-You Note for every Fair Isle sweater she sent you, and you Lost Out on A Very Large Inheritance?

The Etiquette Grrls think this would be Simply Tragic. Here is an example of a good Thank-You Note to An Elderly Relative:

Elizabeth T. Swatterwaithe
375 Linden Lane
Westport, Connecticut 06880

July 10, 2001

Dear Aunt Penelope,

Thank you so much for the adorable pink angora sweater with the cunning little matching stocking cap, scarf, and mittens. I know I shall be quite the envy of all the girls in my class at Vassar this winter. You always know just what I need, and I do so love all of the things you've knitted for me.

I hope all is well with you and Uncle Henry, and I hope that I shall see you both at the House in Bar Harbor on Labor Day Weekend for our annual picnic.

Thank you again for your thoughtful and beautiful gift.

Love always,
Betsy

Writing a short, gracious Thank-You Note is an Easy Task that will not take up much of your time. Even if Small Lies (commonly referred to as "white" lies) are necessary. (Perhaps we don't believe Betsy is really going to be a Vision in head-to-toe pink angora, much to the envy of her friends at Vassar, but Aunt Penelope surely will.) Not only is it THOR to fail to write wee Thank-You Notes, but you will undoubtedly soon become Most Unpopular with all of your friends and relatives, and they will, most likely, soon cease to associate with you altogether. And the Etiquette Grrls wouldn't like to see something like that happen to a Nice Person like you, Dear Reader.

WHAT YOU SHOULD WEAR WHILE WRITING LETTERS

Your letters should be long and meaty and entertaining, possibly filled with Bits of Wisdom, and, in short, Rather Literary. So, to get in the Proper Mindframe, your letter-writing clothing ought to be of a similarly Literary Nature—you might even want to consider dressing like your favorite Literary Figure. (Although, that said, we hope your favorite Literary Figure isn't a Frumpy Creature like Gertrude Stein, Emily Dickinson, or Virginia Woolf.) We recommend striving, say, for more of a Jane Austen-y look—darling little Empire-style dresses in cute tiny floral prints or pretty solid colors.

In Person

In these days of Technological Wonders, a person might go days—months, even—without having any Real Contact with Living, Breathing People. The Etiquette Grrls have noticed that many people seem to have forgotten how to behave when faced with Human Interaction. Thusly, we offer A Brief Refresher Course.

NO ONE'S IMPRESSED BY AN ILLITERATE HICK: GRAMMAR 101

As with Written Communication, it is vitally important that you be able to express yourself beautifully with the Spoken Word. You should speak clearly and in a well-modulated fashion, without mumbling, slurring, or lisping, if you are able. You also should make every effort to make sure your speech is Grammatically Correct. These days, the grammar of the General Public is Simply Atrocious, Dear Reader! How many times a day do the Etiquette Grrls hear "Me and my mom are going to the mall"? Far, *far* too often! Even on television (perhaps *especially* on television), speech is rife with Inexcusable Grammar Mistakes! The Etiquette Grrls are left wondering how most people managed to graduate from Grade School, let alone College.

The Etiquette Grrls realize that some Grammatical Errors in speech patterns are due to a Bizarre Regional Patois, but this is no excuse, Dear Reader. If you should ever find yourself in a place other than The City of the Peculiar Speech Pattern, you will look Extremely Foolish—and we wouldn't want that to happen to you. For several years, the Etiquette Grrls lived in a Lovely and Charming City that was a little Too Far West to be considered the East Coast, and a smidge Too Far East to be considered Midwestern. This perhaps accounted for the Strange Local Patois. The Etiquette Grrls were shocked to discover that even their college-educated friends who were natives of This Fair City possessed the most peculiar, not to mention poor, grammar! Every day, The Etiquette Grrls, cringing, would hear sentences similar to the following:

"The car needs washed! It's so dirty!"
"Where's the library at?"
"Are yinz [you ones] goin' downtown?"

Let's look at what's wrong with the above examples, Dear Reader.

"The car needs washed . . ." You will recall, Dear Reader, that a sentence must contain two things to be, in fact, a sentence: 1) a subject, and 2) a verb. It is Particularly Careless, not to mention Lazy, to leave out the verb "to be."

"Where's the library at?" One does not end a sentence with a preposition. One especially does not end a sentence with a preposition which should not be in the sentence at all.

"Are yinz goin' downtown?" One may not Make Up Words. Furthermore "yinz," as with the Southern "y'all" (which, being a contraction of "you all," at least makes Marginally More Sense than "you ones") is plural, and should never be used to address *one* person.

The Etiquette Grrls, however, are not Elementary-School English Teachers, and we have neither the time nor the inclination to sit down and review the Nuances of English Grammar with you, Dear Reader, although we *are* tempted to make you start Diagramming

Sentences. However, we suggest that you drag out your old War-riner's Grammar Textbook and *The Elements of Style* by Strunk and White and review them. You should pay Particular Attention to the sections on case and tense. You might also read William F. Buckley, Jr., and William Safire, both of whom have written many Interesting and Entertaining Essays on the subject of English Usage.

The Etiquette Grrls are warning you, Dear Reader—despite what you see on television, if you have Poor Grammar, you will not get The Job, you will not win The Prize, and you will not be Rich and Famous. (Well, perhaps you will be. But not the kind of Rich and Famous that the Etiquette Grrls commend.) You will, in short, be A Nobody. And the Etiquette Grrls would never, *ever* want you to be A Nobody.

INTRODUCTIONS AND FAREWELLS

Perhaps you've often found yourself in a position where you must introduce several people to each other. With whom should one start? Does it matter? Of course it matters, Dear Reader. You should know by now that Everything Matters. Introductions are really quite simple. This is the Basic Rule: A Man is always introduced to a Woman first, and Young People are always introduced to Their Elders. For example:

"Miss Hargrave, this is Mr. Smythe."

Or,

"Grandmother, this is Kid Rock."

When being introduced to someone new, you should make eye contact, but not Stare Unblinkingly, as this will lead people to believe that you are probably a Crazed Lunatic. You should shake hands firmly, but not so firmly that you might cause bruising or break any bones in the shakee's hand.

When your superiors (this means Anyone Who is More Important Than You Are, or Someone Older Than You) come into the room, you must stand to greet them. No matter how much you dislike them, you may not slouch down in your chair and mutter, "Oh God, it's *you* again," under your breath as they enter. A Boy must not only stand for a superior, but also when a Girl enters the room, and he must remain standing until the Young Lady has seated herself. Likewise, when a Girl (or a superior) exits the room, the Boy again rises, and waits until she has left before sitting down again. Girls do the same thing when any superior leaves. If someone is Exiting Permanently, it is appropriate at that time to say your good-byes, and if he has only recently been introduced to you, to say something about how pleased you are to have made his acquaintance. You may not, under any circumstances, burst into a rousing rendition of the old jingle that goes, "We're sorry to see you go / We're sorry to see you go / We hope to heck you never come back / We're sorry to see you go." You may think rising to greet your superiors is An Antiquated Custom, Dear Reader, but the Etiquette Grrls beg to differ. The Etiquette Grrls had it drilled into Our Young Heads in Prep School to stand immediately (without slouching, mind you) whenever A Teacher came into the room. This has become Such A Habit that we leap to attention whenever anyone comes into a room where we happen to be. Unlike in Prep School, your boss, your friend's elderly relatives, or strangers are not likely to give you Demerits for failing to rise to greet them, but this doesn't mean that you shouldn't do it. (As an aside—if the Etiquette Grrls had their way, everyone would be given Demerits for Rude Behavior, whether in Prep School or not.)

EDITORIAL COMMENTS ON OTHER PEOPLE'S APPEARANCES
You should keep Your Opinions about others' physical appearances to yourself. The Etiquette Grrls assume (perhaps erroneously) that everyone realizes that they shouldn't go around suggesting that Heavy People should enroll themselves at that Dietary Center at Duke University. Nor would you go around ripping cookies out of the hands of Slightly Chubby Folks, shouting, *"You shouldn't be eating*

that!" However, what most people seemingly fail to realize is that you shouldn't pester a Slim Person about her weight, either. You should not make disparaging comparisons to Kate Moss or Calista Flockhart; you should not ask every ten minutes if she has "eaten yet"; you should definitely not continually pester a Perfectly Healthy, But Slim coworker or casual acquaintance to enroll herself in an eating-disorder clinic, let alone Take It Upon Yourself to Enroll Her Against Her Will. Perhaps you mean well, but not only is this THOR, it could cause Serious Damage to the psyche and General Well-being of Your Dear Friend.

You also should not take every opportunity to point out Temporary Flaws in the appearance of others, such as Wee Blemishes, Split Ends, or Bloodshot Eyes. Undoubtedly, they are already well aware of these problems, and will attempt to correct them as best they can. By pointing these things out, you will only make people uncomfortable, and you will possibly antagonize them to the point where they will be compelled to give you a Good, Swift Kick In The Shins.

One of the Etiquette Grrls' biggest Pet Peeves is when passersby, deli clerks, and the like order the Etiquette Grrls to *"Smile!"* The Etiquette Grrls are Morose Types, and we only smile when we have Good Reason to Smile. Besides, we feel that anyone who goes around grinning like the Cheshire Cat all day is probably Completely Deranged. Utter Insanity is rarely the image you want to project, Dear Reader.

THE LEFT-HANDED COMPLIMENT
The Left-Handed Compliment is A Wonderful Thing, handy for cutting down any Rude, Boorish People who Bother You. Under the guise of graciousness, you may deal out Biting Insults with the aid of the Left-Handed Compliment. For instance: "Oh, you *always* look so nice in that skirt!" or "Gee, I wish *I* could wear *interesting* clothes like that!" or "Not many people could wear that *unusual* shade of green . . ." However, the Left-Handed Compliment should be reserved for people who Truly Deserve It. You should not dole out

LHCs to every living soul who crosses your path. In this instance, you cease to be clever, with a caustic, biting wit, and you are Merely Catty.

TOO MUCH INFORMATION (TMI): CONVERSATIONS YOU SHOULD NOT HAVE

There are some things which simply should Never Come Up In Conversation. The Etiquette Grrls don't especially want to hear about the Gory Details of your Liver Transplant, nor about Your Relatives who are In Jail, nor about the time *you* were In Jail, nor about the time you *should* have been In Jail, nor about any of your Health Problems. The Etiquette Grrls don't want to hear about topics like these from Their Friends, let alone Total Strangers. Any sort of Bodily Fluids, also, should never, *ever* be mentioned in Polite Conversation, and should probably be treated euphemistically even avec Your Doctor. Remember, the Etiquette Grrls are From New England, and we don't talk about such things. Not even in Our Journals, and *especially* not In Public. TMI subjects should, at all costs, be Kept To Yourself. And, this, Dear Reader, is all we are going to say on the matter.

CHAPTER FIVE

At Work

The World of the Gainfully Employed

How dreary, indeed, that Young People in This Day and Age, more often than not, need to Hold Down a Job. How often have the Etiquette Grrls wistfully contemplated Less Complicated, More Pleasant Times, when young ladies such as ourselves would have Lived a Life of Leisure! However, although it is an all-consuming drag to have to find a job, and go to the job, and actually accomplish things on the job, you are not allowed to have a Terrible Attitude or to Perpetrate Rude Acts at Your Workplace. You must always follow certain basic rules of Workplace Behavior.

YOUR BRILLIANT CAREER: WHERE YOU SHOULD WORK, AND HOW TO LAND THE CORRECT JOB

Finding the Right Job requires some soul-searching. Of course, the Etiquette Grrls think you should find a position you think is interesting, challenging, and exciting, both in the short and long term. So please don't go off and become An Accountant just because your Parents think that would be a Good Profession, although math gives you Panic Attacks. You will, most likely, be Thoroughly Miserable, and being Miserable is likely to make you snappy and rude. However, once you've chosen A Profession, unless you're Striking Out on Your Own, you'll need to find a particular job. This means sending out Résumés and interviewing.

Your Résumé should be as stylish and traditional as Your Engraved Writing Paper. (And, preferably, it should be printed on Crane's Résumé Paper, which is lovely, heavy stock and comes in the only two acceptable colors for Résumés: white and ivory. While you may see Orange "Résumé Paper" at the Local Copy Shop, using it will do you More Harm Than Good.) You must also print Your Résumé in a Nice, Traditional Font (and for heaven's sake, keep the italic, bold, and underlined type under control!). Either print all Your Résumés on a laser printer or have them copied onto Good Paper at a Very Reputable Copy Shop—do not, under any circumstances, hand someone a nearly illegible, Photocopy-of-a-Photocopied Résumé, and expect them to Give You a Job. No one is impressed by Entropy in Action, Dear Reader! Any correspondence you have with Potential Employers should also be written upon Good Paper, and all letters should follow strict Business Letter Format. Do not, under any circumstances, dash off a Cover Letter on a Bunny Notecard, not that you should have such notecards in the first place.

Beyond their appearance, though, Résumés and Cover Letters must also have Sensible Substance. One of the Etiquette Grrls hires a fair number of people in Her Day Job, and is Entirely Appalled at the Rude and/or Stupid Things she reads! Dear Reader, do not open a Cover Letter with: "I know what you need. You need the best freelance writer on the face of God's green earth. You need someone who can work from home (Caracas, Venezuela). You need, in short, me." Um, the Etiquette Grrls Highly Doubt that you know what the Hiring Manager needs. Keep the tone polite, respectful, and serious! You're applying for a Job, not writing Creative Nonfiction! And resist the urge to discuss anything that is irrelevant to the Job or Your Qualifications for it. No Potential Employer cares that you "evolved yourself" on an ashram somewhere. You also should not, in your correspondence avec a Potential Employer, discuss information that is TMI: "I need this job. I am getting evicted from my apartment and unless you hire me, I'll be forced to move in with my friend Betsy and sleep on her futon, which is covered with dog hair, to which I'm allergic. Please, hire me so that won't have to happen." And everybody should leave the Personal Details off the Résumé. Your Next Boss doesn't need to know your height, your weight, your dress or jacket size, the fact that you are single/married/divorced/a polygamist, the names of your children, or the names of your pets, no matter *how* proud of any of these things you may be. During your Job Interviews, you must adhere to the absolute Letter of All Etiquette Laws. No sitting down until you are invited to sit; no Clothing Faux Pas (for all jobs, you are safest interviewing in a Business Suit and Good Shoes); no cursing; no tardiness; etc. Of course, by reading This Book, you will soon become Extremely Familiar with all of these things and will exhibit them as A Matter of Course, so Job Interviews, for you, Dear Reader, should present no real Conundrum.

Finally, after an interview, Dear Reader, send a Thank-You Note! The Etiquette Grrls are shocked at how few people take the time to do this!

When You're a Worker Bee

So, Dear Reader, you've recently graduated from college and entered the workplace! Congratulations! We knew a Bright Young Thing like you could do it! The Etiquette Grrls are certain you will accomplish Great Things! However, for the Time Being, yes, that is your desk, which is in a dingy, ill-lighted cubicle you will share with three other people. And yes, you will have to be at work at 8 A.M. and worry about getting back to the office in about an hour for lunch. We sympathize, Dear Reader! Yet we caution you that the Stark Reality of Entry-Level Jobs does not give you an excuse for Behaving Atrociously.

For starters, it is not good to mention your Bright College Years every time you open your mouth in the office. We're sure the memories of how your Fraternity's Winter Formal was "Just so radical, dude, because we just *trashed* the place!" are quite vivid, but we encourage you not to share them, ad nauseam, avec Your Boss and Coworkers. College, in fact, is Over, the Etiquette Grrls remind you.

Even worse than continually referring to Old Nassau or New Haven Technical Community College, though, is continuing to behave as though you were still a student there. This, Dear Reader, must stop right now! Your job is not the 10 A.M. Abnormal Psychology Lecture you frequently skipped or attended avec a Vile Hangover, so you should make certain that your weeknight bar-crawling does not extend beyond the Limits of Your Tolerance. Also, although you may work in a Casual-Dress Office, you must make an active effort *not* to look like a student. This means not using your ten-year-old L.L. Bean backpack, which is covered with patches proclaiming your reverence for the Dave Matthews Band, as a Briefcase. Also, read our advice below on Workplace Attire (pages 101–102).

You must immediately reconcile yourself with the fact that You Are Entry-Level. And that, Dear Reader, means you're going to have to do Entry-Level Things, no matter how annoying they are or how much it bugs you to do them. We're sure you were a splendid Editor-in-Chief of the School Newspaper; however, now that you're at the *New York Times*, the Etiquette Grrls sense that you probably have some photocopying and filing in Your Near Future. And the sooner you realize this, the better. Don't get the Etiquette Grrls wrong, now—we certainly don't hope you get stuck doing too much of the Grunt Work! And we hope you have smart, fair, fun supervisors who follow all of our Advice for Managers.

Finally, if you're not sure how to do something, *ask*. Your Boss will be much happier to explain to you how to proceed in a certain situation than have to straighten out the Untold Catastrophes which might occur if you forge ahead without inquiring. And, as a matter of fact, any smart boss would *expect* you to ask several relevant questions before beginning a new task, rather than simply plunging into it.

When You're the Leader of the Pack

Hurrah for you, Dear Reader! You've just been given that Big Promotion! Now you have people reporting to you! This will be A Piece of Cake, right?

Well, not immediately. The Etiquette Grrls think that when Some People get promoted, they go on Wee Power Trips, making life miserable for those unlucky enough to work for them. Dear Reader, remember, just because you have the power to tell other people what to do doesn't mean you can treat them as Your Personal Servants. This is disrespectful and Horribly Rude. For example, you may not require Your Underlings to run personal errands for you, or tend to your Household Chores. Dispatching the interns to fetch your Dry Cleaning or Water Your Plants is a big no-no! Also, you must not act like a Roman Emperor and force Your Minions to attempt to accomplish Impossible Tasks, just for the pleasure of Seeing Them Fail. It does no one any good, Dear Reader, for you to place unrealistic deadlines on projects. If there's anything worse than looking like a Tyrant, it's looking like a Tyrant with No Concept of Time.

Let us remind you of a few things, O New Manager. Your employees, much like pets, need to eat, sleep, and run around. They will grow to hate you if you deprive them of any of these things. Therefore, please refrain from forcing the Entire Team to Work Through Lunch—if you really can't end the meeting, for heaven's sake, kindly ask the receptionist to Order Sandwiches to be Delivered. Don't schedule meetings between 8 P.M. and 8 A.M.—this is Inhuman. Encourage people to leave the office for a Brisk Walk. Heck, organize a Department-Wide Snowball Fight!

In the spirit of Snowball Fights, remember that you are in a position to Make Work Fun for Several Other People. And to accomplish this is a Wonderful Thing! You should regularly do Nice Things for Your Employees, like bringing in Delicious Pastries from a Really Good Bakery instead of the Ubiquitous Munchkins; organizing an Office Outing to a Baseball Game, or, better yet, A Bar; giving everyone an Afternoon Off right before the Holidays, when everyone needs to do some Shopping; etc. Now, the Etiquette Grrls are not saying that it would be in *your* Best Professional Interests to make your office a veritable playground, with everyone getting nothing done, eating until they're sick, and repairing to A Local Bar, en masse, at 2 P.M., but you get the idea.

And finally, we do hope it is unnecessary to remind you that you must be unfailingly polite, considerate, and kind to your employees, or they will, most correctly, view you as A Monster. Even if you have the power to Fire People, you must observe Basic Etiquette with them at all times!

Your Attire

Different Offices expect, and enforce, widely varying degrees of Formality of Dress. An Investment Banking Firm will require you to look very conservative, while an Alternative Rock Magazine will probably expect you to look more off-beat. Although we assume that you will have some sort of idea of the flavor of your office from your job interview, you may, and certainly with good reason, be unsure of exactly how you should dress.

When you're new on the job, it is better to play it safe and not go too far toward any extreme. Don't spend your life savings on Brooks Brothers suits until you're sure your coworkers don't wear khakis every day. Likewise, no matter how cool you think your new forest-green, crushed-velvet Docs are, keep them at home until you're absolutely, *positively* certain such footwear will be acceptable.

Even in the most informal office, you must abide by certain Unbreachable Principles of Dress. Always, always, *always* make sure your clothes are neat, clean, ironed, and mended. No stained, ripped, frayed, or ill-fitting garments are allowed. If you are inept with a needle and thread (as many of us are), any city or town abounds with satisfactory seamstresses and tailors. Use them. Also, some articles of clothing are simply *too* informal to contemplate wearing at *any* office. Unacceptable items include: sweatpants and sweatshirts; tee shirts bearing any sort of slogan or emblazoned with band logos and/or tour dates; and shorts, *especially* any sort of short that does not fall just above the knee, which even at best, we think is probably only acceptable if you are, say, a courier for a bicycle messenger service. You may, of course, be working on an Archaeological Dig in South America, in which case, you may wear all the Indiana Jones–ish, khaki shorts ensembles you desire, or any other clothing appropriate for the Amazon Basin. But we assume this is an unusual circumstance. (And might we add that Dr. Jones *always* wore trousers and was impeccably dressed at all times—except when he wore a black tie with a wing collar at Club Obi Wan in the opening scene of *Temple of Doom*, but, of course, one can rarely count on a sequel, Dear Reader.) Your shoes should be neat and not scuffed, and the heels should not be worn down. Sandals, sneakers, platform shoes, and combat boots are tricky territory, and you should proceed with caution when wearing these items. Best to avoid them until you are positive they are appropriate footwear. It is also wise to shy away from peculiar haircuts and colors, heavy makeup, and any sort of visible body piercings and tattoos. For general clothing guidance, please see pages 51–59 in chapter 3.

Your Attitude

When you were a Wee Lad or Lass, did your report cards indicate that you Played Well With Others? If you still haven't mastered the art of social interaction, you will need to get your social skills in gear if you are to have a successful Professional Career.

First of all, whether you are an Intern or a CEO, you need to Get Over Yourself. Right now. The Etiquette Grrls feel that it is extremely rude to present oneself as unapproachable—for heaven's sake, no matter *who* you are, you are required to greet everyone in your office pleasantly and to make polite conversation with all. Including the Janitor, Dear Reader, and the Guy Who Refills the Soda Machine.

Keep your Anger in Check. You may not *ever* reprimand someone who reports to you in front of Other People. This is what Offices with Doors are for. If you need to put the Fear of God into someone, and you only have a cubicle to call your office, step into an empty office or meeting room, then call in the Offending Party. (This has the Added Effect of making it seem as if they're taking a trip to the Principal's Office.)

Don't blurt out inappropriate things in front of Bigwigs. The meeting at which the CEO stops in to announce the company's Stock Split is not the time to ask if you can have the afternoon off on the day of the Christmas Party because you need to get your hair done. Also, if you have Strong Opinions about something which is being announced to you by a Bigwig (e.g., your company is merging with your biggest competitor), it is not smart to respond, five seconds after the announcement is made, "What the hell are you executive idiots thinking?" You may very well be right, but you should talk privately with Your Boss about your concerns rather than speak hastily in front of everybody.

Don't try to make other people do your work for you, *especially* if they are not directly subordinate to you. If preparing a Weekly Analytical Report is your responsibility, and you just don't feel like doing it, don't pass it off to your cubiclemate and then attempt to take credit for it. If someone does go out of the way to help you with a project, you should always acknowledge his or her contributions. And, most certainly, the next time you see that person working late to finish something up, you should offer to assist.

Don't be a Brown-Noser. While, of course, it is important not to look slackerly, especially in your first weeks at a job (meaning don't leave early to go to a Phish concert, take three days of vacation time, etc.), don't go overboard in the other direction and be too much of a Striver. It's great (and dare we say, expected) to stay late if something needs to be completed, but if you don't have anything to do, you don't have to loiter in the office until nine o'clock every night just to be sure you're the last one to leave. If there is no Big Project going on, do not, under any circumstances, sit at your desk after hours playing computer solitaire. No one will be impressed; rather, everyone will assume you have No Life Outside the Office, which is not a good thing to have attached to your reputation.

Finally, stop whining. The Etiquette Grrls are sure your job *is* very difficult, time-consuming, and stressful, but you should not Moan and Groan about it to your officemates, or, especially, to Your Boss. Most likely they feel they are in similar positions, and, if they have been Keeping Stiff Upper Lips, will not take kindly to your "Woe Is Me" complaints. You will acquire the reputation of someone who can't put up with anything—a rep that's not likely to Advance Your Career.

Bad Office Behavior

One of the Etiquette Grrls once purchased, and tacked up in her office, a small poster of "Classroom Rules" intended for Elementary School Students. It was eerily applicable to The Workplace. The Etiquette Grrls are not sure why certain kinds of Rude Behavior seem to transpire so frequently in offices, but we think the following Forms of Bad Conduct need to Cease Immediately:

- Being Nosy. If your presence would be beneficial at The Meeting, Dear Reader, you would have been invited to attend it. Just because there's an interesting assortment of people in the Conference Room doesn't mean you need to pop your head in and say hello. Also, it is Bad Manners, not to mention Quite Odd Looking, to stick your head above the walls of your cubicle and spin it around, Periscope-Style, just to see which people are at their desks, who's on the phone, who's not back from lunch yet, etc.

- Stealing other people's desk supplies. You are not allowed to "borrow" items from your officemates and squirrel them away in your desk, Dear Reader. The Girl who sits across from you may have a lovely Waterman pen that she occasionally leaves unattended on her desk, but you may not, in the guise of leaving a note for her, swipe it for your own use.

- Stealing food. Just because you didn't have time for Breakfast doesn't mean you should spend the first hour of your workday

On the Prowl for an Unguarded Bagel. Unless someone has clearly said, "I brought bagels for everyone! Please help your-self!" do not presume that you may take any food you see lying around. It is even worse to purloin Other People's Food from the Common Refrigerator. Even if there is no name on it, the pear-and-Gorgonzola salad in a Tupperware container is proba-bly Somebody's Intended Lunch; it is not for your consumption.

- Bemoaning the Lack of Things You Have to Do. We shouldn't even have to tell you this, Dear Reader. If you find yourself devoid of tasks, you should ask Your Boss what to work on next. If Your Boss has no other project, and you can't easily pitch in on something a coworker is tackling, you should inconspicu-ously sit at your desk and attempt to do Something Construc-tive, like learn a new piece of software, catch up on magazines in your industry, archive your e-mail, etc. Do not, under any cir-cumstances, wander the office, proclaiming, "I'm so *bored*! I have *nothing* to do! I might as well go *home*!" Those who *are* busy will despise you, and deservedly so.

- Perpetuating forwarded e-mail virus alerts (always hoaxes), chain letters, supposedly funny Flash movies that take hours to download, jokes, etc. (This is discussed at length on pages 69–71, but it's worth a special mention here as it happens so fre-quently in offices.) If you do receive a forwarded message, sim-ply ignore it. Do not, in turn, forward it to the Tech Guy as a means of Snitching on the Perpetrator of the Forward. No one likes a Tattle-Tale.

- Repeating everything other people say in meetings in an effort to make yourself look good. If Your Boss wanted to hear her own words thrown back at her, she'd have held the meeting in an Echo Chamber. This just makes you look contemptibly uno-riginal.

- Annoying the Tech Guy. Every office has someone who is responsible for fixing your computer, setting up your e-mail account, etc., and you should never, *ever* waste this person's time. For example, do not ask the Tech Guy to help you "make your e-mail play that little bell noise." He has the power to Make Your Life Hell!

- Irritating Habits. Please, the Etiquette Grrls beg of you, refrain from all of the following practices: cracking knuckles, eating crunchy (read: noisy) foods, eating strong-smelling foods (which might make your coworkers ill), talking at the top of your lungs, conversing with yourself, tapping your pencil incessantly on your desk, etc.

"Optimizing Synergistic Cross-Platform Eyeballs": Tacky Office Speech

Occasionally, the Etiquette Grrls, who have, as you might have noticed, a Rather Strong Grasp of the English Language, hear Linguistic Monstrosities from Corporate Types. To pepper one's speech with neologisms and trendy expressions, just because one *can*, seems Terribly Crass, Dear Reader. Therefore, kindly avoid using any of the following terms at any time: "synergy"; any combination of "bricks," "clicks," and "mortar"; "dot-commie"; "sexy" in reference to technology; "B-school"; "leveraging"; "best-of-breed" (unless you are talking about the Westminster Dog Show); gratuitous usage of "e-" and "i-" prefixes to words; "eyeballs"; etc., etc. To use any of these terms *outside* the office goes Beyond Crass . . . it is Downright Rude to bring up "synergistic best-of-breed bricks-to-clicks e-tailing" at a Cocktail Party. The entire point of Cocktail Parties is to encourage Pleasant, Sociable, Intelligent Conversation avec the Catalyst of a Few Strong Drinks, and talking in Business Jargon is not Pleasant, Sociable, or Intelligent!

Also avoid annoying phrases that tend to come up repeatedly in interoffice communication, such as "FYI" (appropriate when, say, written on a Post-it Note attached to a copy of an article in the *Wall Street Journal*; not appropriate in speech); "So we're on the same page"; "Think(ing) outside the box"; "Let's run it up the flagpole and see how it flies/who salutes it"; "I'll take ownership of that action/item"; "It's on my Radar Screen" (unless, of course, you actually work in Air Traffic Control); etc. These have become as ubiquitous, annoying, and, ultimately, meaningless as early 1980s Valley Girl phrases. We highly doubt that those people who purport to value "thinking outside the box" have the Foggiest Notion of Originality, as they're all tossing around the Same Stupid Phrase.

Under the Weather

So, Dear Reader, you have a case of the Sniffles! The Workplace is like College, right, where you can skip a day and no one will know? Wrong. The Etiquette Grrls sympathize with you, Dear Sick Reader, and wish that your office had a Greater Understanding of illness! We sincerely hate the fact that many of us have to work whilst sick, enduring physical misery and endangering the health of others who happen to share the same office! For shame, Corporate America! Let the sick people stay home! But the Etiquette Grrls digress.

First of all, unless you work in, say, a hospital, where even the slightest bit of a cold could Threaten the Lives of Others, you will have to make a choice about whether or not you should go to work while you are sick. We recommend that, especially when you have first started a job, you drag yourself to work, even though you are at Death's Door. It would be a good idea to, perhaps, telephone Your Boss and say something like, "Hello, Emma, this is Thomas. I'm [slight cough] a bit under the weather today, but I'm on my way in. Is there any way we could move this afternoon's strategic planning meeting to 10 A.M.? If I keep feeling worse, I'd like to stop at my doctor's office this afternoon, and I'd really like to be in on that meeting." This will, undoubtedly, get you Brownie Points. Your Boss might even say, "Thomas, you sound terrible. Stay home and get some rest; I'll e-mail you after the meeting." (However, Dear Reader, we trust that you Know Your Place and would not try to reschedule, say, a meeting of the Board of Directors at which you are merely supposed to operate the Slide Projector.)

When you *must* be at work while sick, please take care to *try* not to infect others. Bring your own Kleenex, Vitamin C, Tylenol, etc., and keep them on your desk, not on the conference table or in the office kitchen. Try to keep coughing, exuberant sneezing, etc., to a minimum, if at all possible. For the well-being of Everyone Else, if you suspect you might have something other than a Quick Bug, you should visit your doctor for treatment.

If you have a Chronic Illness or ailment that will require you to miss work occasionally, it is a good idea to tell Your Boss. Unless Your Boss is a Beast (and we certainly hope not, Dear Reader!), he or she will be understanding, and this will make things much easier for you in the long run.

Office Parties

Ooooooh, it's the company Christmas Party! We hope, Dear Reader, that your company is so Flush Avec l'Argent that it holds fabulous, no-expense-spared, elegant events at places like Tavern on the Green. However, even if this is not your situation, chances are you'll have to attend several Corporate Functions during Your Brilliant Career. Remember: Office Parties are not Real Parties. It is much, *much* more regrettable to get Blazingly Drunk in front of Your Boss than in front of Your Best Friends. Therefore, exercise caution. Even if you work in a Rather Hard-Drinking Office, it really is in Your Best Interest to stop after a few. Trust the Etiquette Grrls on this one. We've witnessed Very Bad Things Happen to Dear Friends (you might care to flip to "Office Hookups," below).

You are not allowed to skip an Important Company Function. It doesn't matter if you are the President of the Leonardo di Caprio Fan Club and *Titanic II: The Musical* is opening on the same night as the Office Party—you are not allowed to Send Your Regrets. Believe us, someone will notice your absence. Unless you are truly Deathly Ill, you have to show up, at least for a little while.

It is always a pleasant, if jarring, experience to see Your Coworkers Dressed to the Nines! Do, however, try to avoid saying things like,

"Oh, my God, is that really *you*, Algernon? You *shaved*! And you're not wearing that rugby-shirt-type thing! You really own a *tie*!?! Wow! *And it's not a clip-on!* Will wonders never cease!" This merely makes poor Algernon feel bad about himself. It is, however, perfectly nice to compliment your coworkers on their outfits. Don't gush, and please don't be smarmy . . . simply say something like, "You look very nice tonight, Algernon." The Etiquette Grrls hope that even in this day of Horrible Political Correctness, we can give each other simple, kind compliments like this, even if we happen to—how shocking—work in the same office!

What, then, should you wear to the Office Party? That depends upon when and where it is, whether a dress code is suggested, etc. If one is not, follow the guidelines on pages 59–64. However, you should always dress more conservatively for a Work-Related Party than for a Regular Party. It is certainly nice to pull out all the stops and Dress Up for a Change, but there is no need to wear some sort of strapless *and* backless *and* short *and* tight outfit to attract attention to yourself. (We don't think you should own anything remotely resembling that, but if you do, please do not wear it to Company Functions.)

If you are invited to a Social Function at Your Boss's House, you should attend (of course), and be on your Very Best Behavior. Take care to avoid Talking Shop too much, especially if the other guests are not from Your Company, and do Take Pains to Converse Avec Your Boss's Spouse, Children, etc., in addition to Your Boss Him- or Herself.

Office Romance

While we all know this is probably not something to be officially encouraged, per se (the Etiquette Grrls Highly Doubt that any Fortune 500 corporations have Friday-Night Mixers, à la Prep School), we all know that Office Romance happens. When you have many Single Young People working Long Hours in the Same Small Space, some kind of romance is guaranteed to start up. The Etiquette Grrls hope that should you Become Involved avec a Coworker, you will continue to Behave Correctly.

To those involved in an Office Relationship, we say: Above All, Be Discreet! No playing footsie in the conference room, no cutting a window between your cubicles so you can hold hands all day, no spending break time in the Server Closet. The Etiquette Grrls despise P.D.A. in general, and consider it grossly, *grossly* inappropriate at the office! Also, do not use e-mail to send Mash Notes, as everyone knows the Company Tech Guys can get into that stuff. Make every attempt to deal with each other in the office exactly as you did before you began dating. Even if your company has a Liberal Attitude toward Office Romance, it will be easier on everyone involved if you always Conduct Yourselves Professionally.

Finally, should you become distracted to the point at which you cannot do your job, then, perhaps, it is time for one of you to Seek Employment Elsewhere.

Office "Hook-ups"

First, let the Etiquette Grrls just say that, being Ladies, we don't particularly care to Discuss This Sort of Thing. However, our attitude toward this is illustrative: If we don't deign to talk about something, Dear Reader, well, neither should you and the Rest of Your Office! This means that coworkers who are not In Love but have participated in what is often termed a "hook-up" must be Silent as the Grave. Chalk your behavior up to a Bad Decision and do not speak about the matter. Ever. Surely, the Office Rumor Mill has plenty of topics for discussion already—why would you want to add yourself to it?

Office Gossip: The Correct Way to Dish the Dirt

The Rumor Mill exists. The Grapevine exists. And, Dear Reader, there is a difference between them. You must avoid becoming fodder for the Rumor Mill and eschew placing Harmful Information into it. However, in contrast, you must try your hardest, from Day One at your job, to become a Necessary Part of the Office Grapevine.

Rumor Mills handle information that is either amusing ("Michael got really drunk last night! He did the *funniest* imitation of the boss. You should see it.") or pernicious ("Michael and Lisa hooked-up because he slipped her Roofies!"). The amusing information is, well, amusing. But because the pernicious information goes this way as well, the Etiquette Grrls think you're wise to listen to the Rumor Mill, as long as you take it with a Giant Grain of Salt and do not add to it. This requires the conversational instincts of a Diplomat, but if you're Really Sharp, you'll get the hang of it. It is truly Rude and Evil to spread Rumors about someone when you know them to be untrue . . . and, even if you only pass along Innocuous Tidbits, the only way you can claim to be "above office gossip" when you find yourself a target of it is to have a Clean Record regarding contributions to the Rumor Mill. Otherwise, Dear Reader, you're Fair Game.

The Office Grapevine, however, is Your Best Friend. Love it. Nurture it. Grapevines deal with Privileged Information, generally about your company—the sort of things that most people don't know about yet, but will affect everyone. The Etiquette Grrls are not telling you to snoop, mind you, but it is invaluable to know things about the company that others at your level are not aware of. Will you be Merging with Your Competitors? Is someone Quitting (especially someone whose job you'd like to have)? So Play Nice, Dear Reader, with trustworthy Grapevine sources. Of course, don't go looking for things it's illegal for you to know, and don't go revealing things that, if widely known, would cause Mass Panic. But it's Not Impolite to Keep Your Ear to the Ground.

"Working Lunches"

When you have a Business Lunch or Dinner at a Restaurant, make certain you follow All Rules of Dining (see chapter 2). Your Table Manners must be Impeccable, whether you are grabbing a quick bite at the Corner Deli with Your Boss or spending three hours at a Four-Star Restaurant with Clients. Furthermore, additional Etiquette Duties apply at a Business Meal, depending upon if you are the Host or a Guest. It should always be clear who is the Host at a Business Lunch or Dinner; this is usually the person who makes the Reservation and has invited everyone (or has had his or her Assistant make the Reservation and Invite Everyone). Everyone else, no matter their company affiliation or status, is a Guest.

When you are the Host, you should make your guests feel as comfortable as possible, just as if they were guests in Your Own Home. Ask your guests about their Smoking Preference before you are seated, and make certain your guests know they may order anything on the menu. One way of indicating this is to make some suggestions about the food: "I'm going to start with the Tomato and Mozzarella Salad, followed by the Salmon, but I can also recommend the Caesar Salad and the Steak au Poivre." (This makes your guests aware that, first, it will be all right if they order both a salad and a main course, and second, that you won't blink an eye if they order the Steak au Poivre, the most pricey thing on the menu.) It is also helpful, while you are perusing the menus, to indicate whether or not this will be a Boozy Lunch. In some companies, this is practically expected; in others, it is Most Uncool. If it's all right for Your Guests to Drink, you should say something like, "The Martinis here are excellent—we always have them," or, if you will not be drinking, "I'm going to stick to iced tea myself today, but they have a great wine list here." (Do not, of course, force Alcohol upon Anybody.) And while we are sure Business is Pressing, the Etiquette Grrls strongly believe Meals Should Not Be Rushed. We know we're doing business avec the Right Sort of People if they like good restaurants and good food.

When you are a Guest at a Business Lunch or Dinner, you must follow Your Host's lead on everything. Unfortunately, if Your Host has not read This Book, you will be forced to Play It Safe on Matters of Drinking, Ordering Expensive Food, and Smoking. This means that unless Your Host orders alcohol, you shouldn't. Even if you, as the Guest of Honor, are ordering first, and you would really like a Drink, you should not order one if Your Host hasn't given the All-Clear. Order sparkling water or something to start; you can always switch to The Hard Stuff if Other People do. Don't order the Most Expensive Thing on the Menu, either, and don't complain if you are seated in Nonsmoking and you'd really enjoy a Cigarette after the meal. Yes, we know, this means you might not have the Most Pleasant Meal of Your Life, but it's better than looking Totally Uncouth in Your Host's Eyes. Try, also, to keep Special Food Requests to a Minimum (as we outline in chapter 2).

It should be clear, at a Business Lunch or Dinner, who's going to Pick Up the Check. This is the Host. However, the Etiquette Grrls do caution you to carry l'argent in case, for some reason, Your Host does The Unthinkable and starts announcing how much each person owes.

Birthday Parties, Gifts, Etc.

Of course you should celebrate your coworkers' birthdays! Not to do so would be Inhuman! Just make sure that everyone in the office gets the same type of party. It's not Polite to order a fifty-dollar cake from the Good Bakery for Your Best Office Friend and have everyone else make do with some blue-frosting-ed monstrosity from the Local Supermarket. Take care, too, that whoever Organizes Parties actually knows everyone's birthday. It's Rude to skip someone.

Some offices engage in a practice of Collecting Money for things like Retirement Gifts, Donations in Memory of Someone's Deceased Family Members, etc. The Etiquette Grrls think that while this is a Nice Gesture, it's often handled by people who view Collecting Money as Their Ticket to All the Power. You must be Extremely Considerate when you ask anyone for money, or they will come to resent you! First, make sure your office agrees on what kind of things deserve a Big Old Collection; then make sure you're fair about this. Here's an example: Weddings may merit collections in Your Office. A very popular coworker is about to get married after a year-long engagement, and you've all met her fiancé. You ask everyone for money for a gift. Great. The next week, someone who barely talks to anyone announces her Upcoming Nuptials to someone she met last weekend. Guess what? You need to Play Fair and collect roughly the same amount of money for her, too. This would also be true if the first person were The Boss and the second An Underling.

Do not ask your coworkers for a specific amount of money, and never, ever ask people publicly. Contributing to a gift should be optional. We recommend sending an e-mail saying, "There's an envelope in my desk drawer containing contributions toward a donation to the Cancer Foundation in memory of Sarah's father. If you'd like to contribute, leave your money in the envelope. There's also a card. Thank you." The donation, of course, comes from "The Marketing Department, XYZ, Inc." And nothing is said to people who do not contribute, or who merely sign the card. That would be THOR.

Electronic Devices at Work

In many of today's offices, something is constantly ringing, beeping, squealing, or buzzing. The Etiquette Grrls are sick of the cacophony! First, everyone needs to turn down the volume on *anything* that makes noise. Nothing your computer does should be audible from the desk beside you. If you work better while listening to music, bring headphones, and connect them to your computer. Kindly do make sure the level of noise coming through the headphones is not annoying to others Of Its Own Accord, though.

When the telephone at your desk rings, you should immediately answer it, or, if your 'phone is capable of it, drop the caller into voice mail. Most office telephone systems have ringers that sound like Car Alarms, and it is extremely annoying to listen to repetitive bleating, just because you're "not at a good stopping point." When you answer your 'phone, say either your first and last name, or something like, "Hello, this is Claudia." Do not bark, "Yeah," or "Whaddaya want," and always follow the 'phone etiquette guidelines given on pages 71–82. If your 'phone has a speakerphone option, you should use it as infrequently as possible. The Etiquette Grrls detest the abuse of speakerphones, Dear Reader! They are useful for Conference Calls, when a few colleagues at one company need to participate in the same 'phone call—but speakerphones used in Conference Calls really must be High-Quality, Expensive 'Phones. It is most annoying to listen to the persistent hisssssssss of static over the line caused by a Cheap 'Phone on Speaker. Furthermore, if you are not on a Conference Call, it is not a Terrible Imposition for you to pick up the Receiver and hold it to Your Ear. It *is*, however, a Terrible Imposition for Your Coworkers to have to listen to you retrieve your Voice Mail, check your credit-card balance, listen to a Muzak version of "MMMM-Bop" while on hold with the Cable Company, etc. It should go without saying that all Private Conversations must never take place on speakerphone—especially if the Other Party is unaware multiple people can hear their every word. We don't think you should be breaking up with Your Girlfriend during business hours, within earshot of everyone, anyway, *let alone* over speakerphone.

Cellular 'phones are another Target of the Etiquette Grrls' Rage. We've discussed their use and abuse elsewhere, but a few special considerations apply to Cell 'Phones at work. Many people use Cell 'Phones as a means of having Private Conversations at work so as not to make Long-Distance or Personal Calls over the company lines. The Etiquette Grrls applaud the spirit of this, but caution you to beware. The more you skulk about looking for a place to make a Private 'Phone Call, the more everyone will think you're Setting Up Job Interviews. The day someone spots you sitting in your car, in the middle of the morning, talking on the 'phone, is the day everyone starts to believe you're thinking of quitting.

You may have been *given* your cell 'phone by your company, which means you will have to give out the number to many people. The number may even be—horrors—on your Business Cards! Obviously, Dear Reader, there is nothing you can do about this, except to be scrupulous about Turning Off the Ringer when you are not in the office. (The Etiquette Grrls don't think that any job should issue you a device that lets Your Boss feel it's acceptable to bother you at home at 11 P.M., but if you have to have the 'phone, try to keep it from bugging Everyone Else.) If you get calls on your Company Cell 'Phone while you are in a Meeting, watch what Other People do when this happens and model your behavior accordingly. If it is general practice to turn 'phones off when meetings start, then do so (the Etiquette Grrls applaud this!). At the very least, you should put the 'phone on the vibrate setting. If you receive a call you feel you should take (e.g., one that is either business-related or of an Urgent Personal Nature, like, "This is Metropolitan Hospital. Your wife has just gone into Labor!"), slip quietly out and answer it. You may quietly say, "Excuse me," before your departure. Under no circumstances should you force a roomful of people to listen to you have a 'phone conversation. When you return to the meeting, either take your seat silently, or briefly apologize; if the call was relevant to the meeting, you may give a recap of it at this time. Finally, Conducting Business on Cell 'Phones while one is on Public Transportation is most irritating to other passengers, and should be kept to a minimum if you are not in an empty train car or bus.

Personal Desktop Assistants, a.k.a. Palmtop Computers or P.D.A.s, bother the Etiquette Grrls for two reasons. First of all, as we grew up reading *The Official Preppy Handbook,* we use the acronym "P.D.A." to refer to "Public Display of Affection" (something we consider Most Vile). Now, upon hearing things like, "I saw this great P.D.A. last night in Circuit City," we experience vexing Cognitive Dissonance. But the Etiquette Grrls digress. P.D.A.s also bother the Etiquette Grrls because, quite simply, too many people have them, and many of these people use them as Toys. Unless you know how to sync your e-mail to your P.D.A., can get directions on it, and have more than fifty contacts in it, you don't really need this device. The Etiquette Grrls don't see much sense in having a glorified electronic to-do list just because it's an expensive little gizmo. However, if you can actually use a P.D.A., and follow the Palmtop Computer etiquette we delineate in greater depth on pages 84–85, we recommend you download a few Classic Books for it and read them at your leisure. It is, the Etiquette Grrls admit, quite refreshing to read a few pages of Katherine Mansfield's *The Garden Party* while waiting for the Train.

Now, let us move from Personal Electronic Items to Electronic Items That Are Shared, such as fax machines, photocopiers, and printers. People are frequently Frighteningly Inconsiderate about using such machines! How many times, Dear Reader, have you had to wait thirty minutes for the printer to finish running a Giant Spreadsheet before the one page you sent it comes out? The Etiquette Grrls think that if you are printing, copying, or faxing a large document, you should do it in small sections. This allows others to "cut in," which is courteous. At the copier, if you see someone waiting with only one sheet of paper in her hand, you should allow her to go before you if you're making five hundred four-page, stapled booklets. (This is especially true if the person waiting is Higher Up in the Food Chain Than You, Dear Reader.) If any machine is Temperamental, do not leave large jobs in it unattended . . . in all likelihood, some Poor Soul will come wandering up, looking to fax one page, and have to spend half an hour removing a nasty paper jam he didn't cause. Yes, it's tedious to stand next to the machine and watch it print all your mailing labels, but it's better than leaving extra blank pages of labels in the paper feed tray and having the CEO start running the Annual Report on them.

Quitting Avec Style and Grace

A new job awaits you, and it's time to bid adieu to your Current Employer! What a splendid forum, you might think, to tell everyone you find annoying, horrible, or mean to See You In Hell! Well, Dear Reader, the Etiquette Grrls caution you to avoid making A Spectacle of Yourself during the process of Quitting. You must actually, formally, quit your job—it is Bad Form to go AWOL for a few weeks. (Your coworkers will likely Contact the Police, and it's very embarrassing to be reported erroneously as a Missing Person.)

To quit your job formally, you will need to deliver a Letter of Resignation to Your Boss. This takes the form of a Standard Business Letter (i.e., in the correct format, typewritten, and signed—you are not allowed to quit via E-mail, Fax, or Morse Code) and should be brief and direct. You must include the last day you will work at the company; it is polite to give at least two weeks' notice, if possible. Most importantly, you must be Absolutely Civil. The following letter shows how you should *not* resign:

> You Incompetent Bitch,
>
> *I am thrilled to report that after today, I will never have to Lay Eyes on Your Sorry Self again. I have a fabulous new job that pays double my salary, and where, I may add, the Management Team are not Insipid Fools. My cat has more knowledge of this industry than you do, and you know what? You look really stupid in that embroidered pink shirt you wear every single day. Indeed, the only thing I have learned in working for you is how not to manage other people.*
>
> *See Me In Hell,*
> Sarah Van Eyck

A better version of this letter would be:

> Dear Sally,
>
> *Please accept my resignation, effective two weeks from today, Friday, August 1. While I have learned a great deal at this company, I have accepted another position which offers me an important chance to further my career.*
>
> *Sincerely yours,*
> Sarah Van Eyck

Is it Cathartic to write the first letter? Of course! The Etiquette Grrls, in fact, think it would be *splendid* if you were to write a resignation letter saying exactly how you feel . . . and simply not send it. It's not polite to insult people, and, more important, you will Burn Your Bridges. What if you and Incompetent Sally are copanelists at an Industry Conference? What if you find out, to your Great Chagrin, that Your New Boss's Boss was Sally's College Roommate? Then, Dear Reader, you will Thank Your Lucky Stars you chose to be Polite. Also, it never hurts to remain in Your Former Boss's Good Graces, as the time may come (and it will, Dear Reader, especially dans Le Monde de Start-Ups) when you will need A Reference. While the Etiquette Grrls can certainly appreciate your desire to make a Dramatic Exit, we also firmly believe that occasionally it's wise to Play It Safe.

It is always, *always* preferable to make a Graceful Exit. On your Last Day, your coworkers may decide to have a Wee Party in your honor. Of course you must attend this! However, do not use this opportunity to Rant About how Awful the Company Is, How Glad You Are That You're Leaving, etc. Remember, Everyone Else still has to work there. Also, even if you've gotten a Phenomenal New Job, with a giant salary increase and all manner of perks, you are absolutely obligated to keep your mouth shut about it. (Discussing money is Rather Vulgar, anyway.) Inquisitive, Rude People may try to press you for actual figures, but the Well-Behaved Person will always murmur something vague and reveal nothing. Merely say, "It's a great opportunity," or something of that nature.

If you are quitting sans New Job, the Etiquette Grrls do not recommend Making Up a Job to Save Face. If you are Found Out, you will look Absolutely Pathetic. Far better to quit and offer a Fabulous Reason—you're going to Travel, or Write Your Memoirs, or Take Some Classes, etc. Believe us, people will be jealous that you're quitting, period, and you will not have to worry about situations like, "My brother *owns* Microsoft! I'll call him right now and put in a good word for you!"

"You're Fired!"

How bloody awful, Dear Reader! The Etiquette Grrls are extremely sympathetic about your situation, and we're here to help you get through your Last Tough Moments at your Soon-to-Be-Former Company. (Note: If you work at any sort of Volatile Company, such as almost any Dot-Com, you should not skip this section. We've all witnessed "unforeseen, nonperformance-based layoffs," haven't we?) First, resist the impulse to do or say Anything Illegal. Don't Defenestrate anyone or anything, and don't threaten Anyone's Life. This is Quite Rude. Second, get to your desk immediately, turn on your computer, and start deleting anything personal. Yes, of course, we all know we really shouldn't keep Personal E-mails archived on our work machines, but we all do, and you should take Great Pains to preserve the privacy of Your Correspondents.

If you are Fired, try, difficult as it may be, to clean out your desk quickly and get out of the office. You'll feel much better anyway, especially if you can call Your Best Friend and ask him or her to meet you for an Emergency G&T. (Note to Best Friends: When one of you Gets Fired, the other one Pays for The Drinks, Listens for Hours, and Handles the Driving.) Remember, Dear Reader: This, too, shall pass. You're also in Very Good Company. It's sort of like getting Kicked Out of Prep School—you just need to dust yourself off, move on, and do something terrific that, in essence, lets those who Fired You know that they can See You In Hell.

CHAPTER SIX

Dating and Breakups

"Let Me Call You Sweetheart": Dating

The Etiquette Grrls are quite sure that many of our Dear Readers' Existential Crises stem from Dating and (perhaps even more so) Breakup Quandaries. The Etiquette Grrls want to say Right Off the Bat that while we are undoubtedly Old-Fashioned, we are Entirely Unlike Those Girls who wrote *The Rules*. We never advocate scheming, conniving, manipulative behavior, especially when the Main Goal is to "Trap a Man." Heavens, the mere phrase absolutely makes the Etiquette Grrls cringe. Are we Old-Fashioned? Yes. Are we Spineless, Codependent, Deceitful Saps? No. *Never.* And we simply won't tolerate such behavior in others, either! In a nutshell, we think that you should be polite, kind, gracious, thoughtful, and courteous at All Times, and Everyone Will Love You. Problem solved. It's as easy as that, Dear Reader.

HOW DO YOU ASK FOR A DATE?

So you, Dear Boy, have met a lovely, funny, very intelligent Girl, and you're thinking about asking her for a date. Splendid! But how, you ask, shall I do this? Fear not, the Etiquette Grrls are here to Walk You Through It.

To begin with, you ought to be clear that you are, in fact, asking for a date, and not merely extending an invitation for this Girl to join your weekly Eighteenth-Century American Literature Discussion Group. For instance, inquiring, "Ya wanna hang out sometime?" in the same tone one would use to offer someone an Altoid is not an acceptable way to ask for a date. "Hanging out" is not only an Inordinately Vague Term (particularly when paired with the word "sometime"), but it also doesn't exactly conjure up any Thrilling Images of a Stylish Evening Out On The Town. "Hanging out" is what one does with one's High-School or College Buddies when one doesn't have anything better to do, or when one is suffering from a case of Light Malaise, and it usually consists of lounging around and complaining about How Dull Your Life Is. This activity has its joys, of course, but it hardly makes for an impressive First Date.

One should, rather, be specific about what Your Plan consists of, and with whom, should the date actually occur. One might say something like, "I have two tickets to see *Waiting for Godot* this Saturday evening at The Playhouse . . . I heard it's really terrific, and I was wondering if perhaps you would like to go with me to see it?" Notice how in merely two sentences, the questions of what, where, when, and with whom have all been answered, providing the Girl with all the information she needs to make a decision. (As opposed to the nonspecific "Do you want to see *Waiting for Godot?*" which not only practically begs for the reply, "Yes, but certainly not with you," but also fails to mention when (Tonight? Tomorrow? Three months from now?), with whom (The one asking the question? His roommate? All by yourself?), or indeed, even if the speaker is offering an invitation to see the play, or only wondering if the person whom he is addressing has any interest in The Theatre of the Absurd.) And indeed, you should always, *always* have a Specific Plan in mind before asking a Girl for a date. Quelle horreur if she should accept your invitation (although we advise against anyone accepting any invitation before one knows of what it consists) and you then can't think of any

Appropriate Activity! You'll be Up The Proverbial Creek, Dear Reader, and then what will you do?

Also, in order to avoid confusion, you should be sure to call and confirm the date, especially if any of the information is vague (e.g., what time it is to take place). The Etiquette Grrls hate it when we're left sitting on the couch on a Friday night, wondering if we are, indeed, supposed to be going out for Drinks because a Passing Reference was made to such an outing a week ago, but we have yet to be informed about what time, or indeed, if we will, in fact, be picked up. Likewise, we are equally peeved when we are not aware of any specific plans for an Evening Out, and while we are busily painting our nails, a Boy arrives on our doorstep, saying, "But I thought you *knew* I'd be over at nine! When I come over, I almost *always* arrive at nine!" Honestly, Dear Reader, not that it's not a Happy Day when one sees A Beau, but A Girl needs to Prepare for These Things, you know!

WHO SHOULD ASK FOR THE DATE?

As previously mentioned, the Etiquette Grrls are Old-fashioned, and while we think that a Girl may certainly feel free to make it clear that she would go out with him were he to ask, we firmly believe that the Boy should do actual asking. Let's take a look at the following conversation between a Boy and a Girl.

GIRL: I haven't been to the Brewhouse yet—I hear it's pretty good, though . . .

BOY: I haven't been either. Would you like to go check it out this Friday at 8 P.M.?

GIRL: Why yes, that would be lovely. Thank you.

BOY: Why don't I pick you up in my Clean, Well-Maintained Automobile? I will be certain to dispose of any garbage that might have Inadvertently Accumulated in said vehicle. May I take your phone number so that if I am delayed, I will be able to call and apprise you of the situation?

GIRL: Of course. Let me write it down for you. (*Takes calling card or business card from her purse, from an Engraved Silver Card Case, of course, and writes down number on back of card.* [Always carry a Paper Product and pen with you, Dear Reader—you never know when you will have to Make Note of Something, and it does look ever so unpolished to scribble on the back of a ATM receipt!])

Note that in the above interaction, there is little opportunity for miscommunication—both parties are Quite Clear about where they are going, when, what time, and who is picking up whom. That wasn't so difficult, was it, Dear Reader? The Etiquette Grrls have absolutely No Idea why some people find it so Terribly Difficult to make simple plans for an evening out!

If an Unexpected Situation arises that will force to you to be late, or even to miss The Date entirely, be certain to call with as much Advance Notice as possible. The only Good Excuse for not calling with Advance Notice of your Tardiness or Absence is if you suddenly Befall a Dreadful Fate, such as, say, a Wee Appendicitis Attack which lands you dans l'hôpital, or, of course, Death. Also, if you find that you must cancel a date, be sure to reschedule at that point, to avoid making the other party feel as though they have been "blown off," which is Positively THOR.

HOW TO REFUSE A DATE, AND HOW TO TAKE "NO" FOR AN ANSWER

Sometimes you will be asked for a date, and even if the thought doesn't make you Utterly Cringe, you just won't want to accept. What to do in such a situation? A Little White Lie (such as "I'm seeing somebody") is okay, but the Etiquette Grrls caution their Dear Readers against doling out Transparent Excuses ("I'm afraid I've *just* Entered a Convent—Darn!"), lies that you can be caught in ("I'm terribly sorry, but I'm seeing Ralph Fiennes, the British Actor"), or that will leave an opportunity for the Boy to keep asking for a date

another day ("Gee, I'm busy Friday . . ."). Nor should you feign illness, especially one of a Chronic or Potentially Fatal Variety, as this
will undoubtedly Catch Up With You, and what are you going to do,
Dear Reader, when eight months down the road, you have not, in
fact, Succumbed to Beriberi?

If, however, something important does preclude dating for a
period (such as studying for Medical Exams, The Bar, etc.), but you
would still like to go out at a Later Date, be sure to provide that information, and say when you will be available. For instance, one might
say something along the lines of, "Gosh, I'd *adore* going to dinner
with you on Thursday, Hobart, but I've got to defend my Disserta-
tion on Monday morning, and I really feel I ought to prepare. I'm
sorry. What are you doing next week?"

Now, on the other hand, Dear Boy, if a Girl is giving you Scads of
Excuses for why she doesn't care to go to dinner, or the movies, or
stock-car races with you, then the Etiquette Grrls respectfully
request that you Take the Hint and also, while you're at it, Take a
Hike. And in the case of stock-car racing, we think that you should
probably reexamine your thoughts on Places Where You Think It Is
Acceptable to Bring A Girl, and indeed, Places Where You Yourself
Should Be. You also should not whine, yell, or otherwise berate
someone for Turning Down a Date with you. You don't know what
the circumstances may be, and you have no right to try to make the
other person feel Terrible, as this, too, is Positively THOR. The Etiquette Grrls know that Rejection is Never Easy, but you should try
your very best to Take Things in Stride, and not throw A Fit, especially if you are In A Public Place. Once you get into the privacy of
your own apartment, of course you may Have a Tantrum if you so
desire. (Just as long as you don't disturb your neighbors or any roommates you may have, of course.)

THE TELEPHONE—WHAT IT IS AND HOW TO USE IT
We fully realize that some forms of Electronic Communication are
not only complicated, but also often intimidating in our Fast-Paced,

High-Tech, Post-Post-Modern World, but the telephone is a common household instrument that should be easy enough, with practice, to master. However, we've noticed that many people, and Boys in particular, seem to suffer from some sort of Dreadful Fear and/or Loathing of the 'Phone. The Etiquette Grrls find this to be Most Perplexing and Exasperating. If using the telephone seems to require a Herculean effort, recall how dreadful it must have been in The Past, Dear Reader! Remember when Push-Button 'Phones *did not* exist? Every time one wished to place a telephone call, one had to use a Rotary Dial 'Phone, which was a Terrible Nuisance, often resulting in Broken Nails and, had we known what it was at the time, probably Carpal Tunnel Syndrome. And plus, it took *forever* to dial a number! And before *that,* every call had to be placed through an Operator! And before *that,* the Etiquette Grrls have been told that most people had Party Lines, and *everyone* in the *Entire* Neighborhood could listen in on your Private Conversations! And you thought it was annoying having Roommates/Siblings/etc. hovering over you while you were on the 'Phone, Dear Reader! Gracious! You ought to consider yourself Lucky that you are dating in an age of Touch-Tone, Push Buttons, and Speed Dial. Hurrah for Modern Technology! We recommend that you attempt to overcome your fear of the telephone by using it, and often. As with all things, Practice Makes Perfect. You will find that the telephone is highly useful in both arranging and confirming dates, as well as for engaging in many Stimulating Conversations on the topic of your choice—always a good activity when not actually on a date.

WHAT CONSTITUTES A FIRST DATE?

A proper First Date should be traditional, and need the Etiquette Grrls even say, Date-like. It should involve Alcohol or Food, preferably both. It should not be an event that one of you is required to attend (Work Parties, etc.), or a Family Function, or anything involving all of your or your date's friends. As the point is to get to Know Each Other Better, you obviously should go someplace conducive to talking. (That means no Very Loud Bars; no movies, unless you are going Somewhere Else as well; no Sporting Events; and no Cloistered Monasteries or Convents.) The First Date should not involve Specialized Clothing or equipment, such as that for wall-climbing, skeet shooting, or skiing. Nor should it be anything life-threatening or illegal. This is not the time to pull That Big Art Heist, Dear Reader! However, there is no need to go overboard and do anything really formal and/or expensive. Dinner and/or drinks are usually a tried-and-true First Date Activity. Again, we emphasize that Specific Plans are essential—of course, you need to tell the other person what you'll be doing so she can Dress Appropriately. Quelle horreur if you, Dear Reader, had been thinking dinner at a Fancy Restaurant, and your date is dressed for An Afternoon at the Amusement Park!

Good Grooming is a must, however Informal the Date. Boys should, at minimum, shower, shave, comb their hair, and wear recently laundered, ironed, well-fitting clothing. (Sans rips, stains, cigarette burns, etc., please, Dear Reader!) Also, if driving, a Boy should take a moment to clean out his car, especially the passenger side, so that the poor Girl will not have to pick her way through a mountain of Big Mac wrappers, Coke cans, cigarette boxes, and other Untold Horrors.

Girls should, of course, follow the same Basic Grooming Rules. Neither Boys nor Girls should douse themselves heavily with Fragrance, as this is apt to cause at best, headaches, and at worst, Asphyxiation. Also, Girls, don't overdo the makeup and hair, and this is definitely not the time to experiment with Outlandish Clothes, either. Remember, Dear Reader, you're just on a date; you are not Appearing In A Cabaret. You should simply look like the Polished, Elegant, Refined Girl that you are. For further details on Your Personal Appearance, see chapter 3.

When meeting someone for a date, tardiness is unacceptable, except, as previously mentioned, in Extraordinary Circumstances. If you do not know where you are going, it is Your Responsibility to find out, either by asking for directions, or by using your Investigative Skills. The Etiquette Grrls have found that Maps are generally

Quite Helpful in these circumstances. We prefer the Boy to pick up the Girl at her home, office, etc. This way, if he is tardy, despite our Copious Warnings on the subject, she is not waiting alone in a Strange Bar, rarely a Pleasant Experience. The only exception is if their date will take place *extremely* close to The Boy's Location, in which case, obviously, the Girl should meet him. (The Boy should then see the Girl safely home at the End of the Evening, of course.)

Also, both parties should complete any Necessary Errands (such as feeding the cat, visiting the ATM, etc.) *before* the date begins, as running your own errands is irksome enough, without being dragged about while someone else runs theirs. Remember, Dear Reader, you are on a date, not Training Your New Personal Assistant. If, despite our Previous Warnings, both parties are not aware of the specifics of the date, the Boy should tell the Girl where he has made dinner reservations, etc., to ensure that she approves. For example, they should not arrive at Legal Sea Foods only for him to find out she is a vegetarian or has a Life-Threatening Allergy to shellfish. Also, if you're at a restaurant, enjoy your food; you're there to have a Fabulous Meal. You can always eat steamed vegetables at home, Dear Reader! Most importantly, relax and have a Smashing Time!

We think the Boy should pay for the First Date. This, Dear Reader, is in the spirit of "the person who invites, pays." We think most Girls would rather go on a date that's within the Boy's means—even if she is the heiress to a Gigantic Fortune—than have him whip out a calculator when the check arrives, and unceremoniously present her with the Grand Total of her share of the bill. If, somehow, no one asks the other for a date, then you may go Dutch, because There Is No Date; you are simply Having Drinks At The Same Bar. This is not to say, Dear Reader, that a Girl who finds herself at a restaurant with a Boorish Boy who is not familiar with the concepts of This Book should have no money and no credit cards with her. (Indeed, Dear Reader, it is never, *ever* wise to Venture Out without Funds—one never knows what sort of Terrible Predicament one might find oneself in!) In this case, you may *have* to pay, as sad as this makes the Etiquette Grrls.

However, we trust that such a Well-Bred Girl as yourself, Dear Reader, would not be caught in this situation. Or at least not twice.

Now, when you enter the phase of the relationship where the Girl is making some plans, she would then, of course, pay for whatever activities she herself arranges for. However, we wish to emphasize, Girls, that just because your Petit Ami is rather loath to Make Plans (as, sadly, so many Boys are), you should not Take Over the Entire Responsibility for Arranging Dates and Paying For Everything. Boys, even when you have been dating a Girl for a while, you should not let the relationship become one of Hanging Out and Watching TV. It's lovely when, apropos of nothing, a Boy Whisks a Girl off to Windows on the World—and, Boys, you should do this frequently, throughout your *entire* relationship, not merely during its Nascent Weeks!

During the date, An Effort at Conversation should be made—by both people. However, neither the Boy nor the Girl should monopolize the conversation, as this is Very Rude. Don't you want to find out all sorts of Interesting Things about Your Date, Dear Reader? After all, you can yammer on about yourself Any Old Time. And of course, as with all New Acquaintances, topics which are overly controversial or "Too Much Information" (TMI) should be avoided.

At the End of the Evening, a Chivalric Boy sees the Girl home, and does not leave her on the sidewalk outside a Restaurant or Bar to find her own way home through the Dark and Dangerous Streets of the City. This means he drives her home himself, calls her a cab (it is very nice if he also supplies her with Cab Fare), or walks her back to her door. He should wait to make sure she is safely inside, even if she does not invite him in (she is, of course, under no Obligation to do so). The Boy and Girl should thank each other, whether the Date was Utterly Smashing or a Complete Disaster. For instance:

GIRL: Thank you so much for dinner. I had a wonderful time.
BOY: Thank you for coming! And for recommending the Brown Derby; it was really keen.
GIRL: I thought you'd like it.

BOY: May I see you again sometime?

GIRL: Yes, I'd really like that. (*Or, if Less Enthusiastic, "Sure, call me sometime" or "I'm sure I'll see you around somewhere."*)

BOY: Thanks again! I'll see you in economics on Monday.

GIRL: Okay, Good Night!

It should be Abundantly Obvious how you both feel about a Second Date. If you do not want to see the person again, you may be noncommittal, but never Downright Rude. You may not, for instance, scream, "You're such a Crass Moron, Buster, I hope you fall off the Face of the Earth!" Ending the first date is all about Conversational Clues, Dear Reader—you absolutely must pay attention. If the Girl would like to make sure the Boy knows she is Very Interested in him, there are ways to clue him in verbally without being Too Overt, which the Etiquette Grrls don't really think is very Ladylike. And, if you really are going to call her, Boys, giving a Time Frame for when you'll call is a good idea so she doesn't think you're "Blowing Her Off." (Such as "I'll give you a call next week," as opposed to the More Vague "I'll call you Sometime.")

A Wee Note to Boys: Well-Bred Girls will trust that you are A Gentleman and will behave accordingly. This means that you have paid for dinner and drinks out of Your Chivalric Pocket without the slightest thought that she has any "obligation" toward you in return. Neither should you pass her drink upon drink, hoping the Disinhibiting Effects of alcohol will kick in, in your favor. If the Girl is not receptive toward any advances that you do happen to make despite our warnings, you should stop. Do not force the issue. There will be Absolutely No Arguments about this, Dear Reader. Period. End of Story.

If, as we sincerely hope it does, the First Date does go well and you continue to see each other, you must continue to be courteous to each other throughout the duration of the relationship. Falling into a Comfortable Routine is no excuse to become "lax" or boorish, whether you are a Boy or a Girl. No matter how well you may know each other, if you Behave Abominably, you may well find that the

Love of Your Life has Walked Out the Door. And the Etiquette Grrls certainly wouldn't want something So Terribly Tragic to happen to any of their Dear Readers.

FORMALS AND OTHER FANCY DATES

It deeply saddens the Etiquette Grrls that gone are the days when Girls in Beautiful Suits and Furs would come down by the trainful to Princeton or New Haven for weekends (which, to the best of the Etiquette Grrls' knowledge, were a *smashing* lot of fun) full of Football Games, Booze, and Formal Dances. Sadly, the Modern Girl's experiences with Formals consist mainly of the High-School Prom (which, the Etiquette Grrls feel they can safely say, from the multitude of Horror Stories we have heard, is usually *ghastly*), and perhaps of the annual "Spring Fling" or Christmas Dance in College. (Also usually ghastly, but possibly made more endurable by the Large Quantities of Alcohol often present.) For the rare occasions when one is faced with a Formal, the Etiquette Grrls offer the following advice:

Dear Reader, you absolutely cannot accept an invitation to the dance and then change your mind when Something Better comes along. This is Terribly Rude and Hurtful. If you really didn't want to go to the dance with the person with whom you first agreed to go, then you shouldn't have accepted the invitation in the first place. Nor can you decline an invitation and then decide at a later point to accept, particularly if The Boy has already made plans with Another Girl. Also, if you have someone in mind with whom you would like to go, and he has not asked you by a certain date, you should investigate and find out if he already has a date. If he does not, of course you may get your friends to encourage him to ask you.

However, the Etiquette Grrls are, in general, Rather Leery of enlisting Third Parties as Go-Betweens. It's Quite Juvenile, and also presents an opportunity for Dreadful Miscommunication Problems. Do you remember playing "Telephone" in Kindergarten, Dear Reader? Do you remember the Final Message ever, *once,* being identical to the Original Message? The Etiquette Grrls are betting not. Although the Etiquette

Grrls are usually hesitant about Girls taking The First Step, we think that perhaps this is sometimes better than getting a Host of People involved, as a Terrible Misunderstanding is all too likely to rear its Ugly Little Head when A Lot of Well-Meaning People start Meddling.

The Etiquette Grrls would like to Go On At Length about what to wear to a Formal, the music which should be played at a Formal, and their thoughts on "themes" for Formals, but they fear that perhaps this might be better saved for Another Volume, as they might be tempted to go on A Bit of A Rant. We will, however, offer some Basic Advice.

Girls, your dresses (and they *must* be *dresses*—no pants, and *especially* no Hot Pants, no matter how Sparkly and "Festive" they may be!) should be of a Decent Length, appropriate to the season (i.e., no velvet in July, no chiffon in January), of an attractive, nongarish color and fabric, and not possess any frilly, poufy, glittery, overly shiny, or holographic qualities. You should also stay far, far away from anything that glows in Black Light. In fact, your Formal should not be lit with Black Lights, anyhow, so this should not even be An Issue.

Boys, listen carefully. Formal = Black Tie. Black Tie = a black dinner suit (not a Tailcoat, which is White Tie—the Most Formal of Dress), white shirt (French-Cuffed, with Wee Studs and Cuff Links—the Etiquette Grrls want to know why every Young Man they see, particularly those in the Entertainment Industry, who has attempted to Clothe Himself in Evening Clothes, seems to have Misplaced his Cuff Links, and has Open Shirt Cuffs hanging down to his knuckles?), black silk bow tie, black cummerbund (with the pleats going up) or a black waistcoat (but never both at once!), and black dress shoes. During the Summer Months, if the soirée is held in a Resort Town or at the Country Club, one may wear a white lightweight wool dinner jacket in lieu of the black. But, of course, black is Always Correct. As with the Girls' clothing, all fabrics must be of a traditional nonshiny fabric (i.e., wool). And it is absolutely imperative that the only colors present be black and white!! *No other color is permitted, ever!* Except *perhaps* if it is Christmas and you are Scottish, in which case you may wear Your Tartan. But this is *Very* Iffy, and the Etiquette Grrls don't recommend it to Novices. Particularly to Novices who are *not* Scottish. For Further Details on Formal Attire, please turn to pages 59–61.

BRINGING A DATE TO EVENTS WHERE EXTENDED FAMILY IS IN ATTENDANCE

The Big Family Dinner is an intimidating, and quite often, Traumatizing Event. Therefore, it is not wise to bring a New Beau to such a gathering. Until he knows you very well, and is already aware of your family's Eccentricities, you might well scare him off. Additionally, by bringing a new date to such an event, you will undoubtedly leave yourself open to prying, and possibly embarrassing, questions from well-meaning, but nosy family members. The Etiquette Grrls know, Dear Reader, that you probably will be mortified when Grandmama starts telling everyone that you're Engaged when you, in fact, could not be any further from such a thing. So, why Tempt Fate? It's best not to subject your Significant Other to Family Gatherings until you're A Well-Established Item.

PUBLIC DISPLAYS OF AFFECTION ("P.D.A.")

We're glad your relationship is progressing so swimmingly that you have begun to express your affection for each other. However, we have no need to witness such acts of expression. Couples who are "all over each other" are Most Boring at parties, and will soon cease to be invited. The Etiquette Grrls simply don't understand how such couples could possibly believe that since they only have eyes for each other, they are somehow in a Magical Force-Field of Privacy. The line at the bank, the beach, the watercooler at the office, and so on are not Appropriate Locales for Your Trysts, Dear Reader! The Etiquette Grrls feel that holding hands is absolutely the limit. And we mean holding *hands*—no other parts of the anatomy, and no hands in Other People's Back Pockets. And even holding hands is sometimes A Bit Too Touchy-Feely for the Etiquette Grrls' tastes, if truth be told. But then, as our Dear Readers know, the Etiquette Grrls, being from New England, are Extremely Reserved.

BABYTALK

Are you really A Preverbal Infant? The Etiquette Grrls don't think so. Is your vocabulary So Very Limited that you can find no other way to order up a fresh G&T than to ask Pooky-Wooky to get you another Drinky-Winky? Dear Reader, the Etiquette Grrls ask, nay, *implore* you to please refrain from using Cloying and Ridiculous Nicknames and vocabulary In Public. Or, for that matter, In Private. Despite what you may think, Babytalk is in no way Cute and Adorable, it is merely Annoying as All Hell. You were given a Real Name for a reason, Dear Reader; use it.

DISCIPLINARY ACTION

Horrors! Boyfriend has been Acting Up, and what's A Girl to do? Turn a blind eye? Stomp out of the room in A Snit? Throw one's hands in the air and sigh loudly in exasperation? Sadly, sometimes A System of Discipline must be enforced in order to ensure that Boyfriend Toes The Line. The Etiquette Grrls vividly recall the rather Elaborate System that was utilized at our Boarding Schools to Keep Order. Infringements of the School's rules would result in (in order of severity) Warnings; "Early Breakfast Check" (EBC)—the privilege of having one's ice-cold morning gruel avec A Member of the Faculty in the Dining Hall at the Crack of Dawn; or Demerits. If one accumulated enough Demerits (or committed a single Great Crime), one would have to meet with the Disciplinary Committee (DC), made up of various faculty and Student Leaders—a scary, secretive, Court-Martial-like affair, which often, for some unknown reason, took place under Cover of Night, and which, more often than not, resulted in Suspension or Expulsion. The Etiquette Grrls have thought a great deal about this, and we think that implementing such a system in Real Life might work wonders to keep Wayward Boyfriends (or other Various and Sundry Persons) from Misbehaving. Below, we list some Common Crimes and Misdemeanors, and their Suggested Punishments.

CRIME	FIRST OFFENSE	SECOND OFFENSE	THIRD OFFENSE
Failure to call or to return a call	Warning	EBC	1 week EBC
Unexplained Tardiness	Warning (a Very Severe Warning, Dear Reader!)	EBC	1 week EBC
Complete Failure to appear as promised (and calls later to apologize; in contrast to being Stood Up entirely)	EBC	1 week EBC	Demerit
Forgets Birthday, Christmas, Anniversary, other Important Day	1 week EBC	Demerit	Demerit and 1 month EBC
Mean-Spirited Behavior, any variety	Meet avec D.C.	It shouldn't happen twice.	Or three times, either.
Goes AWOL	Meet avec DC (if you can ever find him . . . if not, Automatic Expulsion).	Again, there shouldn't be an AWOL Version 2.0.	The Etiquette Grrls sincerely hope this will not be a problem three times over, Dear Reader!
Seeing Another Girl, or other Heinous Crime (e.g. Abusive Behavior, Illegal Activities, etc.)	Automatic Expulsion.	No excuses.	The Etiquette Grrls Really Mean It!

We think that you, Dear Reader, are probably not going to want to Arise Before Les Petits Oiseaux just to ensure that Joe Boyfriend is sitting at the kitchen table Glaring Blurrily at a bowl of Congealed Oatmeal, so feel free to turn EBC into any chore that you desire—perhaps doing your Grocery Shopping, walking the dog, etc. Really, any Odious Task will do quite nicely.

SOME THOUGHTS ON ABANDONING OLD FRIENDS
While the Etiquette Grrls can understand that you are Quite Taken avec your New Beau, Dear Reader, you must always remember that Your Dear Friends may not be quite so charmed by him, and will undoubtedly be Quite Irked if you start bringing Your Attached-At-The-Hip Boyfriend everywhere you go, even to your usual monthly Girls' Night Out. Worse yet, you should never abandon all of your Old Friends once you acquire a Boyfriend, neglect to return their telephone calls, forget birthdays, and otherwise Behave Atrociously. This is an excellent way to Permanently Alienate everyone you know, and is not recommended unless you intend to Thoroughly and Permanently Fall Off The Face of The Earth. You also should never, *ever* permit Your Boyfriend to be mean, patronizing, or condescending to Your Dear Friends. If he would be So Unkind, then he is not someone you want hanging around, and you should Send Him Packing immediately.

Also, Dear Reader, avoid Gratuitous References to your Significant Other! Finding a way to drop the word that you have A Boyfriend in Every Single Sentence you utter throughout the day is Insufferably Rude, and actually, Rather Pathetic. The Etiquette Grrls find it so tiresome to listen to the prattling of a Girl whose Only Topic of Conversation is, "So, I have a Boyfriend, and My Boyfriend thinks this, and My Boyfriend thinks that, and I simply don't have time for you because I have a Boyfriend, and I bet My Boyfriend's trying to call me, so I better get off the 'phone, and My Boyfriend wears socks, and I can't make plans because I need to keep my schedule free, because I have a Boyfriend, and My Boyfriend likes football, and

I can't make any decisions on my own, because I have a Boyfriend, and I'm Unreachable, because I have a Boyfriend, and I have a Boyfriend, and I have a Boyfriend, and I have a Boyfriend, and *did you know that I have a Boyfriend*?!" Such Nauseating Rambling makes it appear, Dear Reader, like you have Misplaced Your Own Mind, and worse, that your life is Horribly, Horribly Empty. And this is definitely Not Cool. Further, some people might get the impression that you are smugly trying to Rub It In that you are Attached when they, perhaps, are not. And this, need the Etiquette Grrls even point out, is THOR.

ENGAGEMENT AND MARRIAGE

The Etiquette Grrls couldn't be More Pleased that you've found Your Own True Love, Dear Reader! It's marvelous, really, and the Etiquette Grrls would adore to guide you though the Upcoming Months of Your Engagement, and help you to arrange a Truly Lovely Wedding Ceremony. However, This Topic could be a book in and of itself! For some reason, Weddings seem to be Fraught with Difficulties; they are A Potential Minefield of Terrible Faux Pas. How can we possibly condense Our Thoughts on Weddings into a Short, Pithy Paragraph? Impossible, Dear Reader! There are, however, many Reliable Books devoted entirely to the topic which will Point You in the Right Direction. However, the Etiquette Grrls will list below some of our Biggest Pet Peeves so you will at least have Some Idea of What to Avoid.

- **Skimpy, Bejeweled, Unflattering, Shiny, Oddly-Colored, Froufrou-ish, and/or Generally Hideous Dresses.** And that goes for both the Bride and Bridesmaids. You are not Vegas Showgirls. (Well, maybe you are, but the Etiquette Grrls can only assume that Your Wedding is not the Floorshow at Caesars Palace.) You are not Little Bo Peep, and you're not even Scarlett O'Hara, so ix-nay on the Frills, Fluff, and Hoop Skirts, please. If you don't believe us, look at it this way, Dear Reader. A Girl does not wear an Outrageous Dress, an Outrageous Dress wears her. Do you want to be Overshadowed on Your Day by A Costume? Of course not. It's also cruel to make your Dear Friends who have promised to be your Bridesmaids wear something which will make them feel Chubby, Short, Gawky, Ridiculous, etc. Obviously, one's friends come in all shapes and sizes, but one can always find a dress which will please everyone. The secret, Dear Reader, is to always, *always,* Keep Things Simple. If you select gowns (and shoes) that are of a very simple cut, color, and fabric, everyone will Look Lovely, and Be Happy, and the Big Day will be Far More Enjoyable by all.

- **Groomsmen dressed to match the Bridesmaids.** Your Bridesmaids and the Groomsmen are not the Bobbsey Twins. Groomsmen should be dressed in a Traditional Manner. Their dress will vary depending on the time of day, location, and level of formality of The Wedding, but this information may easily be gleaned from an Old and Trustworthy Wedding Etiquette Book.

- **Wedding Guests, Bridesmaids, and most especially, Brides clad in black.** *Never* correct. A dreadful, dreadful trend which started sometime in the late 1980s, and which, much to the Etiquette Grrls' chagrin, has failed to die A Quiet Death. You are at a Wedding, all you über-cool Kats and Kittens, not a Funeral.

- **Elopements treated as though they were Church Weddings.** You do not wear Full Wedding Regalia when Sneaking Off to Get Married. You simply wear Street Clothes. Nor do you inform everyone of Your Plans to Elope, as An Elopement, by definition, is done In Secret. Nor do you invite guests to Tag Along. These things all defeat the purpose of An Elopement, and if you want a Formal Wedding, it should be held in a House of Worship, and not in the office of a Justice of the Peace in the Dead of Night, a sleazy twenty-four-hour "chapel" in Vegas, City Hall, or anyplace else where you can be Married in Under Ten Minutes.

- **Invitations/Announcements possessing any cute and/or saccharine qualities.** Invitations are worded Traditionally, and are Engraved (although if one is Counting Pennies, Good-Quality Thermography is acceptable as well) in black ink, in a traditional font, on white or, preferably, ivory-colored Heavy Matte Stock. There should not be any Extraneous Decorations or colors, there should not be confetti or other objects enclosed, and please, *please* remove those tissue-paper fillers! We're not sure what they're for—we think they're what the Stationer uses to keep the ink from smudging or to keep the invitations from sticking together, but in any case, you are not meant to Send Them On to Your Guests, so take them out, please!

- **Pop Songs played during the Wedding Ceremony.** Save them for the Reception, if you must.

- **Gaudy Engagement and/or Wedding Rings.** As with clothing, the simpler, the better. For Engagement Rings, a Very Simple Diamond Solitaire is nice, but despite what the folks at DeBeers have led the Public-at-Large to believe, don't feel that Diamonds are Your Only Option. Actually, they look A Trifle Cold on many Girls—think about Other Stones as well; as long as the design is simple, the Etiquette Grrls don't really care what the stone is (although, personally, we're Rather Partial to Wee Emeralds). Also, Family Heirlooms are often Quite Lovely, but of course one can't really (nor would one want to) Pick and Choose a Husband on the basis of the Quality and Quantity of Good Jewelry floating around his family. And Wedding Bands should be just that—Absolutely Plain bands of gold or platinum, period.

"I Hope You Know That This Will Go Down on Your Permanent Record": Breakups

Sadly, Dear Reader, things can go Fantastically Awry even in the Most Stable of Relationships, and a Terrible Breakup Ensues. Sometimes it's no one's fault. And sometimes it most definitely *is* someone's fault. In any case, things can Get Ugly. The Etiquette Grrls can understand the Temptation to get Nasty and Vindictive, certainly, but doesn't such behavior just cause More Heartache in the Long Run, Dear Reader? As always, even in this Most Trying Circumstance, the Etiquette Grrls ask that you conduct yourself with as much Grace and Dignity as you can possibly muster.

THE GRACEFUL BREAKUP

No breakup may be easy, but there is no excuse not to be courteous about ending a relationship. Of course, the Etiquette Grrls aren't saying that you and the Ex still have to be friends, Dear Reader. However, you should not work to bring about a breakup by becoming an Obnoxious, Drunken, Philandering, Dastardly Bastard. Our advice: If you want to break up, then break up, damn it! Let's look at the following example.

GIRL: I've been thinking about this for a while, and I don't think we should see each other anymore.

BOY: I agree. No hard feelings. You are completely free to see Other People, as am I, and we will not stalk each other, badmouth each other, or enact Violent Revenge.

GIRL: Yes, of course. That sounds very reasonable.

Of course, the Etiquette Grrls realize that the Above Scenario is not likely to ever happen Quite Like That, but the point, Dear Reader, is that it is always best to be Honest, Truthful, and Direct. The Truth hurts, yes, but it hurts less than being Purposefully Deceived. It is THOR, not to mention Cowardly, to manipulate someone into Breaking Up with you, just because you are Too Spineless to do it yourself. And if there's anything the Etiquette Grrls can't abide, Dear Reader, it's Spinelessness.

THE CHEATIN' HEART

Infidelity is a Particularly Abhorrent Quality in a person, and it is Not Something to Be Tolerated, even for a *second,* Dear Reader! The Etiquette Grrls simply cannot *fathom* why anyone would cheat on their Boy- or Girlfriend! Maybe your relationship is Troubled, and maybe you meet someone you Like Better. These things happen, the Etiquette Grrls realize. But why String Someone Along while you Carry On with Someone Else? Shameful Rudeness aside, such deceitfulness is Downright Cruel to all parties involved. And besides, why Complicate Things? Life is Difficult Enough without Sneaking Around, isn't it, Dear Reader?

GOING AWOL

It is also unacceptable to attempt to break up with someone by Abruptly, Inexplicably, and Thoroughly Vanishing. When someone in the Military walks away from the place where he or she is stationed without permission, it is called "Absent WithOut Leave," or AWOL for short. Going AWOL is a Felony, Dear Reader! The AWOL soldier will very likely be captured, then be Court-Martialed (a rather unpleasant experience, we gather), and will then be served with a Dishonorable Discharge, not a good thing to have on one's Permanent Record. The Civilian AWOL Boy may surely expect the same Harsh Treatment. In any case, no matter the state of the relationship, Unexplained Disappearance is apt to cause concern for Your Basic Welfare, and, indeed, Your Life. The Etiquette Grrls implore their Dear Readers to avoid such behavior at all costs!

THEFT AND OTHER TRUE CRIMES

After a breakup, it is proper to return any and all possessions of the other person you may have Lying Around Your Apartment. You may not Hoard these items, either out of Sheer Vindictiveness, or in the hope that you will be able to lure Your Ex over to fetch a dozen CDs and a Palm Pilot. Especially if you are Living Together, you may not go out of your way to take any of the other person's possessions as you move out. This is Larceny, and is Impolite to boot. Heartless as it may seem, we recommend putting your name in your books and your CDs, lest Some Shameless Cad attempt to Make Off With Them. We also recommend replacing at high-end market value, and deducting from the Thieving Ex's portion of the security deposit, anything which he does take.

SEEKING REVENGE

The Etiquette Grrls know that the Temptation to seek Dramatic and Creative Revenge once you have been Jilted is great, perhaps even overwhelming, but you must attempt to Maintain Your Dignity, Dear Reader! Such behavior is Rather Immature, and besides, will undoubtedly Come Back to Haunt You Later, which probably is Not A Good Thing. Once you have broken up with someone, you should then Mind Your Own Business, most especially if you were the one to initiate the breakup. For instance, you have no right to intercept your ex's mail, skulk about his or her apartment or place of employment, plant "bugs" in his or her apartment just to "keep tabs" on him or her, or otherwise exhibit Shifty and Creepy Behavior. If you're that interested in this person's Daily Activities, then perhaps you shouldn't have broken up with him or her, should you have, Dear Reader?

Traveling

First Class, Whenever Possible:
How You Should Get There

Of course, the Etiquette Grrls simply adore Traveling, both in our own Fair Country and Abroad. We, of course, are Always Curious, and for as long as we can remember have wondered what lay beyond our own Croquet Lawn. However, Dear Reader, Traveling is Not What It Used to Be. Back in the Golden Age of Travel, believe it or not, Dear Reader, getting from one place to another was not nearly the Ordeal that it is today. The Etiquette Grrls don't quite understand this. Why is it that in our Post-Post-Modern Age, when everything is supposed to run Smoothly and Quickly, getting from Hartford to New York City requires about as much Advance Planning as the Invasion of Normandy? And the Etiquette Grrls add that the comfort level of being transported between Hartford and New York just about rivals the comfort level, or lack thereof, of those Brave Soldiers who stormed Omaha Beach. The Etiquette Grrls find this so very tiresome, Dear Reader! Wherefore art thou, Parlor Cars? O where have all the Porters gone? O for an Airplane with One Class . . . First! (An Affordable First Class, no less! Yes, Dear Reader, the Etiquette Grrls swear to you, this is true! Well, at least Back In The Day, maybe everyone didn't *exactly* travel by First Class per se, but The Standard was more like today's First Class than the Hell which we know as Coach.) Alas, gone are the days when Every Lady, clad in A Couture Gabardine Suit and Her Sable, could travel in elegance, comfort, and style—and with a steamer trunk or six . . . which no one expected her to carry by herself. The only kind of Coach the Etiquette Grrls like is the one where they get their Leather Goods, but these Bleak Days, even the Etiquette Grrls admit that Traveling by First Class is Prohibitively Expensive. And not even worth the money, in a lot of instances. Sigh. Indeed, These Are the Times That Try Men's Souls, as the Etiquette Grrls' Good Friend Thomas Paine said. However, the Etiquette Grrls are here to tell you how to Make The Most of What We Have, Dear Reader.

AIR TRAVEL

What has happened to Air Travel these days, Dear Reader, makes the Etiquette Grrls absolutely disconsolate! Not only is the Airline Passenger made to feel like part of a Herd of Cattle, not only are the seating arrangements so very cramped that they rival Chinese Water Torture for comfort and pleasantness, but it is a Rare Day indeed when a flight—any flight—arrives anywhere near its scheduled arrival time. Why, the Etiquette Grrls ask, should a less-than-a-one-and-a-half-hour flight between Pittsburgh and Hartford ever take fourteen (or more) hours? And, perhaps Geometry was never exactly the Etiquette Grrls' forte, but we do recall that The Shortest Distance Between Two Points Is A Straight Line. So why do the Airlines tell us that the Shortest Distance between San Francisco and Chicago is through Newark? The Etiquette Grrls would like to have a Word with you, USAir, United, Continental, et al!

While the airlines are busy with their Machiavellian Plans to make Air Travel as inconvenient, expensive, uncomfortable, and time-consuming as possible, the Public-At-Large, it seems to the Etiquette Grrls, has determined that the moment one sets foot in an Airport or upon an Airplane, one is instantly given a license to behave in the Rudest

Possible Fashion! The Etiquette Grrls cannot possibly begin to express to our Dear Readers how Shocked and Appalled they are by this Atrocious Behavior! Why on earth would anyone think that just because you are on an airplane, you may behave in a Rude and Boorish Manner? The Etiquette Grrls have compiled a helpful List of Common Air Travel Etiquette Faux Pas. Never, ever, *ever* do any of the following:

- **Shove your way to the Front of the Line.** As passengers board a plane, the Attendant will call them in sections, starting with First Class Passengers and people who need Special Assistance. This means Handicapped People, Very Elderly and Decrepit Folks, Small Children traveling Alone, and perhaps people traveling with a Tiny Baby. Needing a G&T, stat, the Etiquette Grrls regret to inform you, does not count as "Special Assistance." After this, the Attendant will ask the passengers in Business Class, and then Coach Class, to board the plane. In doing so, she or he will start with the last rows, calling a few rows at a time, and working forward. Hence, if you are to be seated in Row 10, you may not park yourself in line when the Attendant has asked Rows 25 and Higher to board. Nor may you Hover About, getting in the way, while you wait for your section to be called. Sit the hell down and wait your turn, the Etiquette Grrls beseech you, Dear Reader! The plane's not going to leave any faster if you knock over three Little Old Ladies in your haste to get to The Front of The Line. Nor will you win a Door Prize or anything else worthwhile. Likewise, when disembarking, exit in a Tidy and Orderly Fashion—row by row. You'll get off the plane more quickly in the long run if you wait your turn. When a mêlée occurs in the all-too-narrow aisle because everyone's trying to Get Out at once, nobody's going to get anywhere. So, Pipe Down and be patient, Dear Reader!

- **Attempt to bring Too Much Stuff on Board.** These days, Airlines are Cracking Down on Carry-On Luggage. The Etiquette

Grrls guess this is because they are trying to save space so they can wedge a few more passengers on the plane and make an extra dime or two. But the Etiquette Grrls digress, Dear Reader. All Airlines will tell you that you are permitted only two pieces of Carry-On Luggage. You must adhere to this. And by "Carry-On," the Airlines and the Etiquette Grrls mean A Small and Compact Bag, not a damn Steamer Trunk! The Etiquette Grrls get so Exasperated when there is not a Spare Inch in the Overhead Compartment for their Teeny-Tiny Mark Cross Overnight Bag (just like Grace Kelly's in *Rear Window*!) because it's filled to capacity avec An Enormous, Bulging Duffle Bag appearing to contain the Complete Wardrobe of an Entire College Dormitory! Anything larger than a briefcase or a very small overnight case should be Checked. Now, the Etiquette Grrls must say that they think it is Extremely Unfair that a Small Handbag is counted as One Carry-On Item, as a Lady obviously must carry such an thing, and a Man does not. Hence, a Man may carry on board, say, a Laptop and a Valise, but the Etiquette Grrls understand that on some flights a Lady is limited to her Wee Handbag and her Laptop. Life is so unfair, Dear Reader! Alas.

- **Ask for A Peculiar Beverage** when the Flight Attendant comes 'round avec the Beverage Cart. No, it is not at all likely that USAir Flight 1750 will have on hand any Tab or RC Cola that has been Lying Around since circa 1970, or some Strange, Foreign, Sparkling, Kumquat-Flavored Water. Also, the Etiquette Grrls know that Air Travel can Drive Any Normal Person to Drink, but don't ask for a Good Stiff Drink before noon, at least. It's Just Not Done. Unless, of course, Your Flight happens to be serving Brunch Cocktails like Mimosas or Bloody Marys. (And even this is A Little Much at 7:30 A.M.) It's also Very Poor Form to bring your Own Bottle of Liquor On Board and proceed to drink it en route to Your Destination. Even if you do have a Cunning Retro Travel Bar.

- **Violently Jiggle any headrest that you grasp for balance** when rising from your seat or walking up and down The Aisle. Be especially sure that you do not grab a handful of an Unsuspecting Passenger's hair along with the headrest. For that matter, Dear Reader, try not to hold onto Anybody Else's Seat if it can be at all avoided. This is where the Good Sea Legs which you developed from years and years of Sailing will help you out, Dear Reader!

- **Hog the armrests of the Middle Seat** if you're sitting on the end of a row. Heck, in fact, don't hog the Middle Seat itself! If someone is unfortunate enough to be seated between two strangers, and happens to arrive after the Window and Aisle People have taken their seats, she shouldn't be subjected to the Window and Aisle People acting Put Upon when they have to move the stack of Tabloid Magazines they're planning to read on the plane!

- **Allow Your Child to run or play in the Aisles,** climb over seats, or drop food, toys, etc. onto the heads of the people sitting in front of you. This is especially unacceptable behavior for an Adult.

- **Be Rude to Your Neighbors.** When you reach your seat, you should greet the person or people sitting next to you with a gracious "Good Morning/Afternoon/Evening," etc. But if they are obviously Not Keen on Conversing with you, don't pursue it.

- **Be Bored and Fidgety.** You should bring a book or magazine to entertain yourself during the flight. Avoid newspapers unless you are able to read them whilst they are folded up into A Wee Rectangle, as New Yorkers do on The Subway. You may also work on Knitting or a similar project, if you can do it without taking up much room. Projects which involve A Lot of Elbow Room or Messy Things like Paints are to be avoided.

- **Ignore People Who Need Help.** If you see someone—especially an Elderly, Frail, or Petite Person—Struggling Mightily to put something in the Overhead Compartment, give him or her A Hand. This is Especially True for Boys, but an Able-Bodied Girl should Make Herself Useful, too, if presented with the opportunity.

- **Open the Overhead Compartment recklessly.** Be Very, Very Careful in order to keep a Flurry of Briefcases and Packages from Tumbling Down Upon Your Head—or worse, Somebody Else's Head.

- **Communicate with other people in your party by shouting across ten rows,** throwing paper airplanes, or by any other method, should you happen to be seated separately from them.

- **Ignore the Flight Attendants' and/or Pilot's instructions.** Do you want to be on the Plane whose Flight Instruments get All Out of Whack because you wouldn't turn off your CD Player, Dear Reader? No, the Etiquette Grrls didn't think so.

Baggage Claim

One of the Etiquette Grrls' Least Favorite Things about Air Travel is the Holy Terror Which Is Baggage Claim. First of all, the Etiquette Grrls demand to know why, no matter how many Baggage Claim Carousels there are, the Baggage for every single blessed flight is always put on the same blasted carousel? Why, God, why? Is it obvious to no one but the Etiquette Grrls that this causes Nothing Short of Pandemonium? And why is it that The Big, Mean People always shove their way to the front, completely preventing Anybody Else from even seeing if Their Luggage is on its way? And to add insult to injury, these very same people tend to, purposefully, it seems, Whack Everyone in the Vicinity with Their Bag as they Enthusiastically Yank it off the Conveyor Belt! Is it really necessary to Take People Out with your Samsonite? The Etiquette Grrls don't really care how bad your day has been; this seems to be A Bit Much. Also, make certain that you, in fact, have your bag before you Make Off With It. The Etiquette Grrls find it So Tiresome when we have to Sprint After Our

Luggage which is Making Its Way to the Taxi Stand Without Us. This is particularly irksome, as the Etiquette Grrls' Luggage is, of course, Monogrammed! How could anyone possibly Fail To Notice that the suitcase you have mistaken for yours is marked "EG" in tailored brown Embroidery right there on the Front? Unobservant People drive the Etiquette Grrls Positively Batty, Dear Reader! The Etiquette Grrls think we'd all be A Lot Happier when Traveling if everyone allowed Other People to get Their Bags, took care not to cause Bodily Harm to others, and did not Resort to Thievery.

And then there's the Problem of what to do with your luggage once you Do Battle with the Baggage Claim Area, Dear Reader. Much to the Etiquette Grrls' chagrin, skycaps seem to be Un Peu Extinct these days. That leaves only those Wheeled-Cart Things which, in every airport the Etiquette Grrls have ever been in, are hidden away in some Remote, Inconvenient Spot, and consequently, are impossible to find. And then, if you can find them at all, they always seem to be like Grocery Shopping Carts, but with More Personality Problems. How do the wheels simultaneously move in Four Different Directions like that? Despite all the Globe-Trotting the Etiquette Grrls have done in our lives, we have yet to find a Good Way to manage these Silly and Immeasurably Ineffectual Carts, other than hiring A Personal Assistant to worry about it for us. (Or of course, finding the Only Living Skycap.) If we think of anything better, we'll let you know Right Away, Dear Reader!

BY TRAIN

It makes the Etiquette Grrls mournful indeed when we think about what's happened to the State of Train Travel, Dear Reader! Back In The Day, the Etiquette Grrls understand, even the Most Mundane of Train Trips was Something Swanky! For instance, Dear Reader, the "Café Car," was less of an Elaborate Vending Machine, as it is now, and was more like A Good Restaurant, with Real Tables and Linens and Flowers and Silver Teapots and All That Jazz. And, there were Parlor Cars, where you could curl up on An Actual Couch with a

Good Book, and you could even ring for a Waiter to Bring You a Good, Stiff Drink! And if you were taking an Overnight Journey, you could have Your Own Compartment that resembled a perfect, darling, wee (albeit very wee) Hotel Room! Add to all of this that you could easily take The Train to anywhere in the country, even the tiniest, most remote town! As you can imagine, this made getting to things like the Big College Weekend considerably easier than it would be today. (If, indeed, there were any Big College Weekends left to go to. Regardless, have you ever tried to get to Hanover or Williamstown by train lately, Dear Reader? C'est Positively Impossible!) Etiquette Grrls kid you not, Dear Reader! It really was so! And now what have we, the Etiquette Grrls ask you, Dear Reader? Just the chronically late, crowded, and inconvenient Amtrak. It makes the Etiquette Grrls simply want to Cry! Plus, as anyone who's ever seen an Alfred Hitchcock film or read an Agatha Christie novel knows, Back In The Day, one could almost always count on Something Exciting happening on board A Train! The Etiquette Grrls don't know what they're doing wrong, but they've never met anyone as dashing as Cary Grant or become Embroiled dans A Plot of International Intrigue whilst on board the Hartford–New Haven. How wretchedly dull.

In any case, you'll probably find yourself on Good Ol' Amtrak one of these days, Dear Reader, and "how," you ask, "shall I behave?" It's very simple, Dear Reader. All of the rules we described above with regard to Air Travel apply to Train Travel as well. Just because you have more Elbow Room on board a Train does not give you license to run around and Get In People's Way, be Loud and Obstreperous, or be Rude in Any Way. In addition, you'll find that on most Trains there is no Assigned Seating. This does not mean that you get to hog two seats (or four, in the case of the Facing Rows frequently seen at the ends of cars) to yourself if the Train is crowded. One Etiquette Grrl was shocked when on a recent Train Trip, she walked the entire length of the Train, and not a single, solitary soul would move their bags and other accoutrements from a seat so that she could sit down! Meanwhile, as Etiquette Grrl, dragging her Heavy Valise, struggled along miles of Lurching Aisle, the Conductor kept yelling at her Very Rudely to Sit The Hell Down! Yet, when Etiquette Grrl Lodged A Complaint that Everyone was Hogging the Seats, Mr. Conductor Flatly Refused to assist her! Etiquette Grrl vowed then and there to Never Set Foot Upon Another Train until people start behaving in a More Courteous Manner!

　　Lastly, and perhaps Most Importantly, the Etiquette Grrls feel that we must point out the following: Boys, it is Very Chivalric, if you see a Girl standing on a Packed Train, to Offer Her Your Seat. It would make the Etiquette Grrls so very happy if they started to see more of this sort of thing! However, what's More Crucial for Boys and Girls alike is this: If you see An Elderly or Handicapped Person or a Pregnant Woman searching for a seat—whether on Amtrak, or a Commuter Train, or the Subway—you must offer Your Seat!!! There will be Absolutely No Arguments about this, Dear Reader, and that's Final!!!

ON BUSSES

Long-Distance travel by Bus is best avoided entirely, if at all possible. Busses tend always to be very crowded, and one has Absolutely No Legroom, and there's not much space on the Luggage Racks either. Plus, it seems to the Etiquette Grrls that the Bus Station in Every American Town and City is a Very Scary Place, and we don't think they're particularly Good Places for any of our Dear Readers to be Hanging Out. Plus, being on a Bus always makes the Etiquette Grrls feel like we're on a Middle-School Field Trip to the Aquarium or something, and who wants to feel like they're In Middle School again? Quelle Horreur!

BY SHIP

Gather 'Round, Kats and Kittens, it's Story Time: Back before Air Travel was ubiquitous, there was only one way to get to England, Dear Reader, and that was by Ocean Liner. Vast and glittering, The Liner was as Luxurious and Comfortable as the Most Elegant Hotel! One of the most elegant Ocean Liners of all time was the *Normandie,* the star of the French Line, launched in 1935. But, O, she had a short life, Dear Reader, and what a Tragic Day it was when the *Normandie* met her Fateful End that February day in 1942 in New York Harbor! The Most Luxurious and Beautiful Liner in the World burned and sank while she was being made over into a Warship for use in the Second World War. She was later sold for Scrap in Newark. And thus ended The Age of Shipboard Elegance! Sigh. So it goes, as Mr. Vonnegut would say.

There are Two Kinds of Travel By Ship, Dear Reader—the Transatlantic Crossing (elegant, but positively nonexistent since about the mid-1960s, if not before) and Cruises (ubiquitous, and Very Tacky these days, even when going by the So-Called "First Class"). The latter is To Be Avoided at All Costs. Once the epitome of Elegance, Ship Travel has reached the Lowest Pits of Tawdriness. Oh, it simply breaks the Etiquette Grrls' hearts! The Etiquette Grrls have even heard of A Cruise Ship owned by Disney that sails to An Island owned by the same. The Etiquette Grrls can think of No Worse Hell than going to The Isle of Disney on the USS *Mickey.* The mere thought gives the Etiquette Grrls The Vapors!

Traveling Clothes

The Etiquette Grrls long for the days when Traveling was An Occasion, and everyone Dressed the Part! A pox upon this "I Just Rolled Out of Bed" look, which one so frequently sees in Airports and Train Stations! Oh, the Horror, the Horror! It used to be, Dear Reader, that neither men nor women would ever even *think* about venturing out of the house and going somewhere without wearing an Exquisitely Tailored Suit! And a Smart Hat! (Both men and women! And the Etiquette Grrls don't mean a baseball cap with a collegiate embroidered logo, either!) Not only did people Dress Well because it looked nice, and because it was Expected, but because it's a lot easier to be Authoritative when you are dressed in an Impressive Manner. Believe the Etiquette Grrls, Dear Reader. Things being the way they are These Sad, Sorry Days, you're going to need to be as Authoritative As Possible when traveling. When you're bumped off of the twentieth flight today, is that Snotty Airline Clerk going to listen up and rush to get you on another flight A.S.A.P. when you're dressed in Black Watch–Plaid Flannel Pajamas and a torn and stained Penn State Sweatshirt? Maybe, but the Etiquette Grrls doubt it. Will she listen up when you look like you mean Business? Perhaps not, but the Etiquette Grrls assure you that you'll have a Better Chance.

Now, the Etiquette Grrls realize that you're not going to go out of your way to Dress Uncomfortably for Your Trip—but the thing is, Dear Reader, you don't have to! You can look elegant and refined, and still be comfortable during Your Trip, and even emerge Wrinkle-Free! As always, Your Outfit should be clean, neat, and, if needed, mended. (Please, as always, no Uneven Hems or Dangling Strings!) Avoid Light Colors, which will show dirt easily, and wear a fabric that does not get Hideously Wrinkly at the slightest provocation. (This is one of the times when the Etiquette Grrls would avoid Linen, as much as we love it.) If you will be traveling to A Distant City of Another Climate, select an outfit which will be Suitable Attire for both your City of Departure and your City of Arrival, remembering that even Ordinary Street Clothes in Large Cities, especially Large European Cities, may be far more sophisticated than what you, Dear Reader, are accustomed to. The Etiquette Grrls have drawn up A Wee Chart with some Suggestions of Traveling Clothes Which Will Take You Anywhere:

TRAVELING CLOTHES FOR GIRLS

- Plain dress, slacks, or mid-length skirt of light- to mid-weight wool, jersey, or other stretchy/fluid, wrinkle-defying fabric, and in a Medium to Dark Color.

- Blouse, button-down shirt, or Dressy Tee to coordinate with slacks or skirt.

- A nonbulky cardigan—cotton, silk, wool, or cashmere (which is nice) in case you Get Un Peu Cold. (Often airplanes in particular are Rather Frigid. The Etiquette Grrls suppose this is to prevent the passengers from noticing that they are Packed In Like Sardines, or some such, by giving them Something Else to worry about. Like Hypothermia.)

- A matching coat. In the Spring, Summer, and Autumn, a Smart Little Jacket looks nice; in the Colder Months you should wear a Wool Coat.

- Well-polished flat or low-heeled shoes in a Comparable Style to the Rest of Your Outfit, and which are comfortable and fit very well. And don't take them off while you are In Transit! If the Etiquette

TRAVELING CLOTHES FOR BOYS

- Nice, well-fitting slacks. No jeans, and preferably not corduroys, which are best worn in The Country. Khakis are fine, though.

- A nice button-down shirt.

- The Etiquette Grrls would like to see All The Boys wearing ties, too, but we know that's probably Not Going To Happen. Sigh.

- A sports coat.

- A Wool Overcoat (in Cold Weather).

- Nice socks. (That means No Tube Socks.)

- Well-polished loafers, oxfords, or good lace-up shoes, depending on the Style and Formality of Your Outfit.

- No jewelry, save for A Watch and/or Wedding Ring. As always.

TRAVELING CLOTHES
FOR GIRLS

Grrls wanted to look at people's Socks, they'd open a Laundry Business!

·A Handbag—not Too Large, not Too Small. Something which fastens securely is a Good Idea, to guard against Accidental Spills and/or Pickpockets.

·Very Plain Jewelry, if any. (It is never a Wise Idea to call attention to yourself while Traveling, Dear Reader! If you don't want to be Robbed, that is.)

Your Luggage

Like your clothes, Your Luggage is a Reflection of You, Dear Reader, and you should take Great Pains to make sure it is as clean and neat and smart as Your Travel Ensemble. Just as scuffed, worn-down-at-the-heels shoes can ruin your Entire Appearance, An Ugly Suitcase will Completely Destroy the image of the Smart Sophisticate that the Etiquette Grrls know all of our Dear Readers work so very hard at cultivating. Should you have for your suitcase one of those immense metal-framed knapsacks? Not unless you're Setting Off on a month-long trek through the Outback! And should you actually carry Suits in said makeshift suitcase? Most emphatically not! You absolutely must own a set of Real Luggage, Dear Reader, even if you are not a Frequent Flier. You never know when Grandmama is going to ask you to accompany her to London, and you must be Prepared! Now, of course, Dear Reader, the Etiquette Grrls favor Impeccably Maintained Vintage Leather Luggage, but, well, these Gorgeous

Items are damnably heavy and awkward, and what with it being so very difficult to find a porter or a redcap These Dreary Days, the Etiquette Grrls have found that the Modern Wheeled Variety to be Far More Practical.

Your Luggage is An Investment, Dear Reader, and you should buy the best that you can afford. Whereas Cheap Luggage will begin to fall apart after one flight, given the Terrible Abuse it must take from Brutish Baggage Handlers, a More Expensive Set should last a Good Long Time, making it A Worthwhile Purchase. Also, in the case of Wheeled Suitcases, it is very important to buy A Quality Set, as Cheap Bags never wheel properly, which is Absolutely Maddening!

Your Luggage should be of a Matched Set, and it should be very plain, in a solid, dark color, as such colors will not show dirt as easily as light ones, and Your Luggage will remain new-looking for Quite Some Time. Also, it should be noted that it is the Epitome of Poor Taste to have luggage that is Emblazoned avec A Logo. (The Horrible Be-logoed Louis Vuitton stuff leaps to mind, but the Etiquette Grrls have been seeing a lot of This Sort Of Thing lately with Other Designers, too, and we're Utterly Appalled!) First of all, you never wear, or carry, or otherwise own anything with a Monogram other than your own, unless it is an Inherited Piece. Also, it is Extremely Tacky to Announce To The World where you have bought things. Believe us, Dear Reader, the People Who Need To Know Will Know Without Being Told—A Good Eye can quickly assess and assign any clothing/accessories/etc. to the House From Which They Came. Further, these days, it is Not A Good Idea to have Luggage that screams, "I Cost More Than Your House!" Unless you never want to see Your Bag and what is inside it ever again, that is. Luggage may, however, be Discreetly Monogrammed avec your own initials. This is Quite Elegant, and will also help you to spot Your Bag on the Baggage Carousel.

Lastly, The Etiquette Grrls sincerely hope that we don't have to remind our Dear Readers that Their Luggage should never be held together by duct tape, yarn, or any other Makeshift Fastening. If

Your Luggage is in such terrible shape, it's time to invest in a New Set. Also, do not fasten Extraneous Things to your bags. That red bandanna might make it easier for you to spot your bag when it's time to collect it, but it looks Just Terrible, Dear Reader! As the Etiquette Grrls said, a Nice, Subtle Little Monogram is a far more elegant way to Make Your Luggage Distinctive!

Staying at Hotels

Ah, there's nothing like a Good Hotel, Dear Reader! Luxury! Comfort! Room Service! Bring on the Continental Breakfast! The Etiquette Grrls, like Dear Eloise, will say, "Thank you and charge it, please!" When staying dans A Hotel, whether it be Petite Pension or The Grand Hotel, always remember that you are not at Howard Johnson's, and a certain amount of Decorum is required. (Not that the Etiquette Grrls expect our Dear Readers to Raise Hell at Howard Johnson's either, of course!) "Well," you may ask, Dear Reader, "what is A Good Hotel?" A Good Hotel has Room Service, lots of people running around carrying your luggage, a Doorman, and probably A Very Good Restaurant and a Very Swanky Bar where often you can find A Celebrity playing the Piano or Singing. If you do not notice any of these things, you are likely in A Motel, or possibly A Bed and Breakfast. The Etiquette Grrls, of course, expect our Dear Readers will Behave Themselves in these places as well, but they are, by their Informal Nature, Less Intimidating than The Plaza, and the Etiquette Grrls assume our Dear Readers won't need as much Guidance when staying at the Grover's Corners Motor Lodge.

When in Public Areas of the hotel (Lobby, Restaurant, Bar—anyplace but Your Room) you must be Appropriately Dressed at all times. The Etiquette Grrls were saddened and shocked the last time we were at The Algonquin to see Throngs of Tourists loitering around The Lobby wearing Running Shorts, Tank Tops, Sweatsuits, and Other Assorted Horrors! The Etiquette Grrls know that Good Hotels strive to be Your Home Away From Home, but there's No Need to Take This Literally! Rather, A Good Hotel is Your Elegant

Home Away From Home Where You Always Dress For Dinner! When selecting The Outfit in which you will Take Tea down in the Lobby, you must also remember to take into account the Standards of The City Which You Are Visiting—obviously, Street Attire in New York City will vary greatly from that of say, Denver. Resort Towns such as Palm Beach or Newport will call for still a different wardrobe than that which you would wear when En Ville.

Similarly, you should not Take It Upon Yourself to rearrange the Lobby Furniture, prune the Potted Palms, remove lightbulbs from Lamps/Chandeliers, and so on. Nor should you Run Around and make A Lot of Noise. In short, although the Etiquette Grrls are So Very Fond of dear, delightful Eloise, you should not attempt to Emulate her. (The Etiquette Grrls want our Dear Readers to note that it is never correct to Torment The Help.) Even Rock Stars should refrain from throwing furniture/fixtures out the window, setting anything on fire, or hosting Wild Parties in their Suites.

When staying at a Hotel, make sure you have Loads of Dollar Bills on your person, because you will have to tip everybody, all the time, for everything. For instance, if the Doorman helps you out of Your Car and gets Your Bags from the trunk, you should give him a couple of bucks, as you should if he stands in the Pouring, Freezing Rain to Get You A Taxi. It is not necessary, however, to tip him every time you walk in or out of the door if he doesn't do anything in particular for you. You should tip the Bellboy who brings your luggage to your room a dollar a bag, and maybe more if your bags are Extraordinarily Heavy, Awkward, or Plentiful. At the end of your stay, you should leave two dollars or so per day for The Maid. You should place this in an envelope marked "Housekeeping" and leave it Someplace Obvious, like on the Desk. Of course, if anyone does Something Special for You, you should give them a tip commensurate with the service, whatever it was. For instance, give the Maid another dollar or two if you ask for Another Blanket. Asking her to whip up a Wee Patchwork Quilt by tonight, please, would demand A Bit More.

Good hotels have a Concierge Desk, where a helpful person with a Very Good Rolodex will assist you with Travel and Sightseeing Arrangements, Dinner Reservations, Theatre Tickets, etc. Should you urgently need a table at The Hottest Restaurant In Town and a Car and Driver to take you there, the Concierge is the person to ask. He or she will also be able to help with such situations as, "I need to propose to my girlfriend via Skywriting. Can you help?" (although the Etiquette Grrls Sincerely Hope that you are not contemplating Such A Thing, Dear Reader, let alone Requesting Assistance with it!); "Can you set up videoconferencing equipment in Suite 166?"; or "I need a First Edition of *Ulysses* by 10 A.M. tomorrow." The services of the Concierge are free to guests of the Hotel. If tipping is permitted (at some hotels, it is not), you should stop at the Concierge Desk upon your departure and leave five to ten dollars, depending on the service provided, in an envelope, with the name of the person who helped you. If your request was at all Unusual, or you asked for something on Very Short Notice, you should tip the concierge well, and consider including a Brief Note of Thanks.

Staying at a Private Home

So, maybe you're not staying in a Hotel, Dear Reader—maybe you've got a Dear Friend with a Wee Cottage in Little Compton, or a flat on Park Avenue. So what then? The Best Houseguest is an Undemanding Houseguest. Your Main Requirement is to be as Unobtrusive As Possible. Everyone likes A Houseguest who will go off for a walk on her own, or who is content to sit on the porch and read a magazine. No one likes a guest who demands to be Taken Places, Told What to Do, and Generally Entertained 24/7.

Houseguests should be good tempered and easy-to-please at all times. They should make A Genuine Effort to be pleasant to other residents of the house, and any other guests, pets, etc. Guests may not Lodge a Complaint avec the Management about the Quality of the Rooms, Furnishings, Linens, Food, and so on. For this reason, the Etiquette Grrls think that if you are a Very Picky Person, you'd really be happier staying at a Nearby Hotel, Motel, or Inn. At least if you want to keep Your Friends, that is. And, particularly if you are staying for A Great Length of Time, you should do Little Helpful Things: For instance, have you noticed that the Bar is Running Low on Bombay Sapphire? Well, then, slip out, run to the Liquor Store, and pick up another bottle. You should not make an Ostentatious Display of your generosity. Arriving with a fanfare and announcing, "I'm here! And I went out of my way—during the Prime Tanning Hours, no less—to buy more Gin! The rest of you are lazyass bums!" while brandishing the Bombay like a Scimitar is Not Necessary. Simply put The Booze in the bar, where your friends will surely find it the next time you are having cocktails. When someone exclaims with glee over the Miraculous Appearance of More Gin, and says, "Okay, which of you dears is the mystery Gin Fairy?," you can, perhaps, 'fess up. The Etiquette Grrls feel that we should warn our Dear Readers about being Overly Helpful, however. We all know that sometimes that which passes as Helpfulness is actually just a bit of a Hindrance. Maybe you're An Efficiency Expert on a par with Mr. and Mrs. Gilbreth, of *Cheaper by the Dozen* fame, but Your Hostess will likely Not Be Pleased if you rearrange the contents of the refrigerator and kitchen cabinets in order that they be "More Efficient."

The Good Houseguest comes, of course, Bearing Gifts. You must always bring A Wee Something for Your Hostess. Flowers are always lovely (these may be sent ahead if you wish so Your Hostess doesn't have to dash madly about searching for a vase), as are Elegant Food Items. You might bring a little basket full of Exotic Teas, or Fancy Jams, or Madeleines. Or, perhaps a Bottle of Expensive Liquor will do. If you are An Adept Cook, Dear Reader, it is always lovely to bring something you made yourself—cookies or bread, for instance. Or, Something For The House is always nice—a package of Beautiful French Handsoaps, for example. Or, maybe Your Hostess has A Particular Hobby, and you could take this into account. Is her Prize Possession a Vintage Hi-Fi? Bring a great Sinatra LP or two! Or maybe she collects cookbooks from the 1950s—find a nice one at a used-book store, wrap it up in pretty paper, and there you go! It's really quite easy, Dear Reader! As with all gift-giving, it takes just a little bit of thought, but once you get the hang of it, you'll be selecting gifts that are always guaranteed to be The Cat's Pajamas!

THE BREAD-AND-BUTTER LETTER
Within a week of departure, a guest should write his or her hostess a note, thanking her for her hospitality and reiterating what a grand time was had by all. A Sample Thank-You Note (on engraved writing paper) follows:

> Eloise T. Haversham
> 250 Berkeley Place
> Apartment 406
> New York, New York 10028

> June 24, 2001

Dear Emily,

Thank you so much for having me down to the house in Little Compton this past weekend. It was lovely to escape the city for a few days, and I found your friends whom you invited to that Absolutely Smashing Clambake to be Positively Delightful. I am quite sure that I must have gained Several Pounds from all the Delicious Food that you served, but I must say, I savored every single morsel! Thank you again for your hospitality, and do please let me know the next time you plan to be in The City—you know that the Guest Room is always free!

> *Fondly,*
> *Eloise*

P.S. Would you mind sending me the recipe for your delicious Artichoke Dip? Merci beaucoup!!

Note that Miss Haversham invites her friend to visit her in her note. One should always reciprocate, and invite the people who have served as your hosts in the past to come visit you, too. This reassures your friends that you like them for who they are, and not for the places in which they reside.

Getting Your Kicks on Route 66: The Road Trip

The Etiquette Grrls, like most of our generation, and *every* generation who followed Kerouac, love going on Road Trips. What fun to Meander through the countryside on Back Roads! How interesting to Explore different parts of Our Fair Country! Maybe the Etiquette Grrls, City Kids that we are, will never want to Take Up Residence in Smalltown, USA, but we sure don't mind getting a Cup of Joe and some Apple Pie at The Bluebird Diner and having a Lovely Chat with the Locals! If you'll forgive the Etiquette Grrls getting Patriotic for a moment, Dear Reader, there is A Lot to See in the Good Ol' U.S. of A., and we think people ought to Get Out More and Explore. You might even drive to Canada!

But, as with all else, one must be certain that one has outfitted oneself with appropriately snazzy clothing, accoutrements, and of course, most importantly, a Very, Very Stylish Automobile, preferably a mint-condition Vintage Convertible. The Etiquette Grrls are especially fond of MGs, Austin-Healeys, Jaguars, and Thunderbirds from the mid-to-late fifties or early sixties, as well as very early Mustangs and Corvettes. (But please, no late-models of these last two autos! The Etiquette Grrls can't imagine whatever happened to these cars—they are simply Not What They Used To Be!) It goes without saying that your auto ought to be in a Flattering Color. For instance, a redhead should never been seen driving around in a cherry-red convertible, as it will clash with her hair. Generally, black, silver, navy blue, and English Racing Car Green are flattering to everyone.

Girls with long hair ought to fasten their hair back with sweet little stretchy headbands, or, better yet, scarves, à la Grace Kelly. Not only does this look Rather Glamorous with a great pair of tortoiseshell, cat's-eye sunglasses, but it prevents your hair from whipping around in your face, which hurts, and also creates Nasty Snarls. Of course, this also rather impairs one's vision whilst driving, which the Etiquette Grrls dare say is peut-être un peu dangereux. If you are very fair-skinned, like the Etiquette Grrls, you should be cautious with convertibles in Sunny Climates, lest you get Sunburned. Of course, one should use sunscreen liberally, regardless of one's Complexion.

Also, the driving on any long Road Trip should be shared by all passengers in the car. It is no fun at all, the Etiquette Grrls remind you, to have a Dear Friend suggest what sounds like a terrific trip to Key West only to discover that she can't take a turn driving your standard-shift vintage T-Bird.

WHAT YOU SHOULD BRING WITH YOU
While Road Trips are best when they are Impromptu, one must prepare a little bit before Hitting the Road. You should bring with you a large supply of cassettes or CDs of your Favorite Songs. You should also prepare a large picnic basket or cooler (the Etiquette Grrls like those Old Coleman ones) filled with tasty snack foods and bottles of soda and iced tea in order to stave off Starvation should you grow Peckish while you are in the Middle Of Nowhere. Also, you should avail yourself of a cunning little Travel Bar. Don't get us wrong— obviously, The Etiquette Grrls never, *ever,* condone drinking and driving, but you will probably need to make use of your Travel Bar should you need to stop at a Dreadfully Tacky Motel, which does not have a Sufficiently Divey Bar on or near its Premises. (Or worse, an *Overly* Divey Bar on or near its Premises—The Etiquette Grrls would like it Very Much if, whilst on a Road Trip, their Dear Readers did not engage in a Terrible Bar Brawl avec Les Hell's Angels.) But the Etiquette Grrls will forewarn their Dear Readers—it's not likely you're going to find a Ritz-Carlton or Four Seasons in Rural Small-Town America—but then, part of the joy of a Road Trip is Roughing It. We don't necessarily recommend Roughing It as in Camping Out on the

Roadside, but we're sure, Dear Reader, you will be able to find a clean, safe Motel in Most Parts of Our Fair Country!

WHAT YOU SHOULD WEAR

As always when Traveling, one should avoid things which Wrinkle Easily, like linen. (Although the Etiquette Grrls do adore linen ever so much for Summer Clothing!) Cute little cotton Bermuda shorts or capri or cigarette pants, perhaps in a Lilly Print, with sandals, espadrilles, or Keds would be charming. If it's chilly, you have the Etiquette Grrls' permission to wear jeans, for convenience's sake. Also remember to always have a little sweater with you, even if it seems warm, because the weather can Change Suddenly! And, keep a windbreaker or rain jacket within Easy Reach—you won't need it in the car perhaps (unless you have beaucoup de difficulties Putting The Top Up), but you may want to stop unexpectedly for lunch or to see an Odd Roadside Attraction, and be caught dans a Wee Squall, and you'll need A Jacket then, Dear Reader!

WHERE YOU SHOULD GO

Now that you're in possession of a darling little Vintage Roadster, some cute Traveling Clothes, and you're Armed To The Teeth with a stack of CDs and a heavy Picnic Basket, "Where," you ask, Dear Reader, "shall we go?" Let's start by talking about where you *shouldn't* go. First of all, no Major Metropolitan Areas. No one Road-Trips to New York, or Washington, D.C., or Philadelphia, or Boston. This is not going on a Road Trip, this is merely Going To The City. Also, your destination should be nowhere under, say, six hours away. This is not a Road Trip, this is merely being in the car for a Long Time. Road Trips are A Big Commitment, and if you're going to do it at all, you have to do it Full-Force, which means driving for *days*. Also, you simply *must* stay off the Major Interstates! The Entire Point of a Road Trip, Dear Reader, is to See The Country and meet some of the Interesting, Charming, and/or Eccentric Inhabitants of Small-Town America. This will not happen on I-95, Dear Reader!! You must acquire a Sense of Adventure! (And, Dear Reader, you should also be certain to read Kerouac's *On the Road* and Steinbeck's *Travels with Charley*—particularly the latter—Right Away!)

There are really only four *real* routes that you should take for your Road Trip. They are U.S. Route 1, from Maine to Florida, Route 66 (or what's left of it), from Chicago to Los Angeles, the Pacific Coast Highway, and the Cross-Country Trip. Should you decide to drive cross-country, you have to take the Southern Route (you can take the Northern Route on the way back, if you like), which means you can stop in Memphis (i.e., Graceland), Mobile, New Orleans, San Antonio, Roswell (if you're an *X-Files* fan, or a Believer in The Governmental Conspiracy to Cover Up The Existence Of Aliens), and of course, The Big Mac Daddy of all Road-Trip Destinations, Vegas, Baby, Vegas. (As an aside, it Deeply Saddens The Etiquette Grrls that Las Vegas has changed so much from its Rat Pack heyday, but no matter . . . you still have to go there anyway, Dear Reader. You'll just have to *pretend* that you can hear Frank and Dino, God Rest Their Souls, singin' and swingin' at The Sands. Sigh. The Mere Thought makes the Etiquette Grrls Shed A Tear—we love you, Messrs. Sinatra and Martin!)

Road Trips aren't about getting somewhere in a hurry. They're about cruising the open road with your Best Chums, meandering along, and stopping anywhere along the way that strikes your fancy. Therefore, you should stop at every single silly, off-beat, and tacky Roadside Attraction that you come across, and Revel In The Sheer Tackiness of It All. (While the Etiquette Grrls never condone tackiness, per se, let it not be said that we can't Go Slumming once in a while, nor that we can't appreciate the fact that The World's Largest Ball Of Twine is so Indicative of Our Society And Culture. We also think that it is Rather Ironic that the Etiquette Grrls would actually Seek Out Tackiness, and the Etiquette Grrls just *adore* Irony.) If you wish, you could also make your stops thematic—Birthplaces of Famous American Authors, or Sites of Famous Cult Followings, for example. At mealtimes, try to avoid McDonald's and its Brethren if you're able. It's far better to have a Cheeseburger, Fries, and Shake at that chrome-plated burger joint across the street—you'll discover more Local Color, and the food will be better, besides.

On your Travels, it's also Quite A Lot of Fun to keep A Tally of the Silly or Odd Road Signs you've seen. For instance, on recent Cross-Country Drives, the Etiquette Grrls have seen signs like the following, to name Just a Few:

- SOMETHINGSBURG MOTEL: AIR-CONDITIONED—POOL—FIREWORKS!!!!

- INDIANA: AHEAD (Gee, the Etiquette Grrls are So Glad to hear that they haven't Moved it!)

- REST-A-PEST (An Exterminator's Establishment)

- WELCOME TO SMALLVILLE! HOME OF: 5 TRUCK STOPS, 7 RESTAURANTS, 4 MOTELS

- THE YELLOW BRICK ROAD OZ MUSEUM (Spotted nowhere near Kansas, or anyplace having anything to do with Oz or L. Frank Baum, at least as far as the Etiquette Grrls could determine.)

- TINYTON, TOWN OF MOTELS: THE TRAVELER'S OASIS!

Finally, a wee note to Boys Who Are On the Open Road: You should generally not attempt to speak to Girls in Convertibles, unless there is a Genuine Emergency (like you are attempting to point out that A Wheel Has Fallen Off, or some such). Of course, it is the Right Thing To Do to assist in An Emergency. The Etiquette Grrls just mean that one should not Heckle or Leer At anybody in a passing Convertible (or any car, for that matter). Freeways are no place to attempt to have a conversation with strangers, particularly in Los Angeles, where, the Etiquette Grrls understand, Quite A Lot of Angry People on the Freeway are Packing Heat.

Also, Dear Reader, just because you're driving around the Country for Fun doesn't mean that you do not need to follow the same Traffic Laws that you have back home in Columbus. Yes, that Stop

Sign means the same thing in Abilene as it does in Augusta, and you must obey it. But the Etiquette Grrls are positive that all of our Dear Readers don't need to be reminded of this!

Lastly, the most important thing about a Road Trip, Dear Reader, is to Have Fun! You'll probably never have the opportunity to go on a Leisurely Major Road Trip with your Best Friends more than once in your life, so take your time, and enjoy it!

The Etiquette Grrls' Grand Tour

Anyone who's read any Henry James at all knows that Well-Bred Young People simply must take The Grand Tour! The Etiquette Grrls firmly believe that a wee jaunt or three through England and The Continent makes for a Cultured, Refined, and Sophisticated Young Person. But how appalled we are at the Loud, Crass, Boorish, Gum-Snapping, Camcorder-toting, Nike tee shirt–Clad Tourists trotting by the thousand through St. Peter's and to the top of the Eiffel Tower! Such types loudly mock the Local Customs and refuse to eat anywhere but good ol' Mickey D's. No wonder Americans get such a Bad Reputation! Would you like it, Dear Reader, if Throngs of Foreigners came to *your* city, made a Spectacle of Themselves, and in short, Behaved Deplorably? No, the Etiquette Grrls didn't think so! When Abroad, it falls upon Your Shoulders, Dear Reader, to Represent Our Country with Grace, Dignity, and Style.

THINGS TO THINK ABOUT BEFORE YOU CROSS THE POND

The First Thing you absolutely *must* do before you go *anywhere,* Dear Reader, is to check with the State Department and make sure the Country of Your Destination is not having A Wee Uprising or anything. The Etiquette Grrls would just hate it if one of our Dear Readers were Taken Prisoner while en vacances dans The South of France. Call the Etiquette Grrls Worrywarts, Dear Reader, but one can never be Too Careful, you know. Lists of Places which are possibly Dangerous for Americans to visit may be obtained from the State Department's website, http://www.travel.state.gov.

Also, make absolutely sure that Your Passport, and any additional papers or medical requirements, are in Exquisite Order *well* before you Set Sail. (Well, you won't *literally* be Setting Sail, we trust, but you know what the Etiquette Grrls mean.) Nothing gets A Smashing Holiday off on The Wrong Foot like finding out at Customs that Your Passport expired a year ago.

The Etiquette Grrls think that our Dear Readers should avoid most kinds of Organized Tours. True, one can sometimes Economize by going to Europe on such a tour, but the "If It's Tuesday, It Must Be Belgium" Variety of Trip is no way to see the world! First of all, it seems to the Etiquette Grrls that the only reason that people would sign up for such a tour is that they don't trust their Own Good Judgement to seek out that which is interesting or beautiful or historical, even in Europe, where one can't help falling over such places. We know that you are both smart and in possession of Good Judgment, Dear Reader, and thus we think you would find being shackled to such a tour Most Dull. Also, and perhaps more important, such Structure allows for No Leeway in your travels. What if you want to stay in Vienna an Extra Day? What if you'd rather go do some shopping at Galleries Lafayette rather than go to the Centre Pompidou (because you've been there so many times before)? No dice, if you're on An Organized Tour, Dear Reader! Plus, and perhaps worst of all, they always make you wear Those Silly Name Tags. Far better, the Etiquette Grrls think, to go on one's own or avec a Friend or Two or peut-être Mama or a favorite Tante. This way, you can go At Your Own Speed, See What You'd Like To, Skip What You Don't, and you're not stuck avec A Bunch of Crazy Strangers for Your Entire Trip.

While no one is expecting you to be Fluent in Every Language, the Etiquette Grrls think it is A Very Nice Gesture to attempt to learn A Few Important Words in the language of every country you plan to visit. The Etiquette Grrls have found that "Please" and "Thank You" are especially helpful words to know. Similarly, it is Extremely Poor Form to laugh at or otherwise mock the Traditions or Qualities of the Country of whose guest you are, especially while In Public.

Yes, the Etiquette Grrls know that those Mint and Lamb-flavored "crisps" you see at that British Sandwich Shop are an Absolutely Nauseating (not to mention Utterly Perplexing) thought, but keep it to yourself, please, until you're safely in the privacy of Your Hotel Room. The Etiquette Grrls think that you'll find that people will be considerably More Receptive to you, Dear Tourist, if they see that you're Making An Effort to Fit In.

The Etiquette Grrls also encourage you, Dear Reader, to be Adventuresome and wander off the Beaten Track whenever possible. Tourist Traps are the same in any city; the True Flavor lies in the small shops and back alleys. You'll find that the people you'll meet while Adventuring are Far More Interesting than those at the places listed in Baedeker's or Fodor's. For instance, Americans think of Parisians as being notoriously Arrogant and Rude. And perhaps this is true in the parts of the city which are oft-traversed by Horrible Tourists. After all, wouldn't it begin to irk you just a wee bit, too, Dear Reader, if all sorts of Nosy People were traipsing through your neighborhood all day long, pointing cameras at you, and so on? Yes, the Etiquette Grrls think it would. But wander around a little bit, find that Charming Petite Patisserie way over behind the Madeleine somewhere. This is the True Paris, and here are the True Parisians. Of course, though, the Etiquette Grrls warn our Dear Readers to use their Common Sense and always be aware of their surroundings whilst Exploring A Foreign City. The Etiquette Grrls wouldn't want Something Terrible to happen to any of our Dear Readers while they were Abroad. Nor should you do something Foolish and Dangerous, like go backpacking All By Your Lonesome through the Alps, or something.

The Etiquette Grrls are, of course, Experienced Globe-Trotters, and we'd like to give you an Extensive Guide to The World and Our Favorite Cities, Dear Reader, but alas, we're afraid that must wait for Another Day.

CHAPTER EIGHT

Miscellaneous Matters of Importance

Advice for the Collegiate Set

The Etiquette Grrls so enjoyed their Bright College Years! Whether we were curled up in our rooms before a Roaring Fire (yes, Dear Reader, the Etiquette Grrls enjoyed Working Fireplaces in their Dorms! It was swell!), reading Byron and Keats, or in the stands of the Stadium, watching Meaningless Ivy League Football, we had One Hell Of A Good Time! However, it saddens the Etiquette Grrls that for so many Young Scholars, college is a time to display Blatant Tackiness and, worse, Rudeness. We have compiled a few suggestions for our College-Bound Readers, that they might avoid such faux pas and enjoy their Days in the Ivy-Covered Halls of Academe like Young Ladies and Gentlemen.

YOUR ROOMMATE

First, read and follow all of the advice given in Roommates: The Necessary Evil on pages 5–8. However, the Etiquette Grrls recognize that, at least in Freshman Year, most students do not have the luxury of Choosing Their Own Roommate(s). And, sadly, Gone Are The Days when most students enjoyed spacious single rooms! Before you even leave Chez Mama et Papa for College, make certain that you fill out your Roommate Questionnaire honestly. If you smoke, say so . . . if you lie, and your roommate is a Nonsmoker, the Etiquette Grrls are sorry to inform you that you will have to trot yourself Out of Doors every time you wish to enjoy a Cigarette. And we imagine this would get Rather Tiresome.

If your room is small (and, unless you were Extremely Lucky in Room Draw, we're pretty sure that it is), try to make use of other spaces around campus for your socializing if your roommate is not part of Your Social Circle. Everyone deserves some Peace and Quiet, Dear Reader, and furthermore, it is Downright Rude to occupy your room 24/7, so that Your Poor Roommate never gets a Moment of Privacy.

If things get Really Bad avec your Roommate, do not attempt to Enact Revenge yourself. This is what RA's are for. It is not good manners to engage in any of the behaviors listed on the "100 Ways to Annoy Your Roommate" e-mail that we've all received umpteen times. Although even the Etiquette Grrls will admit that there were times when we were Sorely Tempted. We'll understand if you contemplate it, Dear Reader, but you'd best not Put Your Thoughts Into Action.

DECORATING YOUR ROOM

We so hope, Dear Reader, that you've landed a lovely, old-fashioned Dorm Room with Mahogany Trim, Big Closets, a Fireplace, and Cool Windows with Leaded-Glass Panes! Even if you will be spending the next eight months in a twelve-by-twelve-foot square made of concrete blocks and featuring one (1) Electrical Outlet, you can take steps to make your room more comfortable and aesthetically appealing. You must Use Discretion when purchasing any and all "Dorm-Room Necessities" offered at large bed-and-bath chains! Dear Reader, inflatable clear glittery chairs and iMac-esque alarm clocks are not Necessities. They are Monstrosities. Steer clear. However, if you have A Good Eye, you can sometimes find Suitable Items at Such Places, like the pretty little white wooden Laura Ashley lamp bases which one Etiquette Grrl once found On Sale at a Bed, Bath & Beyond. Such stores can also be good for acquiring Basics, like Plain, White, Fluffy Towels. Better yet, take sensible and pretty items to school with you, like the old peach velvet armchair that your mother was going to Put Into Storage. And do buy Curtains and Small Rugs! There's nothing quite like Real Curtains and a Wee Oriental Rug or two to make a Plain Dorm Room more like home.

YOUR WARDROBE

O how the Etiquette Grrls feel we were born several decades too late! It was Quite Disheartening to find that Our Female Classmates did not feel the need to wear Pretty Tweed Suits, Cashmere Twin Sets, and Good Shoes to class! And all the Boys were wearing stained tee shirts with khakis that, by their appearance, had never been *near* an iron! Many people appeared to have Rolled Out of Bed five minutes before class, and were choosing to show The Rest of Us their pajamas! No, no, no, a thousand times, no!

While college attire is more casual now than it was in, say, 1937, you are not allowed to spend four years looking slovenly. Classes are Public Events, and you must, at minimum, wear neat, clean, ironed, mended clothes. You most definitely should not buy seven different sweatshirts bearing your school's name and wear one each day of the week.

BEHAVIOR IN CLASS

Please, don't brown-nose. This is just TTFW. If you prefer to read the book in Its Original German, that's all well and good (although the Etiquette Grrls must say that we Strongly Dislike Strivers) . . . just do not take up everyone else's time by reading aloud long passages from it and expecting everyone else to Follow Along. When you refer to the text in class, you must use the same translation as everyone else. Also, do not fidget, do that silly thing with A Pen wherein you spin it back and forth across your fingers (are you a Majorette?), snack on crunchy food, etc. And always refer to your Professor as "Professor," unless your school's custom is to use "Mr./Mrs./Miss" (as it is at some Eastern Schools) or the Prof introduces him- or herself as "Dr." Graduate-student instructors should not be addressed as "Professor"; rather, they should tell the class how they prefer to be addressed. Do not, on pain of Total Humiliation, ask the Professor, "Can I go to the bathroom?" *Especially* if it is a large lecture class. Dear Reader, are you in second grade?

MAKING FRIENDS AVEC THE FACULTY

Dear Reader, do you realize how boring it is for Professors to hold Office Hours when no one Attends? One of the Etiquette Grrls actually taught undergraduates at a Large University, and she was simply Dumbfounded that no one had the time or inclination to seek out her tiny (yet exquisitely decorated) office in the Far Corner of the English Building! It was like throwing a party to which No One Showed Up! The Etiquette Grrls encourage you to get to know your Professors. Go to the first Office Hour and Introduce Yourself! If you happen to pass a Professor in the halls, or even when you are Dans La Ville, greet him or her pleasantly. Do not, under any circumstances, try to play the "If I Stare at the Ground and Walk Really Fast, I Am Invisible" game. By making friends avec your Profs, you will undoubtedly get invited to Cocktail Parties, etc., Chez Eux, which is Quite an Honor for an Undergrad.

ASKING FOR RECOMMENDATIONS

Ask nicely, and give your Professor enough advance notice. The Etiquette Grrl who taught was extremely irritated, to say the least, when, at the end of the semester, several students felt they could drop by with seventeen Recommendation Forms that "really need to get filled out by you today, or I won't get to go to Grad School/Law School/the Vatican School of Latin." If the forms are to be mailed, provide addressed envelopes with Proper Postage. And do not be upset if the Professor who taught your Introduction to British Literature course, which had five hundred students, does not feel able to recommend you if you did not make an effort to get to know him or her. And after your Professor recommends you, send a thank-you note!

SOCIAL LIFE AT COLLEGE

The Etiquette Grrls avoided Keg Parties like the Plague, Dear Reader, and so can you! If you find the Regular Friday-Night Beer Bashes to be un peu monotonous, then Throw Your Own Cocktail Party. Surely your friends would adore getting All Dressed Up and Tossing Back a Few in Civilized Company!

And remember, Dear Reader, just because you are suddenly Surrounded By Alcohol is no reason to Act Like an Idiot. For example, don't Head-Butt the Lampposts, Boys, simply because they're *there*. This is Rather Childish, and To Be Avoided. The poor Lamppost never did anything to you, did it? And you're likely to suffer a Nasty Black Eye.

At Church

Church is a Solemn and Revered Place. In fact, the Etiquette Grrls are Hard-Pressed to think of anyplace that's *more* Solemn and Revered than Church. Thus, whatever your Religious Background and/or Current Affiliation, you *must* be properly Respectful of the sanctity of any House of Worship, be it a cathedral, temple, mosque, sweat lodge, or what have you. One must be Appropriately Dressed when visiting a House of Worship. No jeans, no athletic attire and/or equipment, no Revealing Evening Dresses, no Frivolous Costumes, no plastic jewelry, nothing that glows (especially if you're at a Vigil Service), and please, Dear Reader, no wallet chains! (They make a Distracting Noise each time you sit down, and for heaven's sake, why do you need to wear them in Church? Are you so Deeply Paranoid you're afraid A Common Thief will Reach Over the Back of the Pew and Abscond With Your Wallet? If so, the Etiquette Grrls suggest therapy, or perhaps seeking out a Church in a Better Neighborhood.) With the exception, of course, of a Seeing-Eye Dog, you should never bring a pet to Church, however well behaved it is. You should not engage in P.D.A. in Church, especially not with the priest. Nor should you arrive In a Drunken State, especially if you *are* the priest. You should not bring snacks or beverages; you should not wear a Personal Stereo; you should not take or place calls on a cell 'phone. In short, Dear Reader, you must be on your Very Best Behavior.

Further, you must maintain A Proper Level of Decorum throughout the *entire* service. Has the priest, in fact, fired a Starting Pistol to signal the beginning of Communion? If not (and the Etiquette Grrls do believe he has *not*), then you should not make a Mad Dash for the front of the Church. You will not get a special gold Communion Wafer as a prize; the priest will not inform the congregation that you are "The Man"; you will not get to stand on a Dais. You should simply proceed slowly to the front and then back to your seat. You should remember where you were sitting and return to the same pew. It will undoubtedly cause Great Confusion when you displace Three Poor Little Old Ladies, who will then displace A Young Couple, etc., etc. The Etiquette Grrls recommend taking a look at your surroundings so that you will not commit this Egregious Offense. Remember the pew number, the leopard coat of the woman in front of you, or some other landmark. Several of the aforementioned Poor Little Old Ladies will leave their handbags in their pew as a Subtle Reminder to Themselves of where they were seated. They have not forgotten their bags; you should not steal them. It would be absolutely THOR for you to gather up all the little old ladies' bags while they are at Communion and place, let's say, twenty-five of them in one row, and the Etiquette Grrls did *not* give you that idea.

Some Religions, such as the Etiquette Grrls', are Rather Fond of Candlelight Vigils, and these are a Lovely, Beautiful Tradition. In fact, the Etiquette Grrls' Prep Schools, which are not in and of themselves Religions per se, are also Rather Fond of Candlelight Vigils, and of course the following rules for Candlelight Services shall also apply to those of the Nonecclesiastical Variety.

- No taking out lighters in lieu of a candle, even if you have some fabulous retro chrome or silver one. You are not at a Who Concert.

- No more than *one* candle per person, please. Remember, no one likes A Glutton!

- No Amusing Yourself by Making Sculptures in the Dripping Wax. If you have An Artistic Bent, you should wait until you are at home to Hone Your Talents.

- Most vigils are not BYOC (Bring Your Own Candle), so unless this is Clearly Indicated in advance, you should assume a candle will be provided for your use.

- Hold your candle within your personal space, so it does not Set Fire to the hair of the Girl sitting in front of you. For some reason, this seems to be Of Particular Concern to the Prep School Crowd. As the Etiquette Grrls reflect upon their Girls' School Days, we recall that almost every single year, some poor Lass had her hair singed during "Candlelight."

- Your candle should not be used to test the Tolerance for Pain of your Younger Siblings, as to drip wax upon their forearms will undoubtedly cause them to screech, which would be Very Rude and Disruptive.

- If the service is one at which the priest lights the first candle and that of each person at the end of an aisle, you should *wait* for the light to reach you. Even if you carry a fabulous engraved lighter, it is quite a faux pas for you to whip it out and light your candle yourself. Also, it is THOR to Act Put Upon when you have to light the candle of the Stranger sitting next to you. This is not A Huge Imposition. Finally, when the candles are extinguished, you must blow yours out, too. The Etiquette Grrls know that holding flaming things is fun, but you can always have a cigarette when the service is over.

GETTING THERE ON TIME

Church is not an open house. Services begin at Regularly Scheduled Times, and you should make every effort to arrive at Church Promptly. Should, however, you arrive late due to Circumstances Beyond Your Control, you should make a Concentrated Effort to Make Your Entrance as subtle and unobtrusive as possible. You should not, for example, run down the center aisle, shouting "I'm *here*!!!!," diving headfirst into to the front pew. Nor are you permitted to intercept the Processional. It is much like a funeral cortège (especially if there is a Coffin in it), and once it begins, you must let it go by you. You should wait quietly near the door which you came in, and once the Processional is over, slip quietly into the nearest pew. Unless, of course, it is full to capacity. The Etiquette Grrls don't want our Dear Readers to go around squishing themselves in places where there's No Room! If the Entire Church is full, you should stand quietly in the back of the Church for the duration of the service.

Also, if you are going to go to Church, then you must make a commitment to stay for the Entire Service. You may not get up and leave in the middle, and no, the Service is *not* considered over once you have received Communion. You *must* return to your seat and wait until the service has ended—that is, until the Final Note of the Final Hymn has been sung. *Then* you are dismissed, and you may take your leave. You should, however, still depart in an orderly fashion, and you should not knock over any elderly or infirm people in your haste to get out of the building.

The Etiquette Grrls also think that one should be quiet and unobtrusive in Church. If you want to join the choir, then join the choir, for heaven's sake. You absolutely should *not* sing harmony to the choir in your Loudest Voice from your seat in the congregation, no matter how fine your voice and sense of rhythm.

VISITING A STRANGE CHURCH

Perhaps you are visiting a Dear Friend for the weekend, and she asks you if you would like to accompany her to Church. You, however, have been Raised By Wolves, and have never Set Foot in a Church. However, the Etiquette Grrls, much like Wordsworth, rather think that even those who are Raised By Wolves are intrinsically moral, and thus, of course, naturally polite, and thus we know that you will accept her offer, even if it sounds like a Really Wacky Church, and that you will show the Proper Degree of Reverence therein.

If you are attending a Form of Service you have never attended before, it does not hurt to Err on the Side of Conservatism in Your Attire and, of course, to Follow Along. If you are accompanying a Friend and have Reasonable Questions about how you should behave (e.g., "This is my first time visiting a Mosque. Should I cover my head?"), you may ask them. Similarly, if you are Traveling and will be visiting a House of Worship as a Tourist, you absolutely must respect Local Customs regarding your behavior. (And, of course, you must *never* disturb Those At Prayer because you want to Snap a Photo of the Famous Frescoes. That is Unspeakably Rude.) Do some research! You will indeed Be Chastised by the Swiss Guards at the Vatican if you attempt to enter St. Peter's in a Sleeveless Dress—yet you could easily avoid Such Embarrassment by Consulting a Good Guidebook. However, you should not ask Stupid, Insultingly Ignorant Questions about a Church, especially regarding its Major Tenets or Chief Code of Beliefs. Such inquiries are readily answered with a Quick Trip to Your Local Library, where the friendly reference librarians will be happy to help you figure out "Who That Guy on the Cross Is." You should not offer comparisons between your Church and your friend's. Communion is not generally given out at a bar mitzvah, and you should not offer the suggestion that it ought to be, simply because you Rather Fancy a Tiny Bit of Unleavened Bread. Nor should you offer suggestions as to how you feel your friend's Religious Services might be Improved . . . you should just be grateful that you belong to a Religion which you like better.

BEHAVIOR AT WEDDINGS AND FUNERALS

The Etiquette Grrls never cease to be Shocked by the fact that So Few People seem to know how to conduct themselves at Weddings and Funerals, Dear Reader! Remember, Dear Reader, you are In Church, and you absolutely *must* behave accordingly, even if you have never set foot in a House of Worship in your entire life! And even if you are at A Civil Service, and consequently not in a Church per se, you still must behave as if you were. As the Etiquette Grrls have said repeatedly, all cellular 'phones and pagers should be Turned Off. And remember, Dear Reader, whether it is a Wedding or a Funeral that brings you to The Church, it is a Solemn Occasion, and you should be quiet and serious (no laughing, jeering, or screaming), and you should not Fidget. Nor should you be jumping up and down, and coming and going, and to-ing and fro-ing, and otherwise Running About. It is not appropriate to bring Small Children to such gatherings. If, for some reason which the Etiquette Grrls cannot imagine, you are forced to bring along A Small Child, you should be certain that The Wee One understands very clearly the Importance of Being Well-Behaved. All children should be still and quiet throughout the Entire Service, just as yourself, Dear Reader. Under no circumstances should they be allowed to Run Around and be Noisy! If Your Child starts Acting Up, he should be Removed From the Church immédiatement, Dear Reader! And we mean *all* the way out of Earshot of The Congregation. Nothing Ruins a Wedding like the high-pitched howling of a Cranky Child having A Tantrum out in the Narthex, his screeches echoing through the Nave of the Church just as the Bride and Groom begin to Exchange Their Vows!

The Etiquette Grrls are Especially Shocked by the varied and often Abysmal Manner in which people dress for Weddings and Funerals. Of course, the Basics of Dress which we outline above (and in Chapter Three) should be adhered to. Further, even at the Most Formal of Evening Weddings, you should dress in a More Conservative Manner than you would for, say, A Prom. Anything strapless or spaghetti-strapped is Completely Inappropriate, as is anything sequined, sparkly, short, fringed, or Loud In Any Way. Flashy Colors should be avoided always, especially Red. (Indeed, Dear Reader, you shouldn't be wearing a Flaming Scarlet Dress *anywhere* . . . it is *always* in Poor Taste!) Also, Wedding Guests should never wear White or Black. The Etiquette Grrls don't care how many people say that this is permissible These Days; the Etiquette Grrls are Putting Their Foot Down! At Funerals, one should wear black, obviously, and one's Manner of Dress should be *Extremely* Sedate. This is No Time to be Radical, Slinky, Experimental, or Anything but the Very Image of Conservatism and Tradition!

It is Always Proper for a Lady to Cover Her Head when entering A House of Worship, Dear Reader! Should a Girl wear a Hat, it must be suitable to her Dress, the Season, and the Hour. Very Informal Hats, such as Stocking, Baseball, or Plaid Wool Ear-Flapped Hunting Caps à la Holden Caulfield and / or Elmer Fudd should be left chez toi, however. Girls also may, and indeed probably should, wear Nice Gloves. These should be of very high-quality glacé kidskin, or cotton in Warm Weather. Never, *ever,* may they be that shiny, slimy, nylon material, or even worse, the hideous and Unspeakably Tacky crocheted or faux-lace variety. Nor should they possess any sort of Sporty, Outdoorsy Qualities, such as Visible Stitching or Bulkiness. Similarly, they should not be made of Wool Knit, or Polartec. Mittens, of course, are also a Poor Choice. Gloves may be kept on during the Service, but you may also remove them in order to easily turn pages in The Hymnal, etc. However, one *must* remove her Gloves before receiving Communion. At a Wedding Reception, Gloves are left on through the Receiving Line, but they should be removed to eat, drink, or smoke. For further guidelines on what constitutes Various Forms of Dress, please refer to pages 63–64. Brides should refer to page 137 for some of the Etiquette Grrls' thoughts on Engagement and Marriage.

All Wedding Guests should remember that a Wedding is a Solemn Occasion. It is not something to which one is entitled to Bring a Date! Unless your Boy- or Girlfriend receives his or her Own Invitation, or unless your invitation includes the words "and Escort" or "and Guest," you must attend Alone. And Mind You, the Etiquette Grrls will not tolerate people who skip the Church Ceremony yet Show Up at the Reception. The Ceremony is the most important part of the Wedding Celebration (indeed, technically, it *is* the Wedding Celebration—the Reception is merely a Celebration of the fact that the Wedding has Taken Place), and you should be Honored to Attend it, if you are invited. If you wish to Spurn this Honor, then you must send Your Regrets for the Entire Affair.

HOW YOU SHOULD BE BURIED
In the Unfortunate Circumstance that you, Dear Reader, are perhaps Un(e) Peu Mort(e), you'll soon be getting A Final Resting Place. Even in Death, you must be certain that Your Plot is in Good Taste. Ostentatious Tombstones have always been Tacky, even more so since the end of The Gilded Age, when Everything was Ostentatious. You should never have A Statue, particularly A Statue of Yourself, erected upon Your Grave, and Obelisks just Aren't Done anymore. Your Tombstone should be absolutely plain and somber granite—it should not have Photographs embedded in it; it should not be elaborately carved or inlaid avec depictions of wee hearts, flowers, teddy bears, cars, or whatever the Favorite Thing of The Deceased is/was. Also, avoid cemeteries which place Artificial Flowers about the graves and which pipe Muzak-y Hymns throughout the Entire Place.

Holidays

The Etiquette Grrls enjoy holidays, as holidays offer a day home from work, an excuse to partake of rich foods, and, often, Lavish Presents. However, we fear that the holidays Contemporary Society chooses to celebrate are Rather Ill-Chosen, and further, the Crass Commercialism of Holidays is beginning to get Wildly Out of Hand. What is the point, the Etiquette Grrls ask, of Thanksgiving Cards? Do we really need to have a Very Boozy Arbor Day Party? And what about The Con Game which is Valentine's Day? This day is, in fact, A

Very Serious Saint's Day, and hence, theoretically speaking, is not a day to Run Out and Gorge Oneself on Cheap Chocolates, but rather, one on which you should contemplate the Martyrdom of Poor Old St. Valentine himself. But clearly, it has lately become nothing but A Ploy by Corporate America to Sell Tacky Rubbish and make the Etiquette Grrls' Dear Single Readers feel Just Terrible. Making people feel terrible is, of course, THOR, and the Etiquette Grrls Do Not Approve. Instead of this St. Valentine's Day Nonsense, the Etiquette Grrls prefer to celebrate Single Persons' Appreciation Day (SPAD, for short) on February 14. SPAD is a time to celebrate One's Independence and Self-Reliance, and it is the perfect occasion for a nice dinner and a few rounds of drinks avec One's Dear Single Friends. The Etiquette Grrls encourage you to have a SPAD party next year! To Hell with the Cutesy Hearts-and-Cupids Nonsense!

Christmas is perhaps the most notoriously commercialized of all holidays, and this makes the Etiquette Grrls Positively Ill. Watch *A Charlie Brown Christmas,* Dear Reader, and you'll Get the Etiquette Grrls' Drift—pay particularly close attention to the words of the Etiquette Grrls' Good Friends Linus and Charlie Brown, who, animated and fictional though they may be, are Wise Beyond Their Years.

You may, Dear Reader, throw A Bash, have a Dinner Party, or Other Similar Gathering to mark any of the following Holidays: Christmas, Independence Day, Halloween, St. Patrick's Day, and New Year's Eve/Day. One does not normally have A Party per se for Easter or Thanksgiving, but it is nice to have a few friends over for Dinner, especially if they have No Place to Go. One Unusual Holiday on which the Etiquette Grrls think that all of our Dear Readers should Have A Soirée is The Anniversary of The Repeal of Prohibition (December 5). Now, if that's not a Reason to Celebrate, the Etiquette Grrls don't know what is! The Etiquette Grrls are Quite Grateful for other holidays that offer them a Long Weekend, but as we do not regularly throw Labor Day Fêtes, or exchange Columbus Day gifts, we consider them as simply Days Off.

Litigious Behavior

It is much, *much* more polite simply to tell someone "See you in hell" than "See you in court." Courts are, sadly, not as much fun as David Kelley would have you believe, as people actually lose cases in the Real World.

However, if you are required to appear in court, you might as well make the most of it. Basically, court is rather like Church, albeit with more Audience Participation. Thus you should dress conservatively—with particular care if you are the Defendant. Arrival on time is a must, and, remember, as with Church, you must leave your firearms, your Small Pets, and your Illicit Substances at home.

Even if you think Court is Fab, please do not resort to Bringing Frivolous Lawsuits in order to get more time in front of the Judge and Jury. Frivolous Lawsuits simply enrage the Etiquette Grrls, as they are generally brought by Idiots who think they deserve Compensation for Their Own Idiocy. And we think that Flaunting One's Idiocy and Obviously Trying to Make a Quick Buck are terribly, terribly rude. Should you be so stupid as to Drive Around avec a Cup of Steaming Coffee Held Precariously In Your Lap, and, of course, Spill It, you should obviously shrink away from all publicity, and, indeed, make up a more reasonable explanation for your injury. You should not hire a lawyer and File Suit. May the Etiquette Grrls remind you, Smarty Pants, that you're the one who decided that driving avec coffee in your lap was a Good Idea.

When You're Famous

Perhaps you're famous. Or perhaps you're not. However, the Etiquette Grrls feel that a current Lack of Celebrity Status is no excuse to be unprepared for Sudden Celebrity Status. Greatness may be Thrust Upon You, and we think you should prepare now for that eventuality, lest you offend Society In General with your Consummate Rudeness.

"WELL, CONAN, IT WAS A FUNNY THING . . .": TALK SHOWS

Now that you are Famous, you will undoubtedly be making the rounds of all the Talk Shows. (*Today, Late Night with Conan O'Brien, The Tonight Show,* et al.) You will, of course want to be an Entertaining Guest who will be asked back. The Etiquette Grrls offer a few guidelines for making Public Appearances.

- When you make your Grand Entrance, you *must* warmly greet The Host and shake hands. You must also remember to greet any other guests or sidekicks who are already sitting on The Couch. Likewise, if you remain on the show for Other People's Segments, you must rise and greet everyone as they come onstage. Never, *ever,* remain seated and Sullenly Glare at the Up-and-Coming Actor, even if you are The Biggest Star In The World.

- You should have at least one amusing, "clean" anecdote to tell that is not too long-winded. Don't be taciturn; it is, you will recall, a *Talk* Show, and it is assumed that you will not reply to all the questions that The Host poses to you with surly one-word answers. On the other hand, don't be so chatty that you take up all of the time allotted to other guests. (If you are a bona fide Legend, say, someone in the league of Lauren Bacall, the Etiquette Grrls think that the producers should allot you the Entire Hour.)

- If you are a comedian, your "chat" with The Host should not obviously be part of your "routine." Similarly, no matter Your Occupation, you should not tell the same story and/or jokes on each television program on which you make an appearance. This is most tiresome. Likewise, even if you're on a Mad Press Junket, Dear Famous Reader, and find yourself paying A Wee Visit to Regis, Dave, and Conan all within forty-eight hours of each other, please make Every Effort to Vary Your Wardrobe! The Etiquette Grrls find it So Very Disconcerting to turn on

Conan on Tuesday and have a Wee Flashback to Dave on Monday!

- Nerve-wracking though television appearances may be, you should not be drunk, or visibly "high" or "strung-out" on drugs. This will make a Very Bad Impression.

- For your television appearances, you must be clean and well groomed, much as if you were going out on a Date. (Refer to Chapters Three and Six.) You should wear a nice outfit that is clean, ironed, and which fits you well. It should be something dressier than what you might actually wear in your own house to watch *Today* or *The Late Show* (i.e., pajamas), but you need not wear a ball gown or black tie, as this, in fact, usually looks A Little Silly. Your outfit should, of course, not only be tasteful, but also appropriate to the season. The Etiquette Grrls were appalled to see an actress who is Old Enough To Know Better show up on a nighttime talk show wearing an off-the-shoulder cropped top, hot pants, and high-heeled shoes. Not only did she look like (at best) A Chorine, not only was she wearing heels and shorts, *it was before Memorial Day*. Unforgivable. The mere memory of it makes the Etiquette Grrls shudder.

- Do not bring photographs of your children or pets with you on-air. Especially your pets. Neither are as cute as you think they are, and honestly, no one cares.

- You should not insult The Host. This is simply THOR. Indeed, it is unwise to insult *anyone,* particularly other showbiz types, on National Television, as it will most likely Spell the End Of Your Career.

- It's sometimes nice to bring a Little Gift for The Host, much as you would bring a gift if you were invited to someone's house. As with normal hostess gifts, it is best, nay, *imperative* that you bring something which your host or hostess will genuinely enjoy and not an item promoting your film/album/book, etc. (You may provide the Studio Audience with free copies of any of the aforementioned, however.)

- You should not wander out onstage during The Monologue or during Another Guest's Segment. Rather, Stay Put dans the Green Room. This is what the Green Room is for.

"THE ETIQUETTE GRRLS WOULD LIKE TO THANK THE ACADEMY": AWARDS SHOWS

Congratulations, Dear Reader! You've won a Grammy/Oscar/ Tony/Emmy/etc.! But oh, what Cesspools of Rudeness Awards Shows Are! The Etiquette Grrls simply don't understand how anyone could act as rudely as Some Celebrities do at these functions! Such behavior would be Nothing Short of Appalling in their own Living Rooms, let alone on a television show broadcast to The Entire World!

- Awards Shows are always Formal. Being Famous is No Excuse to Dress Sloppily/Shockingly/Hideously. For A Guideline to Formal Dress, please turn to page 59. You should also never, *ever* wear any item of clothing which serves in any manner to Advertise your latest film/album/etc., as seen one year at A Music Awards Show when the Etiquette Grrls' theretofore-admired Shirley Manson of Garbage sported that *Version 2.0* Dress.

- When The Nominees are Announced, the camera will pan over each of them. If you are a Nominee, you are not allowed to Look Sullen, or Shoot an Icy Glare at The Competition or The Camera. (Russell Crowe take note!) You also may not Applaud Yourself. The Etiquette Grrls know that Actors and Musicians stereotypically have Enormous Egos, but c'mon. Let's Keep It To Ourselves just a bit, Dear Famous Reader, shall we?

- Never leap Out of Your Seat and head up to The Stage before you have been announced as The Winner.

- If, God forbid, you Lose, you must not appear to be Disappointed or Angry. You may not trip The Winner as he goes to Accept His Award, or otherwise Behave Childishly in any way whatsoever. You must Applaud The Winner, and be Gracious about it. If you happen to be An Actor, this should be easy for you, Dear Reader, because you are, after all, An Actor.

- Keep your Acceptance Speech short, sweet, and to the point. Nobody wants to hear you Prattling On about everybody you've ever met in your Entire Life. Also, Awards Shows are Not The Time Or Place to espouse your Political/Religious/etc. Beliefs. Just thank the Academy and Get On With It, Dear Reader!

DEALING WITH ONE'S FAME

The Etiquette Grrls have little patience for Celebrities who constantly whine about How Difficult It Is Being A Celebrity. The Etiquette Grrls firmly believe that if you are A Public Figure, then you have a Great Responsibility to be kind to The Masses at all times. After all, Dear Famous Reader, if it weren't for The Public, you'd still be Waiting Tables, and that surely isn't as much fun as being a Rock Star. And if you *really* find being In The Public Eye So Very Trying, there are always plenty of waitressing jobs available, so quit your complaining, Dear Fussy, Famous Reader!

"EXCUSE ME, ARE YOU . . . ?": MEETING CELEBRITIES

The Etiquette Grrls know that it's très exciting when you see Your Favorite Film Star dining at the Same Restaurant as you. However, the Etiquette Grrls implore you to just Take A Deep Breath and Collect Yourself. You should never start screaming like a Giddy Teen-Ager no matter how much Jude Law, Scott Wolf, or whoever Makes You Swoon. (For that matter, the Etiquette Grrls don't recommend that you Swoon, either, Dear Reader. It's a long way down to the cold, hard sidewalk, and Swooning being the Rarity it is these days, the Etiquette Grrls think it's Pretty Damn Unlikely that a Chivalric Boy is going to catch your fall.) You should never Give Chase to A Celebrity you spot strolling through SoHo, lest you be mistaken for A Stalker. You also should not demand that A Celebrity give you an Autograph, the Shirt Off His Back, etc. You also should not approach Famous People if they clearly are Busy, are out with Their Family, or are in a similar situation.

Should you find yourself running into A Celebrity, you should treat him or her just like Anybody Else. Celebrities are, after all, Just People. The chicest thing to do probably is to just smile warmly, nod, and continue along Your Merry Way. If you have occasion to speak to A Celebrity, it's best to be Articulate and Sincere. Simply say something like, "I truly enjoy your films, Mr. Norton; I particularly liked *Fight Club*." If, by some Bizarre Circumstance, you find yourself Shooting The Breeze avec a Celebrity You Know Nothing About, don't attempt to feign knowledge of whatever his or her accomplishments may be. Nothing is More Transparent than A Phony, and you'll only look Stunningly Foolish. And the Etiquette Grrls would never, *ever* want any of their Dear Readers to find themselves in that position!

Very Unusual Situations

Allow the Etiquette Grrls to get a wee bit Silly, for a moment, Dear Reader, if you will. The Etiquette Grrls, you see, have Active Imaginations, and like the Boy Scouts, we believe in Being Prepared. And, well, one just never knows when one is going to have to Leap Into Emma Peel Mode, or need to put on your Nancy Drew chapeau. Thankfully, the Etiquette Grrls have given These Things a bit of thought.

SPIES LIKE US

Everyone knows from watching James Bond films and television shows like *The Avengers* that Spying is a very stylish activity indeed. Spies wear very expensive and beautifully cut clothing; have good haircuts; are in possession of lots of Neat-o Gadgets; are often British, with very upper-crust accents; and spend lots of time Drinking Martinis.

What You Should Wear When Spying

As we stated above, good Spies always wear well-cut, stylish clothing, usually in the "Mod" style of the mid-1960s. Obviously, a Spy doesn't want to stand out too much, so one's clothing ought to be in dark, neutral colors. This is not the time to be wearing your lime-green Lilly Pulitzer dress, although we're sure it's very fetching. You should also feel free to avail yourself of several high-quality wigs (should you need to go incognito), and a fabulous pair of sunglasses. Girls, you should model yourself after Emma Peel of *Avengers* fame (this is a good excuse to buy a slinky black catsuit), and Boys, you should obviously base your look on that of Mr. Bond. Oh, and Girls, you'll also have to learn how to run gracefully in high heels should you ever need to beat a Hasty Retreat.

The Basics

When in a restaurant, bar, or other public place, you should always, always seat yourself avec A Clear View of the Door so that you are able to see who is coming and going. Before getting settled in, you should also survey the premises in order to ascertain if anyone you want to avoid is already there, and to find an Alternative Exit should The Bad Guys storm the place. (This will also be handy should there happen to be a Fire.) If you are alone, you should have a newspaper, book, or magazine that you can pretend to read so that it is not obvious that you are, in fact, Spying On People.

A Stealthy Spy is a Good Spy, and you should also learn how to avoid Motion Detectors that turn on lights, or worse, set off alarms. This is something that the Etiquette Grrls became Quite Adept at when we were at Boarding School, and, faced with the need to visit our friends in other dorms after Lights-Out, not only had to avoid Roaming House Parents and Night Watchmen, but had to sneak by the Motion Detectors that controlled the wall sconces in the hallways.

Indeed, one of the Etiquette Grrls' Dearest Friends is renowned to this very day at her Boarding School for her Impressive Ability to scale walls in order to avoid the Dreaded Motion Detectors. We recommend that you watch *Sneakers,* a fine film with Robert Redford, to obtain more tips on The Great Skill Of Avoiding Motion Detectors.

ON THE USEFULNESS OF SPEAKING A FOREIGN LANGUAGE

Everyone knows that well-rounded, intelligent, well-bred people all speak more than one language, preferably (in addition to English, of course) French or Italian, which are both beautiful and useful languages. Dear Reader, fear not, should your Linguistic Skills be A Bit Rusty! There is no need to beat a hasty path to Berlitz for wearisome and tedious language classes! There is Another Option. It is called Franglais.

Franglais is the Etiquette Grrls' Very Favorite Language. The rules of Franglais are very simple. One simply ignores all those difficult French Grammar Rules, like the ever-pesky subjonctif or plus-que-parfait, and instead, use all the French you can think of with Abandon! And here's the best part, Dear Reader: If you can't think of the right French word, you may use the English word, and just make it *sound* French! This usually can be accomplished merely by putting a "le" in front of the English word (e.g., "le gin and tonic"). Once one has become fluent in Franglais, one may begin to occasionally interject other foreign words or phrases into your conversation, such as German ("Ich liebe Random Capitalization!" Or if you want to be Really Tricky and Mix Things Up, "J'ai besoin d' ein Gin and Tonic, schnell!"). Latin is always Quite Nice, too, particularly if one is with an Intellectual Crowd. Besides, the Etiquette Grrls really feel that they should put the Latin which they were forced to study in Prep School to *some* use.

Which Doc Martens?

Every Young Thing needs at least one pair of Docs. Docs, which come in many different styles, ranging from oxfords, to Mary Janes, to all heights of boots, may be worn with everything from jeans to evening gowns (but only if you're The Right Kind of Person to carry this off; the Etiquette Grrls *plead* with our Dear Readers to Proceed With Caution!). Practical for Inclement Weather, Docs are also Badass enough to take you into any Mosh Pit (the Etiquette Grrls recommend the steel-toed variety should you choose to partake of such activities), and are de rigueur for any Goth look. "Which Docs shall I buy?" you ask. The Etiquette Grrls demand only one thing, Dear Reader. They must be black. You may, if you wish, buy a second pair of brown oxfords, or perhaps those cute black-and-white spectators, but you simply *must* have a pair of black Docs. Under no circumstances should you ever wear, let alone buy, Docs (or any shoes, for that matter) in royal blue, pink, or mauve, nor should you ever go anywhere near anything resembling a metallic shade, anything with a printed pattern on its surface, or anything covered in sequins. The Etiquette Grrls remind you that unless you are Dorothy Gale, you should not be wearing any footwear that resembles Ruby Slippers in any way. Always remember, Dear Readers, when in doubt over anything pertaining to Your Wardrobe, Black is Always Best.

Smoking Avec Style and Grace

Okay, Dear Reader, let the Etiquette Grrls just say that we are not necessarily *condoning* Smoking, but let's face it—an awful lot of people *do* smoke, and that's not going to change, so the Etiquette Grrls just want to make sure that nobody's setting anyone else on Fire with their lit cigarette, or letting ashes fall on the Aubusson Rug, or anything. So we don't want to get any Letters about this—all we're doing is Doling Out Information To Those Who Need To Be Told, Dear Reader. If you are not a Smoker, simply Skip Ahead.

First of all, Dear Smoker, What You Smoke says a lot about you. If you are A Smoker, you should avail yourself of Good Cigarettes and Nice Smoking Accessories. Smoking Dunhills (or similarly swanky cigarettes) which live in An Antique Cigarette case and which you light with a Beautiful Silver Lighter seems infinitely more Sophisticated than smoking, say, Merit Menthol Lights out of a crumpled soft-pack, which you light with a decrepit Fluorescent-Yellow Bic. The Etiquette Grrls have always been Somewhat Intrigued by the Holly Golightly–esque quality of a mile-long cigarette holder, but we're afraid that In Practice, such things, as très sophisticated as they may appear, are in truth just a Wee Bit Awkward. Not to mention un peu d'un Fire Hazard in a Crowded Room. Also, the Etiquette Grrls are Deeply Suspicious of any man who uses a Cigarette Holder. (Are you Truman Capote, Dear Reader? The Etiquette Grrls sort of doubt it.) Lighters, as previously mentioned, are nicest when they are Not Disposable. The Etiquette Grrls also really like those Tabletop Lighters which are always sitting around dans Old Movies. They're so Cool, in fact, that the Etiquette Grrls think we might just get one, just for the hell of it! Speaking of lighters, a Boy should, of course, light a Girl's cigarette for her, if given the opportunity. If you are a Smoker, Dear Reader, you should watch lots of Old Movies where Elegant People always Smoke A Lot, and emulate their manner of smoking, lighting cigarettes, etc. No one ever looked Elegant walking around with an ol' cigarette butt hangin' off their lip, least of all a Girl. But Heavy Smoker Bette Davis, for instance, manages to look elegant, *and* refined, *and* intelligent, *and* badass all at once. And how great is that, Dear Reader? We suspect such an attitude is possibly either something You Have or You Don't, but we think it's definitely something worth Striving For.

These days, of course, you can't Light Up Just Anywhere, Dear Reader, so if you find yourself desperately in need of A Smoke while at a Function, you should slip off to the Bar Area if there is one. (Although you should be sure to ask if you can smoke there—if a Makeshift Bar has been set up in a place where there is not ordinarily one, you may not be permitted to smoke at all.) Better yet, step outside. It's especially nice if you have a Smoking Buddy or Two and you can go as a group. While in a restaurant, you obviously should not Start Smoking in a Nonsmoking Section, nor may you excuse yourself in the middle of dinner to have a Cigarette—you'll have to wait until you get outside/relocate to A Bar/etc. If you're in a Smoking Section, you should ask the other people at Your Table if they mind if you Smoke. But, hell, Dear Reader, if you're sitting in the Smoking Section, the Etiquette Grrls don't really see how anyone could say that they minded, as this, obviously, is what the Smoking Section is for.

You should also take care to dispose of your cigarette butts carefully. You should never grind out your cigarette on the floor. The Etiquette Grrls realize this is sometimes Unavoidable on the street, but never, ever do so in any sort of building. Similarly, never leave burning cigarettes lying on furniture, counters, etc. Do not toss Lit Cigarettes into the Garbage, or anyplace else where they will likely Start A Fire.

The Servant Problem

Of course, these days, The Servant Problem is that there Aren't Any. Sigh. The Etiquette Grrls just *know* that our lives would be soooo much simpler if we had a Small Staff . . . gosh, just a Driver, a Housekeeper, a Cook, a Laundress, and a Majordomo would do Quite Nicely! Oh, and maybe a Part-time Gardener. The Etiquette Grrls don't think that's asking too much, really.

But seriously, Dear Reader. Perhaps you yourself do not have any Domestics. But maybe someday you'll find yourself staying someplace that does. It may be a Private Home (which would be nice), but it's even more likely that you will have Hired Help at your Office or your Prep School or College Dormitory. (Or at Good Hotels; see pages 157–159 in chapter 7.) And you will have to know how to treat them. Domestics should be treated with the utmost respect, Dear Reader! It is Inexcusably Rude to be mean and bossy to anyone, even the Cleaning Lady. You should make an effort to find out the names of whatever Help you might have in your dormitory or office, and you should engage them in Friendly Conversation when you see them about. Always be courteous and cheerful, and never, *ever* ask them for Something Unreasonable. (For example, you may not ask the Cleaning Lady in your Dormitory to eradicate the mud from your field-hockey cleats.) Back In The Day, Dear Reader, Prep Schools and Colleges had Maids who would straighten up your room for you. And at some Schools, like a Posh Girls' School which one Etiquette Grrl attended, you could even bring your own Personal Maid from Home, which must have been Awfully Nice. But this is a custom which started to fade in America during World War II, and which had completely disappeared by the 1970s. These days, your school's Housekeeping Staff is responsible only for Public Areas. However, it is Your Responsibility, Dear Reader, to keep these areas as neat and tidy as possible! You absolutely may *not* go around Making A Mess, saying, "Oh well, Gladys is here to clean it up!" Even if you inadvertently make a mess—say, by accidentally knocking over a can of soda, you should make an effort to clean it up as best you can. Remember, Dear Reader, A Gracious Person is as kind and courteous to The Help as they would be to the Queen of England. Further, Happy Help equals Good Help. Miserable Help equals No Help at All.

CHAPTER NINE

The Etiquette Grrls' Patois: A Glossary

23-Skiddoo—v. Scram. "C'mon, kids, we're not going to get any Good Gin here, let's 23-Skiddoo and go to The Stork Club!"

90210—proper n. See *Bev.*

Algonquin, The—proper n. Celebrated Hotel in New York City. "The Etiquette Grrls book rooms at The Algonquin whenever they visit New York."

Algonquin Group, The—proper n. Notable twentieth-century authors, including, of course, the Scorchingly Witty Dorothy Parker, who Held Court at The Algonquin at their famous Round Table. "Everyone should aspire to the Kind of Acerbic Wit that would allow them to Hold Their Own avec the Algonquin Group."

Artichoke—n. *Cynara scolymus*. The Etiquette Grrls' very favorite vegetable, which everyone should know how to eat correctly. "Look at Bunny—she's cutting that poor Artichoke up into pieces and trying to chew and swallow them! Oh, the humanity!"

Artichoke Dip—n. Yummy hors d'oeuvre made from Artichoke Hearts, a lot of mayonnaise, and Parmesan Cheese. "Goody, goody gumdrops! The Etiquette Grrls invited me to their party, and I bet they'll serve their Famous Artichoke Dip!"

At School—phrase. Usually used in a question. How Preps ask where you went to Prep School. "Where were you At School?" "Westover. But my mother was At Porter's."

AWOL—adj., adv. Absent WithOut Leave. State of being Completely Unreachable; to have "dropped off the face of the earth." People (especially Close Friends and Significant Others) become AWOL avec Alarming Frequency: "William won't return any of Claire's phone calls." "Guess he's AWOL again. Poor Claire." Objects also exhibit such behavior: "Oh dear. My left slipper is un peu AWOL." And, unfortunately, even in Swanky Apartment Buildings, so do Utilities: "Dammit. The electricity and the heat are AWOL again." n. One who is AWOL. Great to use in a Nickname. "Captain AWOL deigned to Answer the Phone today! I feel honored!"

Back in the Day—adv. phrase. Wistful reference to an older, better, more enjoyable time. "Back In The Day, a Girl could bring Her Maid to Boarding School."

Bee's Knees, The—adj. phrase. Terrific, all-around. "Big Bad Voodoo Daddy is The Bee's Knees!"

Bev—proper n. *Beverly Hills 90210* (1990–2000), one of the Etiquette Grrls' Favorite Television Programs. Influential on the Etiquette Grrls during their Formative Years. "With *Bev* on FX Four Times a Day, there's No Excuse not to have seen Every Episode!"

Brioche—n. A type of breakfast pastry the Etiquette Grrls are Exceedingly Fond Of. Best bought at Balthazar in New York; best kept in one's handbag as first line of defense against hunger pangs, esp. while traveling. "Pardon me, but you look rather peaked and hungry. Would you like a Brioche?"

Cat's Pajamas, The—adj. phrase. See *The Bee's Knees*. "Bitsy's wooden tennis racquet is the Cat's Pajamas!"

Chivalry—n. 1. Code of gracious, courteous, and thoughtful behavior toward women which used to be practiced nearly universally by Well-Bred Boys. "Back In The Day, Boys knew what Chivalry was." 2. Something the Etiquette Grrls are trying to Revive. "Haven't you ever heard of Chivalry? Why the hell are you letting your girlfriend change that tire?"

Chivalric Boy—n. A Boy who, in the Etiquette Grrls' expert opinion, displays total chivalry. "My beau is, in every respect, the consummate Chivalric Boy!"

Daddy-O—n. What you should call Boys who address Girls as "Kitty-Kat." (see entry for *Kitty-Kat.*) Best used sarcastically to show disdain for Boys who have an overblown sense of their Innate Coolness. "Why don't you make like Kerouac and hit the road, Daddy-O?"

Dastardly Bastard—n. See *Shameless Cad*.

Deutsch, Das—n. German. The Etiquette Grrls' Other Favorite Language. "Das Deutsch sure is A Real Drag to learn, but gee, do I love Those Random Caps!"

Docs—n. pl. Footwear made by Dr. Martens, the British shoe and boot company. What the Etiquette Grrls are wearing on their feet when they're not wearing pretty little delicate pumps. "Boy, the Etiquette Grrls' Docs sure look great with their Cashmere Twin Sets!"

DPS—proper n. *Dead Poets' Society,* the movie which the Etiquette Grrls can recite in its entirety by heart. "Robert Sean Leonard is the guy from *DPS.*" "I don't know what happened to Ethan Hawke . . . he was so great in *DPS*, but I think he Lost His Way somewhere around *Reality Bites.*"

EGs—proper n., pl. Us, the Etiquette Grrls. "Have you heard that the EGs are crusading for Polite Behavior in a tacky, rude world?"

Ennui—n. Boredom, but worse. "Sometimes, I feel I'll just Die of Ennui."

EV—proper n. The Etiquette Volvo. What the Etiquette Grrls get around town in. "In the EV, which has over a hundred thousand miles on it, the Etiquette Grrls travel the world, fighting rudeness with Cutting Remarks, Hilarious Observations, and, always, Elegance and Grace."

Fab—adj. Better than fabulous. "That Leopard Coat is Fab, darling!" "The Beatles aren't called the Fab Four for nothing, you know!"

Fly—adj. Cool, neat. Used facetiously to describe things that residents of "The 'Hood" would not be likely to consider the least bit Fly. "That Edna Ferber short story I just finished reading was really Fly." "Easter Vigil Mass at St. Paul's is Super-Fly!"

Franglais—n. (*FRançais and anGLAIS, FR., French and English.*) A combination of French and English and the Etiquette Grrls' Very Favorite Foreign Language. "Je suis sooooo glad que nous sommes fluent in Franglais, so Les Autres on the Subway ne peuvent pas comprendre what we're parler-ing about!"

From New England—adj. phrase. A Universally Acceptable excuse for opting out of Potentially Embarrassing Situations. Useful when one is, like the Etiquette Grrls, from New England. "The Etiquette Grrls are From New England, and they don't have to answer such Rude Personal Questions."

FSF '17; Scott '17—proper n. The way the Etiquette Grrls refer to F. Scott Fitzgerald, their Favorite Author. "Scott '17 did love his Gin."

G&T—n. *gin and tonic.* The preferred alcoholic beverage of the Etiquette Grrls. Best mixed with a Healthy Measure of Bombay Sapphire. The ideal G&T is strong, cold, and, served with lime, prevents scurvy. "The Etiquette Grrls are probably enjoying a good G&T right now." "Boy, that waitress is so great, she just brought the Etiquette Grrls some G&Ts as soon as they walked in the door, without their even placing an order!"

Gin—n. The Etiquette Grrls' Alcohol of Choice. Preferably Bombay Sapphire, Tanqueray, Gordon's, or Beefeater will do in A Pinch. "The Etiquette Grrls love Gin which comes in a Pretty Bottle, like Bombay Sapphire!" See *G&T, Trav-L-Bar, Zelda.*

Gin and Tonic—n. See *G&T.*

Go AWOL—v. To become AWOL. Implies active effort on behalf of the person who or thing which is AWOL. "What have I ever done to my Vintage Compacts? They Go AWOL at Every Opportunity!" See *AWOL*.

Godlike in His/Her/Their Omniscience—phrase. Über-Omniscient: "Many of the Etiquette Grrls' Dear Friends are Godlike in their Omniscience; they always know when the Etiquette Grrls need A Good Stiff G&T." See *Omniscience*.

Goth—adj. Short for "Gothic," i.e., Morose, Dark, Melancholy. "Your long black vintage dress is rather Goth, Shelby." n. Someone who is rather Morose, Dark, or Melancholy; often self-described as "Goth." Goths may or may not wear head-to-toe black, deathly pale Manic Panic makeup, etc., according to their preference. "The Etiquette Grrls aren't Goths, but boy, are they pale!"

'Hood, The—n. The part of the city the Etiquette Grrls wouldn't care to live in, thanks very much. "The apartment had a great floor plan, but I didn't take it, since it was in The 'Hood." Sometimes The 'Hood is just the Slightly Tackier, Yet Perfectly Safe part of town or even of a campus: "Gee, I hope I get a good number in Room Draw so I don't have to live in the New Quad. It's, like, The 'Hood."

Horrorshow—adj. (*cf.* A Clockwork Orange.) Really dreadful. "That is a Horrorshow Handkerchief Top!"

Keen—adj. Cooler than cool. "Boy, that's a keen cocktail shaker, Philip! Is it Vintage?" Interj. "Oh boy!! I've been invited to 'A Very Boozy Thanksgiving' at the Etiquette Grrls' this year! Keen!!"

Keen On—phrase. Enthusiastic about. Often used in the negative. "The Etiquette Grrls aren't at all Keen On Rum Drinks."

Kitty-Kat—n. A hip, swingin', Martini-swilling kind of Girl. Somewhat sleazy. (See entry for *Daddy-O*.) The Etiquette Grrls may only be addressed as such by the cast of *Swingers* or members of

Big Bad Voodoo Daddy. "Hey, what's up, Kitty-Kat? Would you care for a Cosmopolitan?"

Lilly—proper n. 1. Lilly Pulitzer, Palm Beach designer of brightly colored Posh Summer Clothing. Rumored to be the originator of the infamous Lime-Green and Hot-Pink combo. "Lilly is such a Fab Lady!" 2. An article of clothing designed by Lilly. "Did you see my new Lilly with the Martini Glasses all over it?" "The only time when the Etiquette Grrls aren't wearing black is when they're wearing Lilly." adj. 1. Having the appearance of something designed by Lilly. "Having the table set in all those different colors of Fiestaware is sort of Lilly, don't you think?" 2. Possessed of the "See You In Hell" quality of Lilly clothing. "Great retort, Muffy. That's soooo Lilly."

Malaria—n. A Terrible Tropical Disease. "The Etiquette Grrls will never come down with Malaria, on account of all the Tonic Water they drink, as it contains Quinine, which helps prevent that Terrible, Horrible Disease!"

Malaise—n. A slight, indescribable sickness. "What's the matter? You look a little peaked." "Oh, it's nothing; I'm just suffering from A Light Malaise."

Masher—n. The sort of Boy who makes Improper Advances. "I don't like going to that bar by the University on Saturdays because it's just filled with Mashers." "If you don't leave the Etiquette Grrls alone, You Masher, you're gonna get Decked!"

Money—adj. (*cf.* Swingers.) *Really,* truly, *unspeakably* cool, like Frank Sinatra. "Eugene O'Neill is *so* Money!"

New England—proper n. 1. The region of the United States which reigns supreme in terms of attitude, accent, intellectual nature, and quality of Private Schools. "New England should really have followed through on its threat to secede." 2. Where the Etiquette Grrls call home. adj. Pertaining to a state of mind, encompassing intense privacy, high esteem for education, a Strange Fondness for L. L. Bean, and a certain severity of spirit found in the Northeastern states above New York. "Great skirt. Very New England." Also see *From New England*.

Offer It Up for the Souls in Purgatory—phrase. "Deal with it." What Nuns and the Etiquette Grrls' Mothers say when you whine about something to them. "I can't believe there's nothing vegan on the menu here!" "Offer It Up for the Souls in Purgatory."

Olive, A Big Damn—n. What the Etiquette Grrls expect to come in their Martinis. "I'll have a Martini, Bartender, and I'd like A Big Damn Olive in it please, and none of that nouvelle Craisins-on-a-Toothpick business!"

Omniscient—adj. All-knowing, all-seeing. Sometimes used facetiously. "Omniscient Sally asked if the Etiquette Grrls know anything about Etiquette."

Patois—n. Special vocabulary of a particular group. "The Etiquette Grrls' Patois contains many Literary References!"

Peachy—adj. Great, super. Often with "Keen." "Those Etiquette Grrls are Peachy Keen kids!"

Pimm's—proper n. What the Etiquette Grrls drink in the Summertime when they're not drinking Gin. "Why do the British put cucumber in Pimm's?"

Prep—n. A person who attended a Preparatory School (usually in New England, usually a Boarding School). "I know he looks Goth now, but Holden is a Prep; he was At School with me." adj. Something which is characteristic of a Prep. "Madras is very Prep." v. The act of attending Prep School. "I'm so glad I Prepped at Portsmouth Abbey rather than Canterbury." Capitalized, or not, in order to distinguish what is *truly* Prep from what is not. A lowercase *p* indicates a pseudo-prep, a prep poseur, somebody who did not attend Prep School. (See entry for *At School*.)

Random Capitalization—phrase. Method of emphasizing Particularly Important Words. Always appropriate in writing. If one is Quite The Expert, as the Etiquette Grrls are, the capitals can also be heard in one's speech. "Despite their liberal use of Random Capitalization, the Etiquette Grrls are not German Scholars."

Scurvy—n. One of the Etiquette Grrls' Favorite Diseases. "The Etiquette Grrls Prevent Scurvy by having a Big Slice of Lime in their G&Ts."

See Me In Hell/See You In Hell—phrase. The Etiquette Grrls' all-purpose phrase to tell people who have trifled with them Where They Can Get Off. "USAir lost my luggage again. They can See Me In Hell!" adj. phrase. Used to describe clothing, etc. that will make people sorry that they Wronged You. "I found the perfect See You In Hell skirt to wear when I see my ex-boyfriend, that Dastardly Bastard!" "I think this nail polish really says, 'See You In Hell,' don't you?"

Shameless Cad—n. A really terrible, awful, moralless sort of Boy. Not A Gentleman. "Helen told me that the Boys in That Fraternity are nothing but Dastardly Bastards and Shameless Cads; you'd best stay away from them!"

Smashing—adj. Chiefly British, esp. when used by anyone other than the Etiquette Grrls. Great, fabulous, beyond praise. "I always have a Smashing Good Time with the Etiquette Grrls!" "All of Frank Sinatra's records on the Capitol label are Smashing!"

Soigné(e)(s)—adj. Calm, cool, collected; very polished and sophisticated. What the Etiquette Grrls are. "Wow, those Etiquette Grrls sure are Soignées!"

Subversive Nail Polish—n. Nail polish, preferably manufactured by Urban Decay in unusual and odd colors, preferably with witty, cynical names. Makes the biggest Statement when worn with conservative clothing, as it will make people think twice about you. "My Subversive Nail Polish in Urban Decay's 'Cult' looks totally cool with my Audrey Hepburn–ish black shift dress."

Swell—adj. "Gee, that's a swell mink coat! Where did you get it?" See *Keen*.

That_____Person or T.__.P.—phrase. Fill in the blank with the first name or initial of someone you're not sure you like. The abbreviation is useful for e-mail. In reference to an officemate named Linda, you might write, "T.L.P. is whining. Again."

THOR—phrase. The Height Of Rudeness. "Refusing to give a seat to a Pregnant Woman on a train is THOR!"

TMI—phrase. Too Much Information. When someone tells you more than you needed to know. "Sally rambling on about her ingrown toenail troubles was just TMI!"

Too Clever By Half—phrase. Extraordinarily Clever, a Really Good Idea. "Look, Eloise, the Etiquette Grrls made Wee Turnovers by wrapping Puff Pastry around their Famous Artichoke Dip! Isn't that simply Too Clever By Half?"

Toss Back a Few—phrase. To drink Alcoholic Beverages, esp. dans A Bar, and esp. avec the Etiquette Grrls. "Boy, I've had a Rotten Day! I sure hope the Etiquette Grrls are free to Toss Back A Few!"

Trav-L-Bar—n. The Brand Name of the Etiquette Grrls' Trusty Travel Bar, which is how the Etiquette Grrls Carry Their Gin Around. "Boy, am I glad the Etiquette Grrls brought the Trav-L-Bar along on our Road Trip, because the Bars in This Place Stink!"

TTFN—phrase. Ta-Ta For Now. "Oooh, I'd better dash, or I'll be late for Nuclear Physics class! TTFN!!"

TTFW—phrase. Too Tacky For Words. "Good heavens, those microwaves that resemble iMacs are TTFW!"

UNIX—n. The Etiquette Grrls' very favorite Programming Language! "We love UNIX because, like Catholicism, it is rather Retro and Severe."

V.—adv. (*cf.* Bridget Jones's Diary.) Very. "*N Sync is V. Annoying."

Version___.0—adj. Used to describe Something Which Has Already

Been Done or Existed in a Previous Incarnation. "I heard that Penelope is transferring to Carnegie Mellon next semester. Guess it's College Version 2.0 for her."

Vile—adj. Extremely disgusting. Most effective when used for Exaggerated Effect. "How's your yogurt?" "Vile."

Vintage—adj. What a lot of the Etiquette Grrls' clothes are. To qualify as Vintage, an object must be *at least* thirty years old—your Rubik's Cube is not Vintage, and neither is your Collection of Benetton Rugby Shirts from 1985. "The Etiquette Grrls' Vintage Coat Collection is threatening to Take Over the Closet."

Wee—adj., of Scottish origin. Very small. "I thought a Wee Convertible would be perfect for summer."

Zelda—proper n. FSF '17's wife. "That Zelda sure was wacky, but like Scott '17, she did love her Gin."

PROFILES IN ETIQUETTE: ABOUT THE AUTHORS

Lesley Carlin is a New Englander—in terms of both Her Birthplace and Her Temperament. After seven years of Catholic School, which she fondly compares to Chinese Water Torture, she enrolled at a small Massachusetts Prep School, whence she graduated as a member of the last all-girls class. Lesley continued her studies at Princeton, where she majored in English Literature and Creative Writing and learned how to Mix a Mean G&T. She picked up her A.B. in 1995, packed up the Etiquette Volvo, and moved to Ann Arbor, Michigan, to begin Graduate Work in Creative Writing, courtesy of a Jacob Javits Fellowship. Her poems have been published in several journals and nominated for the Pushcart Prize. After earning her M.F.A. in 1997, Lesley embarked upon what is obviously a natural career path for a Trained Poet; she is now the Managing Editor and Site Producer for an Internet Start-Up. Lesley lives near Boston, Massachusetts.

Honore McDonough Ervin, who was raised in Washington, D.C., London, and Massachusetts, attended the all-girls Westover School, but transferred in order to be one of the first girls to graduate from Portsmouth Abbey School in Rhode Island, where she tried her damnedest to instruct her classmates, nearly all of them Boys, in The Art of Gracious Living. She then settled at Chatham College in Pittsburgh, Pennsylvania, where she majored in Art History and English, graduating in 1997. While pursuing Graduate Studies at the University of Virginia, she discovered that contrary to popular belief, and much to her Bitter Disappointment, Southern Living does not, in fact, entail quaint activities such as sipping Mint Juleps on the verandah and singing songs about the Swanee River. Honore has since returned to Pittsburgh, where in between still more graduate classes, she Holds Court at the Etiquette Flat, à la the Algonquin Round Table's Mrs. Parker.

The Etiquette Grrls enjoy traveling (First Class, whenever possible), drinking stiff G&Ts (with Bombay Sapphire, please), and shopping for Vintage Clothing. "Accomplished" young women in the Jane Austen sense of the word, they were taught at very young ages how to play the piano, dance divinely, eat Artichokes properly, and spot Good Jewelry. They are vicious Badminton Players! You will find the Etiquette Grrls listening to Cake, road-tripping to exclusive ocean-front towns, and collecting Lilly Pulitzer dresses. The Etiquette Grrls throw Fabulous Parties, renowned all over the Eastern Seaboard, from the classic A Very Boozy Thanksgiving to impromptu soirées for which even poor, starving graduate students wear their smartest clothes. A frequent response from a first-time guest at one of the Etiquette Grrls' parties is, "I had no idea a party without a keg and tequila shots could be so much fun!" In the Etiquette Volvo, which has over a hundred thousand miles on it, they travel the world, fighting Rudeness with Cutting Remarks, Hilarious Observations, and, always, Elegance and Grace.

The Etiquette Grrls are Not to Be Trifled With.